A *Supernatural* Politics

A *Supernatural* Politics

*Essays on Social Engagement,
Fandom and the Series*

Edited by Lisa Macklem *and*
Dominick Grace

McFarland & Company, Inc., Publishers
Jefferson, North Carolina

This book has undergone peer review.

Library of Congress Cataloguing-in-Publication Data

Names: Macklem, Lisa, 1962– editor. | Grace, Dominick, 1963– editor.
Title: A Supernatural politics : essays on social engagement, fandom
and the series / edited by Lisa Macklem and Dominick Grace.
Description: Jefferson, North Carolina : McFarland & Company, Inc.,
Publishers, 2021 | Includes bibliographical references and index.
Identifiers: LCCN 2020054955 | ISBN 9781476675879 (paperback : acid free paper) ∞
ISBN 9781476641195 (ebook)
Subjects: LCSH: Supernatural (Television program : 2005-2020) | Horror television
programs—United States—History and criticism. | Horror television programs—Social
aspects—United States. | Politics on television. | Fans (Persons)—United States.
Classification: LCC PN1992.77.S84 S879 2021 | DDC 791.45/72—dc23
LC record available at https://lccn.loc.gov/2020054955

British Library cataloguing data are available

ISBN (print) 978-1-4766-7587-9
ISBN (ebook) 978-1-4766-4119-5

Front cover image © 2020 Joe Therasakdhi/Shutterstock

Printed in the United States of America

*McFarland & Company, Inc., Publishers
Box 611, Jefferson, North Carolina 28640
www.mcfarlandpub.com*

Table of Contents

Part Three—The Politics of Fandom

Introduction

LISA MACKLEM *and* DOMINICK GRACE

A television genre show about two brothers hunting monsters might seem like the last place one would find political commentary of any kind, yet *Supernatural* delves into the political on a number of levels. This collection examines how the show engages with American life, the social dynamics of intertextuality, and the politics of the show's fandom itself. While *Supernatural* has received a surprising amount of critical response, including several essay collections (some refereed, some not), only relatively recently have collections focusing on specific aspects of the show begun to appear, suggesting that *Supernatural* is sufficiently complex to stand up to in-depth analysis of particular aspects and features of the show. More general collections include such volumes as *In the Hunt: Unauthorized Essays on* Supernatural (2009), compiled by Supernatural.TV; Abbott and Lavery's *TV Goes to Hell: An Unofficial Road Map of* Supernatural (2011), or George and Hansen's Supernatural, *Humanity, and the Soul: On the Highway to Hell and Back* (2014). More tightly themed volumes include Zubernis and Larsen's *Fan Phenomena:* Supernatural (2014), which as its title suggests engages specifically with fan practices and the show; Edmundson's *The Gothic Tradition in* Supernatural: *Essays on the TV Series* (2016); Taylor and Nylander's *Death in* Supernatural: *Critical Essays* (2019); and our own Supernatural *Out of the Box: Critical Essays on the Metatextuality of the Series* (2020)— in addition to other books and critical articles on the show, as well as innumerable volumes targeted at non-academic audiences. This volume extends and deepens the discussion by taking several different approaches to how the show engages with real-world social and political issues.

The show, which concluded with its 15th season in 2020, continually touched on political and social topics throughout its run. For instance (and perhaps in response to ongoing concerns about misogyny in the show), in the episode "Ouroboros" (14.14), a gorgon, Noah, is about to eat a male victim. The victim wants to know why the monster is picking on helpless men.

Noah tells him, "'Helpless men'—that's rich. No, I do eat ladies, too, but women have become so cautious lately. Must be all that finally waking up from centuries of misogynistic oppression. Good for them. Bad for you." The gorgon's answer touches upon the #MeToo movement, but also touches upon a particularly contentious concern within fandom as well as among scholars (see, for instance, Victoria Farmer, "'Sweetheart, this *is* Gender Studies': Jo Harvelle, Female Strength, and Fandom in *Supernatural*"), and the horror genre generally, that women are too often the victims. It is debatable whether the show's somewhat cavalier treatment of the issues in this case results in a satisfactory answer to any of these debates, and indeed that debate continues in several essays in this volume, but the issue is certainly one that the show's writers are aware of on multiple levels within the politics of their interactions with fans and within the politics of the entertainment industry. The essays in this volume seek to explore *Supernatural*'s political and social concerns, broadly defined—the ways the show engages actively with the real world in which it is produced and consumed.

Television viewing theory has come a long way from the time when viewers were thought to be simply passive consumers whose brain activity mimicked that of sleep. Today, even the passive viewing theory suggests that what people watch still has an effect on them, and active viewing suggests that viewers interact with what they view to create meaning. Genre television often engages viewers because it is, or seems to be, an escape from the world which confronts them every day. This distance offers a safe, liminal space in which to examine issues which may be more difficult to tackle in a more real-world setting. Of course, because it is a more fictional world, it also creates the potential for more disputes over the facts of that reality. In fact, this world-building aspect of genre fiction often results in viewers becoming both involved and invested in its parameters, inciting, in turn, its own political battlefield within fandoms.

In his original pitch for *Supernatural*, Eric Kripke described the show as "*X-Files* meets *Route 66*. [...] Two brothers, cruising the dusty back roads in their trusty 64 Mustang, battling things that go bump in the night" (Highfill). While the show has arguably evolved over the years, these seeds focusing on cultural politics—the American west, the American Dream, family values—remain at the heart of the show. The story of two brothers raises questions of family politics, a theme to which the show itself returns regularly, and this familial aspect was taken up whole-heartedly by fans of the show who are known collectively as the SPN family. This leads to yet a third area of cultural politics: the relationship between fans and producers of the show. Stuart Hall identifies two ways of looking at cultural identity: "The first position defines 'cultural identity' in terms of one, shared culture, a sort of collective 'one true self'" (223). Because the central characters,

Dean and Sam Winchester, are essentially quite different, viewers can identify with the familial bond and often identify strongly with one or the other brother. The second element of Hall's theory of cultural identity "recognizes that, as well as the many points of similarity, there are also critical points of deep and significant *difference* which constitute 'what we really are'" (225). It is these differences that have sparked so much on-going discussion of the show over its long run. These theories speak not only to the fan/producer relationship but also to the questions of intertextuality and larger concerns of communication in today's society, as is discussed in Part Two of this collection. Across its three sections, this book explores several of the ways *Supernatural*—the show itself and its social context—is engaged in a complex exploration of social and political dynamics.

Noted Stephen King scholar Tony Magistrale has argued that "[n]o literature, not even the literature of supernatural terror, can be understood as discrete from the culture out of which it arises" (150). We would go further and argue that this is especially true of the horror genre, with its capacity to metaphorize real-world problems and to render more starkly and clearly the implications of social ills. King himself has likened modern horror to "the morality plays of the fifteenth, sixteenth and seventeenth centuries" (368), with their explicit agenda to comment on transgressions against order—a divine rather than a human order, to be sure, but the parallel is clear, and morality plays do indeed consistently ground their concern with supernatural superstructures in transgressions against social as well as moral codes. Horror is, as Edward Ingebretsen argues, "a vehicle for the presentation of social ills" (5). The ancient metaphor of the body politic underscores the fact that "[t]he political is, and always has been, a bodily, affective affair" (Knudsen and Stage 1), so it is perhaps unsurprising that horror, the genre more than any other concerned with the formation, fracturing and othering of the body, is also a productive site for political explorations.

Horror has a long history of providing a fertile ground for political commentary, and *Supernatural* has proven to be no exception. John S. Nelson posits that "[p]olitics that emerge from a creative focus on scenery, sound, story, characters, or even sales can be more provocative and informative than any intentional messages about parties or ideologies" (5). According to Nelson, not focusing on a specific ideology or policy allows creators to offer more insight into everyday politics that affect audiences. This trend is seen in the successes of movies at the box office over the last few years, including one of the biggest success stories: Jordan Peele's *Get Out* (2017), which deals with racism. Aviva Briefel and Sam Miller point out that after 9/11 "the horror genre emerged as a rare protected space in which to critique the tone and content of public discourse" (3). Linda J.

Holland-Toll asserts that "[h]orror fiction [...] actively denies and resists the more affirmative cultural models which we use to tell reassuring stories about ourselves and our communities" and goes on to point out that horror discusses the human condition through the construction of the monster (2). However, the true monster very often wears a human face. The protagonist in *Get Out* leaves the city and the comfort of his own cultural space to meet his girlfriend's parents in what should be the pastoral countryside, but it is a pastoral countryside of a white American Dream. As Holland-Toll points out, "horror fiction is a fiction of the margins, a fiction of the outer limits of humanity, a fiction of 'Otherness'" (7). The America of the American Dream is, of course, a multi-faceted one that takes different forms depending on who is describing it.

The American Dream perishes in horror fiction. Dean and Sam Winchester are the disenfranchised, living outside of society even while infiltrating it and protecting it. They live outside of the white picket fences of suburbia, yet this is still a dream that even they often seem to yearn for. However, when one of the brothers seems to achieve some semblance of the American Dream, the other arrives to pull him back out of it. In the "Pilot" (1.01), for instance, Dean arrives in Stanford to take Sam away from his girlfriend and his university studies (significantly, he hopes to be a lawyer, an arbiter of societal justice, but instead of working *within* the system, he ends up working *outside* it) to find their missing father. When Dean thinks Sam is dead at the end of Season 5, he tries to live a "normal" life with Lisa Braeden, only to have Sam arrive and pull him out of it ("Exile on Main Street," 6.01). In fact, when given the opportunity to fantasize about another life when captured by a Djinn, Dean dreams of a life in which their mother is still alive and they'd never heard of monsters—in effect, a conventional middle-class life. The title of the episode, "What Is and What Should Never Be" (2.20), underscores the wrongness of this life for Dean. Yet as recently as Season 14, when faced with the horrors of their existence, Sam takes refuge in the white picket community created by a powerful psychic ("Peace of Mind," 14.15). It's telling that in this episode the "monster" is once again human. In the end, Dean and Sam always return to their mostly solitary existence, outside of mainstream society, but this allows them a distance to observe from without—the same distance afforded the audience with horror.

Distance affords fans space in which to construct their own narratives and deconstruct the narrative of the show. However, distance itself can create fan politics, both when the gap may be large and when it may be small. Fans may agree with each other and the show's writers and producers, or they may disagree among themselves or with where the show itself seems to be headed. Paul Booth and Lucy Bennett list only a few of the attributes of fans: "A fan may be creative, productive, transformative, influential, affirmational, antagonistic, or any other of the hundreds of ways that media fans have been described" (1). One of the reasons that television shows like *Supernatural* attract such passion from fans is, according to Rebecca Williams, that "[t]elevision offers opportunities for sustained emotional connection that other media, such as cinema, cannot" (10) because of its long-form serial narratives. Becoming a fan is almost always an important milestone in a fan's life. It becomes an important aspect in both their sense of self-identity but also in their cultural identity, and a strong fandom, such as that created around *Supernatural,* offers multiple ways for fans to engage with both the show and other fans. This investment in both the show and fandom creates strong reactions as fans wish to see their vision of the show come to fruition and also to see their own cultural capital increase. Paul Booth points out that sometimes this investment leads to dissatisfaction "not because they hate a show but because they feel *betrayed* by a show they once loved" (78). This dissatisfaction can lead to a number of responses from fans. Some turn to Twitter to try to influence the writers and producers directly. Others turn to fan works to comment on the show and discuss the show through those fanworks. Well-known *Supernatural* fan and vidder Ash48 explains that she is "often inspired by things outside of the show—the fan campaign to send thousands of rubber ducks to set, the winning of awards [*Supernatural* and the lead actors have won multiple People's Choice Awards], etc. 'Soapernatural' was [her] way of dealing with the utter frustration [she] was feeling during the first half of Season 8 with all the 'soapy' elements in the show" (70). While the show clearly has its own agenda in its storytelling, dictated by copyright concerns in the media industry, Booth and Bennett point out that "fandom is more than just a particular subculture, it has become a major economic force in its own right" (3).

While fan studies is not a new pursuit, the awareness of fans has increased among media personnel with the advent of social media and the Internet. Social media tends to create a false sense of closeness, which can be seen at times in fan communities themselves, but also in understanding between media insiders and fans. In meeting the producers or actors, fans may experience cognitive dissonance, resulting in the fan giving more weight to the encounter. For their own part, producers and actors may not understand the fan perspective. *Supernatural*'s depictions of fans within its own storytelling represents, at least on some level, an ongoing learning experience by the writers and producers, as they try to engage back with those who have engaged so heavily with the show. Portrayals of fans have not always been positive or well received even when not intended to be necessarily negative. Much has been written on the fanbase and the depiction of fans within the show. There has been little acknowledgment of the development of that relationship within the specific crucible of the growing power of fandom and the learning curve that was required of fans and producers/writers alike, an oversight that the final essays in this volume begin to address.

Supernatural manages to examine the politics of family, fandom, and America writ large in its storylines, often seeing these politics as intersecting rather than as discrete. The authors of the essays within this collection use different methods and approaches to the subject matter, but each shines a light on interesting facets of the topic.

Part One of this collection, "Being American," explores the specifically American nature of *Supernatural*. In the first essay, "Post-Crash Politics: Supernatural Masculinities in the Mid-West," Leanne McRae applies quantitative analyses of Republican and Democrat television viewing preferences. *Supernatural* is one of the top three shows widely enjoyed by registered members of both parties; this essay argues that different aspects of the show appeal to different demographics, with the show's conventional renderings of biblical justice, southern masculinity, largely conservative renderings of family, and a clearly delineated Heaven and Hell on the one hand and non-conventional narrative trajectories, subversive and self-reflexive masculine tropes, and ironic production values on the other hand providing something for conservative and liberal alike. McRae argues that *Supernatural* exists in tension and in cohesion with the complexities of contemporary masculinity, faith, religion and the mid-west of the USA.

In the second essay, "'I killed Hitler': American Exceptionalism and Triumphalism in *Supernatural*," Cait Coker focuses on the conservative side of the show, rereading "*Supernatural*'s engagement with popular culture, history, and myth as meta to explicate how it uses Sam and Dean to illustrate American exceptionalism and triumphalism through metaphysical adventures" (29).

The next essay, Camille DeBose's "Dean's *Yellow Fever*: Acts of Forgery in Genre," argues that *Supernatural* problematizes concepts of American masculinity by presenting in the mise-en-scène and narrative frame a distinctly American, male sensibility while the performances within the show disrupt the surface conformity to the unstated political assumptions of the show, and instead create Deleuzian forgeries of the hyper-masculine, American man in a horror show, especially in Jensen Ackles's depiction of Dean.

Focusing on Season 7, in "'You guys getting hungry?' On Leviathans, Consumption and American Politics in *Supernatural*," Angélica Varandas reads the "big bads" of that season, the Leviathans, as serving to condemn "the consumer habits of the American population" in the season's "denunciation of political propaganda and demagogy as a means of conveniently maneuvering people" (70), drawing parallels between the monsters on the show and specific corporate and political practices in the real world.

Part Two, "Text and Context," focuses on the relationship between intertextuality and textual knowledge, and their real-world implications. In the essay "Re-Constructing Monstrosity: Faces of Evil, from Mary Shelley's *Frankenstein* to the TV Show *Supernatural*," Tatiana Prorokova-Konrad discusses *Supernatural*'s intertextual relationship with *Frankenstein* in Season 10, analyzing how "the image of the creature from *Frankenstein*, being an embodiment of evil, has been transformed in the 21st century with the help of *Supernatural*, now personifying multiple evil groups—from the Nazis to terrorists and beyond" (75); that is, this essay addresses how horror tropes resonate with real-world conflict and political action.

In a very different vein, Paula S. Kiser, in "Knowledge Is Power: Informational Literacy in *Supernatural*," demonstrates the importance of information literacy if one is successfully to combat threats to one's world and way of life—a point that has acquired special urgency in recent times and the increasing predominance of deliberate misinformation campaigns, the manipulation of records (e.g., the modification of video recordings to misrepresent events), and accusations of "fake news." Kiser here explores this less-widely appreciated weapon in Sam and Dean's arsenal: knowledge of the true facts, not the alternative ones.

Finally, in "'There is no singing in *Supernatural*!' Fan/Producer Relationships, Metanarrative and *Supernatural*'s 200th Episode Special," Keshia Mcclantoc provides an essay that transitions into Part Three's specific exploration of fan engagement. Mcclantoc explores the politics of fan/producer relations, reading *Supernatural* as a show that "mediates participation in a way that invites and celebrates fans while still maintaining balanced consumer boundaries" (103). Mcclantoc reads the 200th episode as paradigmatic of how the show allows interpretive space for fans while insisting that the show's narrative itself remains the domain of the producers.

Part Three, "The Politics of Fandom," engages more extensively and specifically with the complex and fraught territory of *Supernatural* fandom, presenting essays that address how fans interact with the show, with its producers, and with each other. Emily E. Roach's "Slash Fiction: Homoerotics and the Metatextual Fangirl" addresses the complicated tensions between homoerotic subtext, fan service and queerbaiting in order to suggest that *Supernatural* is at the forefront of an increasingly fractious and difficult dialogue in the sphere of fan studies, especially in the politics of representation of fandom in the show.

Continuing this theme, Kimberly Lynn Workman's "Breaking the

Fourth Wall: Fandom Representation in *Supernatural* Canon" explores the boundaries of fan/show interaction, analyzing the possible positive and negative ramifications of border-crossings; Workman argues that the show's "breaking of the fourth wall erases the safe boundaries that exist between creator, creation, and fan. Without these boundaries in place," she argues, these "interactions can become extreme and unhealthy" (155), as for instance in the case of Becky Rosen, who arguably serves as a representation of the over-invested fan. On the other hand, both within the show and in the real world, "fans can make connections with the canonical text and align it to their own lives" (158).

By contrast, Megan Genovese's "Monsters Make Gender Trouble" argues that the show's sexual politics are problematic; the "ideological assumptions that define *Supernatural*'s narrative paradigm hinge on a binary, pseudo-biological understanding of gender as a strict dichotomy between male and female characteristics and roles deriving from dimorphic physiology" (163), which leads to the show's construction of monsters and monstrosity through a "discourse of the monstrous" (164) around gender trouble.

On a more optimistic note, Laurena Aker's "'Driver picks the music': Tracing *Supernatural*'s Long Road Trip to Discovering Fan Identity" argues that *Supernatural* has across its run revealed "distinct strategies and evolving stages in the show's view of itself, its relationship with its fans and the creative tension they exert on the show" (180); her essay explores the ways *Supernatural* and its fandom have negotiated an enduring relationship, with the show exploring fandom from multiple perspectives, both explicitly (e.g., in the overt depiction of fans) and implicitly (e.g., in how it defines such relationships as those between leaders and followers such as Cas and the other angels, or God and the Winchesters).

Finally, the coda, "Engaging with Engagement: Following a Creator/Creating Followers," explores some of the ways the show speaks back to fandom complexly, casting fans as problems, even as villains, but also offering up possibilities for mutual accommodation. The final season, in the middle of its run as of this writing, has chosen to cast God/Chuck, Kripke's avatar in the series and the spokesperson for authorial control, as the Big Bad, no doubt providing considerable new fodder for discussion of how *Supernatural* engages with its audience. This, however, remains to be seen.

Supernatural as a show about two American brothers, as a text, and as the object of a passionate fan base provides several fertile grounds for social and political discussion. This collection of essays seeks to explore some of the interesting ways that a genre show provides an excellent vehicle for these discussions.

WORKS CITED

Abbott, Stacey, and David Lavery, eds. *TV Goes to Hell: An Unofficial Road Map of* Supernatural. ECW Press, 2011.

Ash48. "Fan Appreciation No.1: Ash48: The Vidder." In *Fan Phenomena*: Supernatural. Eds. Lynn Zubernis and Katherine Larsen. Intellect, 2014. 56–75.

Bennett, Lucy, and Paul Booth, eds. "Introduction: Seeing Fans." In *Seeing Fans: Representations of Fandom in Media and Popular Culture*. Bloomsbury, 2016. 1–10.

Booth, Paul. "Fan Euthanasia." In *Everybody Hurts: Transitions, Endings, and Resurrections in Fan Cultures*. Ed. Rebecca Williams. University of Iowa Press, 2018. 75–86.

Briefel, Aviva, and Sam J. Miller. "Introduction." In *Horror After 9/11: World of Fear, Cinema of Terror*. University of Texas Press, 2011. 1–10.

Edmundson, Melissa. *The Gothic Tradition in* Supernatural: Essays on the Television Series. McFarland, 2016.

Farmer, Victoria. "'Sweetheart, this *is* Gender Studies': Jo Harvelle, Female Strength, and Fandom in *Supernatural*." *Supernatural Studies* vol. 3 no. 1 (2016): 85–98.

George, Susan A. and Regina M. Hansen, eds. Supernatural, *Humanity, and the Soul: On the Highway to Hell and Back*. Palgrave Macmillan, 2014.

Hall, Stuart. "Cultural Identity and Diaspora." In *Identity: Community, Culture, Difference*. Ed Jonathan Rutherford. London: Lawrence & Wishart, 1990. 222–237.

Highfill, Samantha. "*Supernatural* Creator Erik Kripke Shares His Original 2004 Pitch for the Show." *Entertainment Weekly* Feb. 7 2019. https://ew.com/tv/2019/02/07/supernatural-creator-eric-kripke-show-pitch/

Holland-Toll, Linda J. *As American as Mom, Baseball, and Apple Pie: Constructing Community in Contemporary American Horror Fiction*. Bowling Green State University Popular Press, 2001.

Ingebretsen, Edward. *At Stake: Monsters and the Rhetoric of Fear in Public Culture*. University of Chicago Press, 2001.

King, Stephen. *Danse Macabre*. Everest House, 1981.

Knudsen, Britta Timm, and Carsten Stage. *Global Media, Biopolitics, and Affect: Politicizing Bodily Vulnerability*. Taylor and Francis, 2014.

Kripke, Eric. "Kripke's Original Pitch for Supernatural." Supernatural Fan Wiki. http://www.supernatural-fan-wiki.com/page/Kripke%27s+Original+Pitch+for+Supernatural

Macklem, Lisa, and Dominick Grace, eds. Supernatural *Out of the Box: Critical Essays on the Metatextuality of the Series*. McFarland, 2020.

Magistrale, Tony. *Stephen King: The Second Decade*. Danse Macabre *to* The Dark Half. Twayne, 1992.

Nelson, John S. *Politics in Popular Movies: Rhetorical Takes on Horror, War, Thriller, and SciFi Films*. Paradigm Publishers, 2015.

Peele, Jordon, director. *Get Out*. Universal Pictures Home Entertainment, 2017.

Supernatural.TV, ed. *In the Hunt: Unauthorized Essays on* Supernatural. Benbella Books. 2009.

Taylor, Amanda, and Susan Nylander, eds. *Death in* Supernatural: *Critical Essays*. McFarland, 2019.

Williams, Rebecca, ed. "Introduction: Starting at the End." In *Everybody Hurts: Transitions, Endings, and Resurrections in Fan Cultures*. University of Iowa Press, 2018. 10–16.

Zubernis, Lynn, and Katherine Larsen, eds. *Fan Phenomena*: Supernatural. Intellect, 2014.

PART ONE

Being American

Post-Crash Politics

Supernatural *Masculinities in the Mid-West*

Leanne McRae

> **Sam:** Dean, I might have done … who knows what. And you want me to just forget about it?
> **Dean:** You shove it down, and you let it come out in spurts of violence and alcoholism.
> **Sam:** That sounds healthy.
> **Dean:** Well, it works for me.
> —"Mannequin 3: The Reckoning" (6.14)

> **Castiel:** Yes, well … before I was very self assured. I was convinced I was on this righteous path. Now I realize that there is no righteous path, it's just people trying to do their best in a world where it is far too easy to do your worst.
> **Claire:** Wow, deep.
> —"The Things We Left Behind" (10.9)

In 2020 *Supernatural* completed a run of 15 seasons. This achievement is of particular note considering that *Supernatural* screened on the CW and was the only show to survive from the CW's predecessor, WB. Creator Eric Kripke has always affirmed he only ever had a five-year vision for the narrative and left the series as showrunner when he had concluded this trajectory. Despite major changes to showrunners, network heads and writers, it retained "steady ratings of over 2 million viewers" (Luksza 180) and evolved into a fan favorite often used to usher in new shows like *Arrow* (2012–20) and *The Flash* (2014–) which have gone on to greater success. *Supernatural* is a show about monsters, the mid-west, and gothic horror with its target audience firmly entrenched in the 18–49 male demographic. Most surprising, however, is the large and sustained female audience that is drawn to the show, conveying the nuanced, conflicted and

12

subversive tendencies of the program that may also be instrumental to its long-term success.

In 2016, E-Score (*EPoll Research*), an online marketing company specializing in entertainment industries, conducted a survey among viewers who "identified themselves as Democrats and Republicans" ("Which TV Shows Do Republicans and Democrats Rate the Highest?") to rank their favorite shows. While the survey made no attempt to address the complexities and nuances of political affiliation, particularly as it evolves and unfolds over a lifetime, the starkly binarized framework presented a curiosity of commonality: *The Walking Dead* (2010–), *The Big Bang Theory* (2007–2019), and *Supernatural*. For Republicans, *The Walking Dead* was the second most favorite program. For Democrats, it was listed at number six. *The Big Bang Theory* was at number six for Republicans but number four for Democrats. *Supernatural*, however, was listed as the favorite program among Republicans (Democrats selected *Game of Thrones* as their number one), and the third most favorite program for Democrats. This high ranking of *Supernatural* for both Democrats and Republicans is the focus of the argument in this essay. The remarkable longevity of this program speaks to its ability to mean many things to multiple interest groups and audiences. The cogent masculine, mid-west tropes mask the complexities that have seen it gather diverse and disobedient audiences. The apparent simplicity of the program is belied by this ability to straddle and transgress borders and boundaries—a trait in the production of the program—that perverts, sustains and corrodes convention. The objective of this essay is not to uncover why both Democrats and Republicans like *Supernatural*, but to offer an analysis of the program that might offer a pathway into understanding the ways in which complex and contradictory meanings can coexist, circulate and perpetuate. In particular, it suggests that in a post-crash period where the infrastructures of capitalism are being dislodged, corrupted and revealed as corrosive to those very identities that have invested in it, *Supernatural* provides a site for dialogue between comfortable and complex ways in which to navigate these changes. It does this through a rendering of masculinity that is both conventional and creative, sedate and subversive. Sam and Dean Winchester may deploy archetypes of heterosexual heroics, but they also undermine these constructs. They prod and provoke the iconographics of Heaven and Hell, but also of masculinity and femininity, gay and straight, right and wrong.

Our current age offers up many conundrums, not only about how a show like *Supernatural*—seemingly embedded in pulpy pleasures and popular punctuations—has such longevity and such an ability to reach multiple audiences and interests, but also how social structures, meaning systems and stabilities have been turned on their heads. This shift is deployed not only in the rise of anti-vaccination ideologues and flat-earthers, but in widespread attacks on social institutions that have been at the heart of democracy, such as the rule of law, and financial institutions, as well as in the reactionary backlash against progressive attitudes and institutions such as the welfare state, and in the fear of difference deployed in Brexit debates and "build-a-wall" rhetoric. One of the biggest conundrums is Donald Trump. Though—perhaps not. As John Fea has claimed: "I[We] should have seen this coming" (6). Part of the reason we did not see this coming is a widespread disengagement from the lives of people bearing the brunt of the callousness of capitalism in an age of abundance. These contradictions have plagued people as they seek to make sense of their lives in a time of acceleration, mobility, deindustrialization, perpetual war, global financial crisis, and consumption. *Supernatural* provides a crucible for articulating and circulating the widely differing subjectivities and experiences that coexist.

In particular, a vision of the American Mid-West, and the rise of evangelicals as the major Trump voters, needs deeper interrogation—not to demonize these people as racist or sexist, but to encode the complexities of global fallout that have impacted these communities in damaging ways. It is these communities that are rendered, represented and circulated through *Supernatural* and provide a counterpoint to the prevailing concerns about democracy, the rule of law and elitism currently punctuating popular debate.

This essay makes no attempt to offer a nuanced assessment of the differences between Republicans and Democrats. Instead, it leans towards generalizations about the values of left and right politics without accounting for subtle variances in ideology. It situates Republicans as asserting conservative Christian family values, free-market economics, the rights of the individual, and small government. Democrats affirm diversity, big government, the good of the collective, and economic liberalism. Over time, the polarities of left and right politics across the globe have migrated towards the right with conservatism now characterized along the lines of an increasing fundamentalism. In the U.S., this has seen an amplification in the overt insertion of religion into politics, increasing manipulation of the rule of law to pervert its intent, tightened regulation of women and black people's bodies through violence and persecution, and an increasing intolerance of difference. As a result, left leaning political parties are no longer on the left but instead have come to mouth a rhetoric similar to but softer than that of the right: fiscal responsibility, national pride, and economic rationalism. It could be argued that the inability of the left to articulate a strong and sustained resistance to the rise of the right has led to its capitulation or at the very least collaboration with the right in a grab at power. For the "rural underclass," the persistence of liberal elites in marginalizing their concerns and reifying the identity politics of "others" at their expense has corroded their commitment to robust and regulatory democratic institutions. Jason Cervone affirms, "the rural underclass views this as the interests of others being placed before them, and their own struggles being ignored and mocked while also being told they are the ones responsible for the oppression" (3). *Supernatural* provides for a robust rendering of this underclass and an evocative site to interrogate these interactions and engagements.

Supernatural appears as a conventionally conservative text. It features two young men, Sam and Dean Winchester, crossing the country in their 1967 Chevy Impala, fighting demons, monsters, vampires, witches and werewolves to protect the innocent from evil. Season 1 situates this journey as part of the "family business" of "hunting" stimulated by the boys' father, John Winchester, who is missing. Their journey is motivated by their desire to discover what happened to him. The dark hues, rock 'n' roll soundtrack, abundance of flannel, persistent absence of women as meaningful foils to the boys, and brutal violence all situate the show within a conservative ethos punctuated by a vision of white, heterosexual, heroic masculinity. Analysts have pointed to the generic convergence of western, horror, and road movie, as a nexus for contemporary mobilization of the frontier myth. For instance, as Joseph M. Valenzano argues, "The frontier myth emphasizes the importance of the hero, personified in the character of the cowboy who erases those vestiges of cultures that do not conform to the American way of life through individual acts of aggression on behalf of the community he protects" (557).

The Winchesters hail from Lawrence, Kansas, in the "heartland of the United States" (Valenzano 558), and their name "invokes the famed American gun manufacturer the Winchester Repeating Arms Company, whose Winchester rifle is known in popular history as 'The Gun That Won the West'" (559). This premise sets them up as quintessential American heroes protecting a mythological origin of U.S. identity located in taming unruly landscapes and protecting people (mainly constructed as European-descended) against evil others (mainly constructed as Native Americans). The ideology of American Exceptionalism threads through the show whereby a unique and predestined ethos of a divinely ordained "special nation" (556) is embodied in the Winchesters' ability to act as border guards to right and wrong, good and evil. This positioning is amplified in Season 4 with the introduction of Angels into the plotline. Until this season, the Winchesters exclusively dealt with demonic as well as pagan forces, Christian and other religious icons and evils, and they existed within a diegesis that had a distinct and codified absence of anything divine or related to Heaven. As Dean affirms in Season 2, "There's no higher power, there's no God. There's just chaos and violence and random, unpredictable evil that comes out of nowhere. It rips you to shreds" ("Houses of the Holy," 2.13).

The introduction of the angel Castiel in episode one of Season 4 creates a binarized biblical context for the conflict in the show that leans heavily on Old Testament mythology involving the creation of the Earth, Heaven, and the Fall of Lucifer.[1] The angels, however, are not situated within the narrative as benevolent guardians of humanity, but instead are depicted as malevolent soldiers—warriors happy to bring about the Apocalypse to cleanse the earth. This allows Dean and Sam Winchester to embody humanity's favored status in the eyes of (an absent) God and to intervene and check both divine and demonic realms:

> Americanism—as as espoused in these two myths—as not only a manifestation of a divinely ordained status in the world, but, through the depiction of its brother protagonists, as evolving into a mythos that places America on an equal plane in terms of power with the divine [Valenzano 554].

The introduction of divine alongside demonic entities enables the Winchesters to enact mythologies about America as a special, unique, and superior nation responsible for intervening in injustice and protecting innocents against aggression. Importantly, this locus is found in the Mid-West and in a white, working class, heterosexual masculinity that assuages the elitism of the liberals via an evangelical undergirding of the United States as a Christian nation that must buttress itself against attacks (internal and external) that may compromise its moral core. Increasingly, it is Sam and Dean who get to decide what is right and wrong. The brothers affirm that angels cannot service the moral and protective needs of the U.S., and that it must be humans who "win back or restore the culture" (Fea 6). Sam and Dean, and not angels, define the moral codes and constructs of the United States. By aligning angels along the same continuum as demons, Sam and Dean compose American exceptionalism as a human responsibility and duty to protect and maintain. Dean diminishes archetypal understandings of angelic attitude by simultaneously affirming and disavowing the relationship between Christianity and the American founding narratives: "I thought angels were supposed to be guardians. Fluffy wings, haloes—you know, Michael Landon. Not dicks" ("Are You There, God? It's Me, Dean Winchester," 4.02).

The U.S. shapes itself as a deeply religious nation in keeping with the origin myths of exceptionalism and divine providence. Recent PEW research reports 55 percent of Americans claiming to pray daily, "compared with 25% in Canada, 18% in Australia and 6% in Great Britain" (Fahmy). This religious fervor is less precisely mapped in terms of denomination.

However, for politics there are significant consequences, with earlier (2014) PEW research showing that "the most Republican-leaning group in America is white Mormons, 76 percent of whom favour the GOP and 16 percent of whom favour Democrats" (Blake). This is mapped against a background of declining Christianity in the general American population since the 1970s. Evidence demonstrates that "white Christians are no longer a majority in America, but they still make up nearly three-quarters of the Republican Party" (Singer). By 2017 "the GOP remains about 73% white Christian" (Singer) with 35 percent identifying as evangelical, and "on November 8, 2016, 81 percent of self-described white evangelicals helped vote Donald Trump into the White House" (Fea 5). This data maps the resurgence of a predominantly white, evangelical Christian identity at the core of the Republican party. This is paralleled with declining educational qualifications of members and a reversal of party percentages with those obtaining higher levels of education gravitating towards the Democrats:

> In 1994, 39% of those with a four-year college degree (no postgraduate experience) identified with or leaned toward the Democratic Party and 54% associated with the Republican Party. In 2017, those figures were exactly reversed [Pew Research Center].

This is mirrored in the conditions of and for education in the rural United States where the stripping of funding and increasing push towards skills-based education in preparation for a global marketplace has led to a decline in critical literacies that might offer tools for making sense of political economy, cultural tensions and oppression. This impoverishment of analytical skills results in a "lashing out at a perceived other, whether it be a racial other, immigrants, or the 'godless'" (Cervone 8) who are coded as responsible for the decline in their own conditions and capacity for success. This attitude is funneled into and via an evangelical fear of the wider decline of the U.S. as an exceptional nation.

What this means for viewership of *Supernatural* is that the high levels of Republican-affiliated viewers can be correlated to the Old Testament binaries between Heaven and Hell with the American brothers situated as foils for both sides—demonstrating the U.S. exceptionalism coming from a devout, special and moral core—even more devout than the angels who persecute, manipulate, torture and murder humans. The entities that are supposed to be "on our side" turn against humans—much like the institutions of capitalism that were supposed to deliver prosperity but only delivered crisis and an economic crash. This is paired with an underclass and an evangelical morality that has been dismissed and diminished, even hidden from contemporary consciousness, but that Sam and Dean and their fellow hunters embody: protectors against moral and social decline.

There is also a significant class-based shift with the traditional working-class affiliations of Democrats swapping to Republican. Those with lower or limited education that might have once made up the working classes and now increasingly the working poor, now align themselves with the party of big business. This may be related to the uncomplicated ideologies offered up by Republicans to explain and solve social crises reduced into rhetoric advancing better/more efficient economic management and annihilation of enemies. But it is also fundamentally connected to the failure of the left to provide a rigorous and righteous intervention into the exploitative global practices that have created the precariat underclasses. The nuances of diversity, identity politics, and tolerance ring hollow for workers being laid off as a result of widespread deindustrialization. All they want is a return to stability where an honest day's work did result in an honest day's pay. What these working classes see is that respect for difference and tolerance of diversity has lost them their living wage and done nothing to improve social conditions. Steve Hall and Simon Winlow (2013) demonstrate the specific "social distance between subjects who were forced to engage every day in a socioeconomic struggle against each other in a shrinking economy" (82), adding further credibility to their assertion that "there is no 'natural' connection between working-class life and right-wing politics" (Hall, Winlow, and Treadwell 11). Rather, this connection has been born out of a rampant neoliberalism motivated by accelerated capitalism and a failing left that refuses to articulate the conditions experienced by millions of working-class and working poor people across the U.S. and instead champions the rights of the "other": immigrants, multiculturalism, LGBTQI etc. And understanding the nuanced economic, military, classed and powerful structures that have systemically impoverished ordinary people is exhausting, soul destroying and crushing work; to see how the very system that is supposed to support them has dramatically failed, been neglected, or even manipulated to the benefit of the powerful takes its toll. Donald Trump and the Republicans offer simple solutions—a return to halcyon days—to make America great again. It is binarized, displaced blame, and shrouded in boosterism—easy to identify with and adopt when all is lost.

Neoliberalism liberated the working classes, ushering in an era of unprecedented prosperity in the 1990s, seen as a "golden age" (Horsley 2). Though in reality, this was funded by credit and facilitated investors and rentier capitalists instead of workers earning a wage. Yet the perception remained and therefore the neoliberal juggernaut was not seen as the enemy but rather, was seen as the solution—a way out of the quagmire and back to the halcyon days of less regulation, more market freedom, smaller government—as if this offers some magical and equal playing field that nestles quietly and easily into the free-enterprise and individual spirit of the U.S. as a special and exceptional nation that has divine success and status.

Sam and Dean Winchester represent this wholesome working-class earnestness, honesty and common sense. Their solutions to crises are simple. It is to be found in their identities as white working-class men who act from a place of righteousness and clarity. Consider, for instance, the hunter Gordon's explanation for why he "love[s] this life" of the hunter: "It's all black and white. There's no maybe. Find the bad thing, kill it. You see, most people spend their lives in shades of grey. 'Is this right, is that wrong?' Not us" ("Bloodlust," 2.03) This attitude confirms a binarized and coherent rendering of the world and the universe, good and evil, monsters and humans. Sam and Dean act within this space. They are confronted with evil and they destroy it. This clarity, the Old Testament biblical righteousness for the supernatural elements of the show, combined with the marginalization of religions outside of Christianity as deviant, as well as a strong working-class ethic of white heterosexual masculinity conveyed through violent defense of humanity, all serve to situate a structure for explaining high levels of Republican viewership. However, the show is also successful because it is "able to forward a Catholic version of Christianity without being a Catholic show" (Engstrom and Valenzano 81). It taps into the icons of religion that are deployed within filmic and televisual conventions, but also offers space for the dominance of the evangelical exceptionalism that is core within Protestantism. In an age in which mainstream television deploys "a self-censorship of overt depictions of religious faiths" (Valenzano 553) so as not to offend viewers, *Supernatural* saturates itself in Christian mythology and iconography tempered with an American humanism. The ambivalence and nuance with which these meanings are constructed and deployed are at the core of what opens space for multiple readings and viewerships of what appears to be a strongly heterosexist, masculine and conservative text. *Supernatural* is not afraid to call attention to its own construction and call upon the intelligence and media literacy of its viewers. Spaces inside and outside the text flow through the readings and meanings deployed. Play with reality and fiction also punctuate the trajectory of the show. The actors who play Sam and Dean are situated within a celebrity discourse that bleeds into the show. Their attractiveness is both overtly and subtly deployed within the discourse, and it also reflexively engages with the core demographic of the CW: young (heterosexual) women. This is perhaps not an anomaly within an industry defined by celebrity and beauty, but it is more connected to women than men on mainstream television. Both Jensen Ackles (Dean Winchester) and Jared Padalecki (Sam Winchester) represent idealized archetypes of white heterosexual working class masculinity. It is an aesthetic that the show recognizes and deploys, as is reflected in this exchange from "Tall Tales" (2.15):

STARLA: My God, you are attractive!
DEAN: Thanks. But no time for that now. You need to tell me about this urban
    legend. Please? Lives are at stake.
STARLA: [*staring at Dean*] I'm sorry, I just … I can't even concentrate. It's like
    staring … into the sun.

Such dialogue is just one example of the delightfully rollicking and joyful reflexivity of *Supernatural*. The stark contrast between the somber and sedate biblical absolutes of the *Supernatural* world and the hyperbole within which Sam and Dean often confront it is a source of complexity and celebration that might explain its popular ranking by Democrats.

While the Democratic party does not have such a high percentage of those who align themselves with religion, PEW data does show that 55 percent of Democrats believe in God (with absolute certainty), and that 21 percent are "fairly certain," making 76 percent of those affiliating with the Democrat party believers, compared to a combined score of 90 percent in the Republican party. Both parties score strongly on belief in Hell with 80 percent for Republicans and 66 percent for Democrats. This confluence is no doubt due to the strength of the belief that the "United States was founded as, and continues to be a Christian nation" (Fea 9), supported by the post–World War II initiatives of adding "the words 'under God' to the Pledge of Allegiance, and to place the words 'In God We Trust' on U.S. coins and paper currency" (48). Yet, while 47 percent of Republicans hold that there is an absolute standard for right and wrong, only 23 percent of Democrats share such a belief. This flexibility is mirrored in the greater diversity of identities that affiliate with the Democratic Party. Significant numbers of women, Black, Hispanic and Asian people identify as Democrat, contrasted with an overwhelming homogenous whiteness of Republicans. This diversity of identity and outlook spotlights a complexity of perspectives and a deeper nuance that works in contrast to the binarized Old Testament constructs within *Supernatural*.

The serious Apocalyptic events, exorcisms, possessions, violence, murder and torture that punctuate *Supernatural* belie the irreverent subversions. The show is intertextual, perverse, emotional, and funny. The jokes in the show play on generic conventions and poke fun at television as an entertainment system. There are numerous in-jokes and references to other popular media as well as plays on constructs of race, class, gender and sexuality. While Sam and particularly Dean operate to ground and reify a stable white, heterosexual masculinity, when the show chooses to upend this grounding it does so in ways that are ironic, playful and celebratory, rather than ridiculing or malicious. *Supernatural* is full of self-deprecation, irony, and complexity that works to break down the distinctions between representation and reality, producers and audiences, actors and fans, genres and conventions. It pulls back the curtain and offers a peek at the unruly meanings, memories and moments that comprise the everyday. Therefore, a dual ethic exists: one of finality, clarity and absolutes, and the other of plurality, inversions, perversions and struggle over meaning. The main characters embody both tropes. Dialogue conveys both an intense conservatism and a radical inversion. Narrative constructs follow the conventions of television, and then play with them, calling attention to and perverting them.

Dean Winchester embodies a conventional, hard and heroic masculinity while Sam Winchester conveys an intellectual, sensitive and intuitive one. There is a litany of popular culture references from across a broad spectrum of contemporary and historic texts both within the horror genre and outside of it. Rock and roll music is presented as a core literacy, while the male tropes attached to it are also parodied. A running joke within the series is the aliases adopted by the brothers as they impersonate various agencies of authority to gain access to crime scenes. Most often they present themselves as FBI agents with names mined from popular culture, as this partial list of their aliases attests:

Ford and Hamill (Harrison Ford and Mark Hamill from *Star Wars*)
Bachman and Turner (Bachman Turner Overdrive)
Campbell and Raimi (*Evil Dead* series)
Angus and Young (AC/DC)
Tyler and Perry (Aerosmith)
Babar and Stanwyck (Barbara Stanwyck)
Smith and Wesson (gun manufacturers of the Colt pistol rival to the Winchester rifle)
Bonham and Copeland (Led Zeppelin and The Police)
Page and Plant (Led Zeppelin)
Cliff and Marley (Jimmy Cliff and Bob Marley)
Smith and Smith—no relation (*Die Hard*)
Rose and Hudson (Axl Rose and Slash)
Crosby (Dean) Stills (Sam) and Nash (Castiel)
Tandy and Lynne (Electric Light Orchestra)
Hicks and Ripley (*Aliens*)
Stark and Banner (Iron Man and The Incredible Hulk in the Marvel comics and films)
Nicks and McVie (Fleetwood Mac)
Wilson and Fisher (Heart)
Spears and Aguilera (Britney Spears and Christina Aguilera)
Gabriel and Collins (Peter Gabriel and Phil Collins)
Grohl and Cobain (Nirvana)

Elliot and Savage (Def Leppard)
Penn and DeNiro (*We're No Angels*)
Stark and Martell (*Game of Thrones*)

These plays and perversions are mapped on top of structures and conventions of comfort: predictable displays of masculinity and heroism that are then turned awkward or emotional to allow Dean and Sam to mobilize a whole range of meanings that circulate, play on and pervert their style of masculinity. Their masculinity is policed by a rejection of the feminine and the homosexual. Dean can be both sexist and homophobic. He enjoys watching pornography, goes to strip clubs, sometimes refers to women as "sweetheart" and accuses Sam of being "gay" when he displays any inner turmoil, insight or emotional repertoire. Simultaneously, these forays into the offensive are muted by a self-deprecation and embrace of the masculine as hyperreal as well as a reflexive insight into the values of brotherhood, and family. Emotional literacies are on display, and the intimacies between the brothers provide the subversive undercurrent to the overt masculine tropes. Both Sam and Dean are able to display a remarkable depth of emotional insight that simultaneously activates and counteracts the archetypal masculinity. Despite his exaggerated masculinity, for instance, Dean is able to recognize other values, as when he tells Jo Harvelle, "Jo, you've got a mother that worries about you, who wants something more for you. Those are good things. You don't throw things like that away. They might be hard to find later" ("No Exit," 2.06)—as he knows from hard experience, given that the loss of his own mother when he was a child was a formative event in his life.

Supernatural offers a diversity of identities, critiques and experiences that are not just about fighting demons and saving the world. There is a thread of rebellion, resistance and critical engagement with the contemporary that flows through embodiment, dialogue and mise-en-scène to establish an always fluctuating and fragmenting universe where truth, reality, expectations and binaries twist and turn in on themselves. Where Sam conveys an intellectual subjectivity, it is Dean's radical skewering of the everyday that offers up a subversive and redefined masculinity. He slices through the façade of sense-making to peel open the double meanings and crises of selfhood and society that circulates through power structures. The following exchanges provide examples of Dean's critiques of idealized orders:

SAM: Dad said they always had the perfect marriage.
DEAN: It wasn't perfect until after she died ["Dark Side of the Moon," 5.16].
DEAN: We're humans. And when humans want something, really, really bad ... we lie.
CASTIEL: Why?
DEAN: Because. That's how you become president ["Free to Be You and Me," 5.03].

The show plays with what it means to be alive and dead, human and non-human, empowered and disempowered. Human agency is offered to non-humans, and those that are divine behave as if they are evil. Demons, devils and outcasts are favored, and the marginal, odd and unseemly buttress the forces of evil. Authority is rejected as is divine prophecy about what is right and wrong. People as well as monsters are complicated—able to exist within multiple meanings, contexts and discourses simultaneously. Categories can be subverted and inverted. The right to exist, to be seen and coherent can be recoded in the tensions between catechism and capitalism:

> DEAN: You're a zombie.
> CLAY: I'm a taxpayer ["Dead Men Don't Wear Plaid," 5.15].

Generic conventions are inverted as elements of soap opera creep into the program via brotherly love as Sam and Dean often confess their feelings to each other in emotional displays. Furthermore, long-term additions to the core cast are rare. While Katie Cassidy (Ruby), Lauren Cohan (Bela), Mark Sheppard (Crowley), and, more recently, Mark Pellegrino (Lucifer) and Alexander Calvert (Jack) have been series regulars, the only interloper who has not only been permitted to stay any longer than a few episodes but who has also been fully embraced by fans has been Castiel, who was introduced in Season 4 and remains a fan favorite and is now a regular cast member. Castiel enjoys particular intimacy with Dean, and this connection is both emotional and physical, depicted in the hand-shaped wound Dean possessed after Castiel "gripped [him] tight and raised [him] from perdition" ("Lazarus Rising," 4.01) when he rescued Dean from Hell. This intimacy is poked and prodded as Dean summons Castiel when Sam can not:

> DEAN: C'mon, Cas. Don't be a dick. We got ourselves a … plague-like situation down here. Do you…. Do you copy? [Nothing happens]
> SAM: Like I said, the son of the bitch doesn't answer. [*Castiel appears behind Sam, Dean sees him.*] He's right behind me, isn't he?
> CASTIEL: Hello.
> SAM: [*to Cas*] So what you—you like him better or something?
> CASTIEL: Dean and I do share a more profound bond. I wasn't going to mention it ["The Third Man," 6.03].

Similarly, Balthazar's "Sorry, you have me confused with the other angel. You know, the one in the dirty trench coat who's in love with you" ("My Heart Will Go On," 6.17) comments explicitly on the erotic undertones to Dean and Cas's relationship.

This tendency to explore, evoke and provoke the relationship between intimacy and masculinity is an important part of the diegesis. Because Sam and Dean do not develop heterosexual relationships with women (and if they do, many of those women end up dead), the "romance" in the show is "bromance." There is a great deal of flexibility in these tropes with the brothers walking a thin line between the diegesis and acknowledging the fandom that exists around it. In the meta-episode "The Monster at the End of This Book" (4.18), when Sam and Dean discover that they are the subject of novels written about their adventures, they also discover fan fiction being written about them—mirroring the fandom that embraces *Supernatural*. In a nod to the fans of the show, Sam and Dean interact with this material.

> DEAN: And what's a slash fan?
> SAM: As in Sam-slash-Dean. Together.
> DEAN: Like "together" together?
> SAM: Yeah.
> DEAN: *[pause]* They do know we're brothers, right?
> SAM: Doesn't seem to matter.
> DEAN: Aw, come on, that—that's just sick! ["The Monster at the End of This Book"]

It is a trope that is peppered throughout *Supernatural*, offering a dialogue with social conventions as well as opportunities to provoke interrogation of beauty, intimacy, masculinity and queer potential. These flexibilities are counterpointed by Dean's porn-loving and women-objectifying, racially exoticizing characterization. He embraces and strains the boundaries of conventional masculinity that define him and permit the flexibilities in reading strategies around him. The following exchanges suggest the complexity of the depiction of the brothers' relationship:

> DEAN: Of course, the most troubling question is why do these people assume we're gay?
> SAM: Well, you are kind of butch. Probably think you're overcompensating.
> DEAN: *[uncomfortable chuckle]* Right ["Playthings," 2.11].

> BOBBY: You're bickering like an old married couple.
> DEAN: No, see, married couples can get divorced. Me and him? We're like, uh, Siamese twins.
> SAM: *[angry]* It's *conjoined* twins.
> DEAN: See what I mean? ["Tall Tales," 2.15]

> SAM: Dude … were you on my computer?
> DEAN: No.
> SAM: Oh really? 'Cause it's frozen now, on, uh, bustyasianbeauties.com? *[Dean says nothing]* Dean! Would you just—don't touch my stuff anymore, okay?
> DEAN: Why don't you control your OCD? ["Tall Tales," 2.15]

These constructs are punctuated by general critique of the status quo and deconstruction of the meaning systems that maintain them. These are filtered through popular culture and present nodes of disruption in contrast to the biblical fight between good and evil. These moments are not only provided by Sam and Dean but by a range of supporting characters as well, who provide points of intervention into the normalities and conventions of the *Supernatural* universe. The goddess Kali, for instance, offers this comment:

> KALI: Westerners, I swear, the sheer arrogance. You think you're the only ones on Earth? You pillage and you butcher in your God's name, but you're not the only religion, and He's not the only God. And now you think you can just rip the planet apart? You're wrong. There are billions of us, and we were here first. If anyone gets to end this world, it's me ["Hammer of the Gods," 5.19].

What all this maps is a fundamental division between viewership and political party affiliation. It is impossible to track readership from a Democratic or Republican perspective in any way that might offer nuance, or even accuracy. What can be traced is how left and right manifest in popular imagery and how they leverage power. The rise of an inflexible evangelical right wing that has placed Donald Trump into the presidency of the United States (Dick Roman in Season 7 might be seen as an anticipatory parody of the blending of the corporate and political that achieved its apotheosis with Trump's election) is based on an inability to process crisis with reflexivity and without fear. Binaries, absolutes and moral virtue provide places of refuge for the profound injustices and disturbances in the status quo. Nuance, argument, and perspective are empty vessels when social stability is upended. What is yearned for is a return to the past where the status quo ensured whiteness, heterosexuality and masculinity at the apex of power, and even if one did not occupy that position, one could aspire to some semblance of it through hard work and struggle. These strategies have been destroyed for the illusions that they are in the post-financial crisis era. The social structures are being up-ended, and we lack a popular literacy for understanding this. The left has reveled in difference and diversity, but has not connected this language to one of economy and power that is not marginalized as "Marxist" or worse, "communist." Instead, the right has colonized this with rhetoric about immigrants taking jobs. Connecting diversity, complexity and nuance into a dominant rendering of national interest has been lacking on the left. Instead, those on the left are accused of being bleeding hearts and do-gooders, unable to make these experiences relevant and potent to understanding the deep structural inequalities in the social system. The literacies of race, class, gender and sexuality that pepper the left are only present in pithy portrayals in the popular. Irreverent escapism in popular culture provides no placebo. Viewers may revel in the joyful perversions of *Supernatural*'s play with borders and boundaries, expectations and experiences, race, class, gender and sexuality. Pithy dialogue, subversive representations, double meanings, and layered intersectionality with the real and representation, masculinity and sexuality, intimacy and family, authority and resistance are empty tropes. They are moments of glee, but they lack a way forward into new meanings because they are always anchored to the old ones.

Supernatural's longevity is due in part to the fact that it offers two pathways to make sense of the world: one that is filled with sophisticated readings, multiple meanings, and radical subversion, and another that is straight and clear and unambiguous. These two pathways currently stand in for the rhetoric of Democrats and Republicans, while also playing off each other. While Democrats hail difference, complexity, and diversity, the perception of competing interests and mealy mouthed do-gooding limit real and meaningful change. On the right, the Republicans advocate for simple, clear and largely uninformed strategies for change that reify the status quo and resituate the power structures that already exist. The Democrats are unable to articulate their pathway to change and offer no real resistance or dialogue with the trajectory of the Republicans who de-complicate a world that is profoundly difficult with comforting ideals that return to a past much like the old testament that was clear, righteous and just. *Supernatural* plays between these binaries representing, challenging and changing both—offering radical reflexivities and engagements with masculinity that reaffirm whiteness and heterosexuality, violence and heroism while also subverting and rewriting these constructs through emotional literacies, intimacies, and provocative rebellion.

NOTES

1. It is important to note that while *Supernatural* began in 2005, the transition into this new trajectory in Season 4 was in 2008, the same year of the Global Financial Crash.

WORKS CITED

Blake, Aaron. "The 10 Most Loyal Demographic Groups for Republicans and Democrats." *The Washington Post*, 8 Apr. 2015, www.washingtonpost.com/news/the-fix/wp/2015/04/08/the-10-most-loyal-demographic-groups-for-republicans-and-democrats/?utm_term=.a4d58a599af7. Accessed 27 Jul. 2018.

Cervone, Jason A. *Corporatizing Rural Education: Neoliberal Globalization and Reaction in the United States.* Palgrave, 2018.

Engstrom, Erika, and Valenzano, Joseph M., III. "Demon Hunters and Hegemony: Portrayal of Religion on the CW's *Supernatural*." *Journal of Media and Religion*, vol. 9, no. 2, 2010, pp. 67–83, doi: 10.1080/15348421003738785.

EPoll Market Research. www.epollresearch.com/corp/products/escore-celebrity. Accessed 12 Jul. 2018

EPoll Market Research. "Which TV Shows Do Republicans and Democrats Rate the Highest?" 20 Jan. 2016, www.prnewswire.com/news-releases/which-tv-shows-do-republicans-and-democrats-rate-the-highest-300301143.html. Accessed 12 Jul. 2018.

Fahmy, Dalia. "Americans Are Far More Religious Than Adults in Other Wealthy Nations." *PEW Research Center*, 31 Jul. 2018, www.pewresearch.org/fact-tank/2018/07/31/americans-are-far-more-religious-that-adults-in-other-wealthy-nations/. Accessed 18 Aug. 2018.

Fea, John. *Believe Me: The Evangelical Road to Donald Trump*. William B. Eerdmans Publishing Company, 2018.

Horsley, Mark. *The Dark Side of Prosperity: Late Capitalism's Culture of Indebtedness*. Ashgate, 2015.

Luksza, Agata. "Boy Melodrama: Genre Negotiations and Gender-bending in the *Supernatural* Series." *Text Matters*, vol. 6, no. 6, 2016, pp. 177–194, doi: 10.1515/textmat-2016-0011.

Pew Research Center, "Wide Gender Gap, Growing Educational Divide in Voters' Part Identification." 20 Mar. 2018. http://www.people-press.org/2018/03/20/1-trends-in-party-affiliation-among-demographic-groups/. Accessed Aug. 18 2018.

Singer, Paul. "White Christians Decline in the U.S., but Still Dominate Republican Party." *USA Today*, 6 Sept. 2017, www.usatoday.com/story/news/politics/2017/09/06/white-christians-decline-but-still-dominate-republican-party/634536001/. Accessed 27 Oct. 2018.

Valenzano, Joseph M. "Cowboys, Angels, and Demons: American Exceptionalism and the Frontier Myth in the CW's *Supernatural*." *Communication Quarterly*, vol. 62, no. 5, 2015, pp. 552–68.

Winlow, Simon, and Steve Hall. *Rethinking Social Inclusion: The End of the Social?* Sage, 2013.

Winlow, Simon, Steve Hall and Treadwell, James. *The Rise of the Right: English Nationalism and the Transformation of Working-Class Politics*. Polity Press, 2017.

"I killed Hitler"

American Exceptionalism and Triumphalism in Supernatural

CAIT COKER

Eric Kripke has said that he was inspired by Jack Kerouac's *On the Road* (1957) to write *Supernatural*, as two men roadtrip across the U.S. and into popular myth. However, it would be more appropriate to read the show's expansive roadtrip across the country as a conservative reply to Neil Gaiman's 2001 novel *American Gods*, a fantasy that retells the history of immigration through folkloric myth along America's backroads. *Supernatural* is mythic, too, in that it recasts Christian mythology into a family drama, with explicit parallels made between God and his two favorite archangelic sons, Michael (the obedient elder) and Lucifer (the prodigal younger) and the Winchester brothers who are fated to re-enact a tragic story. However, Dean and Sam Winchester are apparently exceptional enough to rewrite the Bible (if one counts the purported "Winchester Gospels" of a future that may never materialize): they live, they die, they are resurrected, and repeat for well over a decade. Indeed, American Exceptionalism is written as the aversion of Armageddon on American soil, with Manifest Destiny revised as (Team) Free Will. *Supernatural*'s "immigrant story" focuses on white male saviors who need little more than a GED and a give 'em hell attitude. While the extra- and in-textual trappings of the show play with genre and fannish response, its textual boundaries are strictly delineated into the cultural and physical space of the continental U.S., particularly its literal and metaphorical heartland, where the norms (even the supernatural norms) are overwhelming white, heterosexual, and working class.

In the latter seasons, *Supernatural* doubles down on this rhetoric by providing a series of challenges and confirmations that reiterate specifically American Exceptionalism and triumphalism. Chuck Shurley is confirmed to be God—purely American from his "safe space" of a bar to his "World's Greatest Dad" mug, as are his angels (in contrast to the British demon/King of Hell Crowley and Irish witch Rowena)—while a new series of threats appear from overseas, including the Germanic Thule, surviving Nazis who wish to resurrect Hitler, and the British Men of Letters, who at first want to convert American hunters to their ranks and, when this fails, exterminate them. Again, the Winchesters save the world, literally killing Hitler and, later, expelling Lucifer from the body of an American President partial to Trumpisms in a rare nod to real-world politics. This essay will reread *Supernatural*'s engagement with popular culture, history, and myth as meta to explicate how it uses Sam and Dean to illustrate American Exceptionalism and triumphalism through metaphysical adventures.

(Anti)Immigrant Song

Rachel Rubin and Jeffrey Melnick's *Immigration and American Popular Culture* (2007) explores the history of American popular culture as inextricably interwoven with the succeeding phases of immigration in the 20th century, from Jewish refugees in 1930s Hollywood to global music and cyberculture movements. They explicitly link the "founding traumas" of racism and colonialism to problems of identity in popular culture, which are enacted repeatedly as a problem that must be "solved" and yet never can be. Since its inception, the United States has had conflicting attitudes towards immigration, despite the fact that, of course, all of the Founding Fathers were either immigrants themselves or their immediate descendants. Anxieties regarding succeeding waves of immigrants from across the world often take center stage in history textbooks; whether the people in question are Irish, Eastern or Western European, Chinese, or another nationality, they are always coded as a dangerous Other to the current population—at least until they are assimilated and the next wave becomes the new threat. In science fiction, fantasy, and horror, these iterations of the foreign Other often become codified as literal monsters. This pattern arguably started with Bram Stoker's novel *Dracula* (1897), in which the plot is set in motion as the titular Count purchases multiple pieces of land in England and then moves to London. Interestingly, Dracula needs the earth of his homeland to survive and ships boxes of sand and dirt from Transylvania to his new lairs; the heroes of the novel will later effectively destroy them by putting sacramental bread inside the boxes, making them useless. Most tellingly, Dracula sexually menaces the women of the novel, Lucy Westenra and Mina Harker, transforming Lucy into a vampire herself and nearly doing the same to Mina before he is destroyed by the heroes.

Monstrous immigrants also suffuse genre fantasy shows such as *Buffy the Vampire Slayer* (1997–2003) and *Constantine* (2014–2015). *Buffy* takes place on the literal borderlands of Southern California in the small town of Sunnydale (which nonetheless has an international airport and shipping dockyards). In the episode "Inca Mummy Girl" (2.04), the high school protagonists host visiting international students, with Peruvian "Ampata Gutierrez" staying with Buffy. Ampata is the avatar of an Incan princess whose remains were part of a traveling museum exhibit until she escapes, kills the real Ampata and takes his place, and must feed on the life force of others to stay alive. Though Ampata is ultimately dispatched by Buffy by episode's end, her story is presented as semi-tragic and parallel to that of our heroine: both have been taught that they must sacrifice their lives and personal happiness to save their people. By refusing to do so, Ampata becomes a villain. Her brown skin and exoticized origins contrast with the "good immigrant" Rupert Giles, an educated white man who is Buffy's mentor and teacher. Despite the feminist narrative of sharing power that the show pushes, it specifically celebrates whiteness and literally demonizes the other throughout its lengthy run. More recently, the show *Constantine*, adapted from the long-running comic *Hellblazer* (1988–2013), pitted the British white hero John Constantine against Papa Midnite, a black voudon priest who has been alive since at least before the American Revolution. Papa Midnite uses his powers to call forth spirits and control zombies for a price, but more than once, Constantine is shown to have superior knowledge of voudon magic, even explaining the importance of showing respect to ancestral African spirits to the Afro-Caribbean man.

Supernatural continues these patterns with an escalating rhetoric that reflects the show's longevity and the political landscape as it transformed across the terms of three presidents while the show has been on the air. First airing in 2005, the show began during George W. Bush's "War on Terror" with plots that drew on horror and urban legends; in 2008, its fourth season took on a newly metaphysical turn in which an ongoing War in Heaven is concurrent with the election and two terms of Barack Obama, and in late 2016 the show began to engage with real world politics in response to the Electoral College's concession to Donald Trump and his notoriously xenophobic campaign. Anxieties around immigrants, whether as humans or as supernatural entities, are an ongoing concern on the show, as are the tensions that stem periodically from the old gods and spirits of a colonized land. Indeed, as Leow Hui Min Annabeth argues in her essay on "Coloniality and the Chicana Gothic: Traveling Myths from the Pilot" (2016), these themes appear in the very first episode, when Sam and Dean encounter a spirit reminiscent of, and yet never identified as, La Llorona. La Llorona is a famous figure in the southwestern borderlands, from California to New

Mexico and into Texas, but the spirit in the pilot is mysteriously devoid of racial or ethnic identifiers. The introductory story is also bookended by the murders of women—Mary Winchester and Jessica Moore; the mystery/monster plot of the week is resolved when Dean shoots the spirit, and the ghosts of her murdered children take their mother back to the netherworld. Leow concludes that "colonialism lingers and haunts the discourse of *Supernatural* just as it does the stories" (99).

The recurring problems of colonialism, racism, and especially (violent) misogyny repeatedly inform the show's plots as well as its readings. In his essay "'All I Saw Was Evil': *Supernatural*'s Reactionary Road Trip" (2014), Brian Ireland argues that the first four seasons (2005–2009) are conspicuously reactive to post–9/11 America, from the recurring emphasis on family values (the nuclear unit represented by the lost Winchester parents) and nostalgia for a time gone by (when the brothers still had their parents and were not engaged in an everyday "war"). These underpinnings are "relentlessly conservative," Ireland says, but the "conservative tone is softened and masked by the portrayal of its two main characters as blue-collar everymen" who are "apolitical and appear tolerant of socially marginal characters" (136). "Tolerant" is probably overly kind given Dean's tendency towards homophobic and sexist language, as well as gay characters' tendency to die horribly in episodes like "Ghostfacers" (3.13) and "Dark Dynasty" (10.21). But the problem of immigrants specifically first emerges in "A Very Supernatural Christmas" (3.08) when the brothers track a series of grisly murders linked to Christmas wreaths and, seemingly, Krampus. They eventually find that the wreaths are made by Madge and Edward Carrigan, a friendly older couple that Dean likens to "Ozzie and Harriet." It turns out, however, that they are the weakened remnants of (unidentified) pagan gods who have been lying low since the rise of Christianity. Madge says, "We kept a low profile; we got jobs, a mortgage. Wh-What was that word, dear?" and Edward replies, "We assimilated." Assimilation here is about presentation, giving off the appearance of being one thing while being another; it speaks directly to anxieties as to who is "really" American, from the Red Scare of the 1950s and its anti–Communist hysteria (perhaps best invoked by the 1965 film *Invasion of the Body Snatchers*) to contemporary divisions on the Dreamers.

As seasons progress, the issue of immigrants transforms from the metaphor of "pagan gods" to actual immigrants as human beings—and whose deaths are frequently required to solve the problem of the week. In the Season 6 episode "My Heart Will Go On" (6.17), the angel Balthazar prevents the famous Titanic from sinking, saving hundreds of people and changing history. As Sam puts it, "Those people and their kids and their kids' kids, they must have interacted with—with so many other people, changed so much crap. You totally Butterfly-Effected history!" "Those people" were largely immigrants in steerage who made up the bulk of the passenger manifest and the bulk of the casualties in the disaster. The Fates try to restore the timeline by systematically killing these immigrants' descendants, before the boys convince the angels to restore the original timeline. "Those people" have thus died for the greater good of history.

"Those people" also become a single person in later episodes, specifically, Crowley's human son Gavin MacLeod. Gavin is introduced in "King of the Damned" (9.21) as he prepares for his journey to the American colonies in the early 18th century, only to be kidnapped by Abaddon. Gavin is supposed to die when the ship sinks on its voyage; his appearance in the present day has the possibility of skewing history in ways similar to the Butterfly Effect of "My Heart Will Go On," and therefore the focus is on returning him to his rightful moment in time. However, the episode ends with Crowley saving Gavin by keeping him in the modern world, hiding him from the Winchesters. He returns three years later in "Family Feud" (12.13), when the Winchesters investigate ghost-related murders, ultimately linking them to the remains of Gavin's lost ship, which are on display in a nearby museum. The vengeful spirit is Gavin's former fiancée, Fiona Duncan; alone on the ship without Gavin, she was abused and raped before the ship sank in the storm. In order to end Fiona's violence, Gavin is returned to the 18th century, where the couple live happily together before dying aboard ship. This again restores time, and the murders never happen. Again, the "happy ending" of the episode requires the deaths of people trying to emigrate to America.

Threats from Abroad

Threats from abroad beyond hopeful immigrants become of increasing concern in the later seasons of the show. In "Everybody Hates Hitler" (8.13) the plot revolves around the conflict between the descendants of Nazi necromancers known as the Thule and the slacker grandson of the last survivor of the Judah Initiative, Jewish magicians from the resistance who were allied with the Men of Letters. Aaron Bass, who inherits his grandfather's Golem, is non-practicing in both faith and magic, understanding only some Hebrew, not keeping kosher, and comically if problematically having literally smoked the "owner's manual" for the Golem, as the pages were perfect for rolling papers. In contrast, the Thule members all speak with German accents—and know enough Hebrew to put the Golem temporarily out of commission. This same episode introduces the former bunker of the American Men of Letters to the show, subsequently emphasizing the class, education, and ideological differences between them and the Hunters that will also be points of contention in the series. This plot is also parallel to the magical and intellectual decline of Aaron's family, as Sam and Dean have effectively lapsed from tradition themselves: though they remain "legacies" of the Men of Letters that their grandfather was a member of, they have grown up detached from and ignorant of these roots.

The Thule reappear in two other episodes, "The Vessel" (11.14) and "The One You've Been Waiting For" (12.05). In "The Vessel" Dean is sent back in time to retrieve a lost Hand of God in the midst of World War II, set during another conflict between the Men of Letters and the Thule. Dean meets a French Woman of Letters, Delphine Seydoux, who is preparing to deliver the artifact to the Allies, but Dean convinces her to give it to him instead as it is needed in the future. Agreeing to this, she uses its power to destroy both the American submarine they are on and the German destroyer that is pursuing them in accordance with the timeline of the past. The episode emphasizes that the moral necessity of defeating Nazis is worth whatever the sacrifice. In "The One You've Been Waiting For," the Thule seek to resurrect Hitler—and succeed. Hitler is both comical and evil, giggling about buying "doggies" to feed his enemies to and loving modern technology. "I sold 10 million copies of *Mein Kampf*," he says, "What do you think I can do with Twitter?" (This line is a possible nod to then American President-Elect Trump; more on that below.) After the obligatory fight, Dean kills Hitler for good, first with a bullet to the head and later by burning the body. "I killed Hitler! I killed Hitler!" he repeats with disbelieving glee, "I think that entitles me to free drinks for the rest of my life. I'm gonna get t-shirts made!" In fact, a number of t-shirts, both licensed and not, have been made for sale on this very theme. Dean also brags about this feat throughout the rest of the season, to many characters' disbelief and bemusement.

What is particularly notable about the Thule is the low profile that they maintained for decades; when Dean calls fellow Hunter Garth Fitzgerald to see if he has heard anything about them, neither research nor his contacts turn up any information. Like the menace of the unnamed pagan gods, the Thule have effectively assimilated into modern society, patiently waiting for the right moment to return to power. Though the Winchesters seemingly kill all of the remaining Thule High Command in "The One You've Been Waiting For," it's hard to believe that they are truly gone for good, especially when they seem adept at hiding in plain sight both in Europe and in the U.S.

The other threat from abroad that the Winchesters must tangle with are the British Men of Letters; their conflict takes up the majority of the 12th season. While it is unclear whether the American branch seceded from the British, or the British from the American, by 2016 they are effectively set to enter the U.S. with the explicit purpose of either converting or killing American Hunters. They claim to have been keeping tabs on the Winchesters since they averted the Apocalypse, but only chose to interfere after the chaos that was spawned when Dean freed Amara/The Darkness. Their organization, Lady Toni Bevell assures Sam (while also torturing him) in "Keep Calm and Carry On" (12.01), is a massive, high-tech security group that has all of Britain warded. "There hasn't been a monster-related death in Britain since 1965 because we are good at our job," she claims, and proceeds to demand information about the American Hunters so that they can "teach" them how to "make America safe." When the episode first aired in October 2016, this line had a particular political resonance to the rhetoric of then-candidate Donald Trump. Viewed afterwards, it seems to foreshadow many of the explicit references the show will go on to make.

Bevell's assumptions regarding how the Hunters function are striking, couched as they are in the language of international intelligence operations: amongst other questions, she demands to know the "organizational hierarchy" of Hunters, the location of dead drops, and a list of names. As we know, even if she doesn't, American Hunters work as independent free agents, their network connections limited to friend-of-a-friend meetings. They are also largely blue-collar workers who live in rural areas. In contrast, Lady Bevell and Arthur Ketch are coded as upper-class, and all British Men of Letters attend the Kendricks Academy in London, a sort of Hogwarts institution with an emphasis on occult lore and fighting skills. Indeed, Mick Davies is conspicuous as one of the only non-upper-class members in the association, as shown in "The British Invasion" (12.17). The British Men of Letters, it becomes apparent, view everyone not like them as a threat. In "Who We Are" (12.22), the Winchesters gather together a small band of Hunters, including Jody Mills, to take the offensive to the British command base on American soil. Sam explains to them that, as seductive as the British tech and training systems are, they

> want control. They want to live in a world where they can sit in some office and decide who gets to live and who gets to die. And they've killed people. They've killed innocent people just because they got in the way. They think the ends justify the means. But we know better. We know hunting isn't just about killing. It's about doing what's right, even when it's hard. So we go by our gut, right? We play by our own rules, and that scares them. That's why they want us dead, 'cause we're the one thing they can't control.

The British Men of Letters functionally represent colonial and corporate genocide, willing and able to kill all of the American Hunters along with American monsters. This is of course made problematic by most of the American Hunters being white and male (of the 64 Hunters seen/referenced on the show, 40 are white men, 17 are women, and seven are people of color, as the "Hunter" superwiki page documents), versus the British having a few people of color on their side. The Hunters' "rules" have an unfortunate tendency towards, as we have seen, something like white supremacy. While Sam's speech is meant to invoke the classic American idealism for freedom—alongside the other favored narrative that comes to mind with American versus the British forces from the Revolution, that of the Biblical David and Goliath—it reinforces the other stereotypical messages regarding threats from abroad as being inherently inimical to American citizens. Though later seasons portray Arthur Ketch as more of an ally to the Winchesters, it is at the expense of his competence: In "Exodus" (13.22) he is disarmed by the rampaging angels of the Apocalypse World, and later he is made the butt of a joke in "The Spear" (14.09) in which he makes the dubious decision to send one of the only weapons useful against the Archangel Michael to the team by mail. To the Winchesters' and Castiel's dismay, he states confidently that he "paid extra: Certified priority express!" This scene speaks to the tradition in American cinema of having the British be comically inept when they aren't evil, thus neutralizing their "foreignness."

Threats from Within: Trumpism Hits Home?

Ideological threats from within are coded differently than those from abroad. In some cases, they become jokes, as when the archangel Raphael is introduced to Castiel in "The Man Who Would Be King" (6.20). He is sitting in Ken Lay's Heaven, gazing thoughtfully at a portrait of President George W. Bush with an American bald eagle and an unfurled American flag rippling majestically in the breeze. When he demands that Castiel "pledge allegiance" to him, Castiel comments that he "still questions [Lay's] admittance," to which Raphael responds with the slightest of shrugs, "He's devout. Trumps everything." Lay was of course a close friend of the Bush family, founder of the Enron company and inextricably bound up with its massive bankruptcy scandal. Humor aside, he is an analog for machinations on both sides of the Angelic War, from backdoor deals to a manufactured conflict for power to the inflationary creation of souls needed for ammunition. It is worth noting that this implicit criticism was written into the show a safe three years after the end of Bush's tenure in office rather than during it.

In more recent seasons of *Supernatural*, these threats from within are also read as explicitly political. Perhaps most telling is the episode "LOTUS" (12.8), in which Lucifer possesses American President Jefferson Rooney, pitting the Winchesters against the U.S. government. In a meeting with aides, the Lucifer-in-Chief responds to a question about international relations and whether to contact the U.N. by saying, "That or we can just go ahead and nuke 'em." The exchange is a clear reference to then President-Elect Donald Trump, who single-handedly raised the specter of nuclear war for the first time in decades as both a candidate and a sitting official. While the "real" President Rooney is a textbook conservative who likes to read from the Bible and have sexual affairs with secretaries, President Lucifer likes to privately order the torture and deaths of American citizens "off the radar." Of course, Lucifer likes the sex too; it's unclear if he had planned to impregnate Kelly Kline from the beginning or if he was only inspired when she told him he would "make an amazing father." However, what is particularly notable about these episodes is how they take the stereotype of the corrupt government official not only for granted, but repurpose it for specific commentary on the real world outside of the show in the present.

Another 12th season episode, "American Nightmare" (12.04), plays on and subverts the same nostalgia for the "American dream" that the show's early seasons had canonized. Here Sam and Dean investigate the death of a Child Protective Services worker, and initially assume she was murdered by her Wiccan coworker. This initial storyline speaks to the religious anxieties that have preoccupied rural America for decades, the threat posed by literal witches to a Christian God-fearing populace. That this version of puritanical Christianity bears so little resemblance to that practiced in the rest of the world is not coincidental; American Evangelical Protestantism historically has very little to do with other branches in precepts. The twist in the story is that the death was an accident caused by an imprisoned psychic child begging for help: Sam and Dean have to rescue the girl, Magda Peterson, from her own ultra-religious family who are keeping her prisoner while telling the public she has died. Concurrent to this storyline, the boys must deal with their growing estrangement—by her choice—from their own mother, Mary, as she grapples with her return from the dead and her adult children. The happy nuclear family is an ideal and not a reality; indeed, reality asserts that sometimes the nuclear family is better off apart rather than together. Children should not be forced to stay with abusive parents; sometimes the federal government absolutely *should* interfere in the private family's lives; members of minority religions are not to blame for shocking crimes.

A year later, a 13th season episode comments on the increasing oligarchy of the American government. In "Breakdown" (13.11), the boys' investigation of a series of disappearances reveals that an FBI agent has been both covering up and acting as a dealer in selling human body parts. The episode also aired only months after the conclusion of an extensive exposé on the underground body part trade by Reuters journalists that was published serially between October and December 2017 (see Grow et al). When Sam is captured, FBI agent Terrance Clegg provides the obligatory evil mono-logue explaining why he does what he does:

> How many monsters do you think are out there, Sam? … See, those freaks that you and your brother chase, those are just the ones that can't pass, either because they're too mean or they're too stupid, or both. But most monsters, hell, they could be your next door neighbor. They work a regular job, mow the lawns on a Saturday. And they need to eat, which is where I come in.

As it happens, the easiest people to "disappear" are minorities; those kid-napped, menaced and/or murdered on screen include a Hispanic man and a young white woman. Predatory white men in power abusing those vulnerable to our society is nothing new, exactly, but the ways in which bystanders can "assist" are—in this case a young white male gas station clerk, Marlon, who identifies possible victims and then enjoys watching the auctions and dis-memberment online. Marlon's predilection for this kind of snuff is analogous to the real world of online trolls, and his description of the site as "like eBay, kinda" presents it within the norms of digital commerce. Marlon enables the worst impulses of others online as an everyday sort of monster—literal as well as metaphorical—when he is revealed to be a vampire at the end.

Another Season 13 episode, "Scoobynatural" (13.16), plays with every-day monsters—and Trumpism—in an unexpected format: through an ani-mated crossover with *Scooby-Doo*. Framed by a live action plot in which a shady real-estate developer uses a real ghost to scare away shop-owners so he can buy land cheaply, the Winchesters encounter the Scooby gang and spectacularly deconstruct the tropes of both shows. As he is arrested, Jay, the crook, even yells at the brothers, "And I would have gotten away with it, too, if it wasn't for those meddling kids!" The episode also aired only days after the massive March for Our Lives protests were held across the country (and world) and just as Robert Mueller began handing out indict-ments in his legal probes; "those meddling kids" continuing to hamper the agenda of another shady real-estate developer in real life. A few weeks later in "Bring 'Em Back Alive" (13.18), a frustrated Lucifer sits on the throne of Heaven, frustrated by the lack of worship from both humans and angels, before storming away in disgust. In case the parallels weren't clear, by "Exo-dus," Lucifer dismisses the "stories" of his evil intentions as "Fake news!" and explains to Jack that God and the angelic family are a dysfunctional but powerful group, just like "the Tudors, the Trumps, [and] the Jackson Five." Finally, in the season finale "Let the Good Times Roll" (13.23), the boys explain to the alternate universe refugees the problems of their Earth, con-cluding with "Businessman billionaire mogul turned President, embroiled in yet another controversy." Bobby baldly responds, "Let me get this right […] that damn fool idjit from *The Apprentice* is President, and you call where we come from 'Apocalypse World'?"

The willingness to take Trump on directly in these episodes is especially noteworthy given that this also introduces a minor plot hole between our real world and the Winchesters' fictional one. Though President Bush is "seen" in an image from Season 6 and President Barack Obama is referenced in "Time After Time" (7.12) and "Paper Moon" (10.04), it is unclear how and when the fictional "President Rooney" of "LOTUS" came to replace him, nor how and when Rooney was replaced by Trump. While *Supernatural* isn't exactly known for its continuity, it *is* known for its metatextual commentary, but the usages here seem to mark a new era for political relevance—and something like conservative reclamation—for the show.

Conclusions: A Melting Pot of Myth?

The choices *Supernatural* has made in recent years underscore ongoing political anxieties in American culture. America is itself its own kind of myth; as Odin notes in the televised version of *American Gods* ("Head Full of Snow," 1.03, May 14, 2017), America is "the only country in the world that wonders what it is…. I mean, no one wonders about the heart of Norway or goes searching for the soul of Mozambique. Mozambique knows what it is. They all know what they are." The human America of *Supernatural* has a tripartite identity: the blue collar, rural, working class that engages with monsters on a daily basis; the suburban middle class that is largely oblivious yet consistently under siege; and the powerful upper class and government officials who are complicit. At the same time, America's Exceptionalism and triumphalism are continuously confirmed through Dean and Sam's adventures; they are the only ones who can consistently save the world from angels, demons, and the very gods themselves.

The mythic America, however, is seemingly disempowered: Does it make sense that the Native American gods and monsters, from Cacao to the Wendigo, that we see are lesser than the "true" Judeo-Christian God that is Chuck, in all his nebbish white male fragility? Or that other cultures and histories are erased altogether under the vaguely broad umbrella of "pagan lore"? The show makes a gesture at solving this problem in the fifth season episode "Hammer of the Gods" (5.19) when surviving deities that include Baldur, Kali, Mercury, and Zao Shen hold a makeshift convention at an out-of-the-way hotel to address the looming Apocalypse, and wonder what they need to do about it. The episode is reminiscent of a sequence in Gaiman's *American Gods*, as Odin takes center stage at the proceedings to the bemusement to members of the other pantheons. Ideologically, both scenes are about much-diminished gods trying to survive in the modern world; in both stories, a bloodbath ensues in which many gods meet their permanent death. However, in Gaiman's version, the gods kill one another on equal terms, while in *Supernatural*, the angels kill the gods with significantly greater powers. The text of the show demonstrates that as far as the writers considered, Chuck and the angels have power that the other entities simply do not. In both *Supernatural* and *American Gods*, powerful beings require human belief and worship in order to survive; consequently, those figures who are deemed purely "mythological" continue to live on in increasingly mortal forms with mortal limitations. That *Supernatural* contains a "real" God whose power does not wax and wane but remains stable if stagnant pushes against Gaiman's multiplicity.

Further, the show seems to ape the *American Gods* adaptation itself deliberately in "Unfinished Business" (13.20). In this episode, Gabriel makes his semi-triumphant return in an episode homage to Tarantino's *Kill Bill*, as he goes on a vengeful killing spree against the Norse demigods that sold him out to Asmodeus. The visual appearances of Fenrir, Sleipnir, and Narfi recall those of the *American Gods* portrayals of Mad Sweeney, Media, and Czernobog respectively. In the end, Gabriel (and the Winchesters) kill the demigods, even as he dismisses "the whole Norse pantheon" as "its own weird thing. Think of 'em more like, uh, god-begotten monsters." In case we were in doubt, non–Judeo-Christian beings are just more fodder to the Winchesters and their allies.

Supernatural's story, therefore, is not just the roadtrip of two brothers saving people and hunting things, but of American ascendance writ large. American ascendance, however, is predicated on the problematic grounds of white supremacy, colonialism, Christian theocracy, and corrupt government. In short, the show engages with the exact problems that haunt the politics of today, making Sam and Dean's adventures (and misadventures) potently relevant to an audience that may, or may not, be aware of the real monsters that surround them.

Works Cited

Cerone, Daniel, and David S. Goyer, developers. *Constantine*. Ever After/Phantom Four Productions, 2014–2015. CW. Television.
Fuller, Bryan, and Michael Green, developers. *American Gods*. Living Dead Guy Productions, 2017.
Gaiman, Neil. *American Gods*. William Morrow, 2001.
Grow, Brian, John Schiffman, et al. "The Body Trade: A Reuters Series." Reuters.com. October 24, 2017–December 27, 2017. www.reuters.com/investigates/section/usa-bodies/. Accessed 16 Feb. 2018.
"Head Full of Snow." *American Gods: Season 1*. Lionsgate, 2017. DVD.
"Hunter." *Supernatural Wiki*. http://supernatural.wikia.com/wiki/Hunter. Accessed 29 Dec. 2018.
"Inca Mummy Girl." *Buffy the Vampire Slayer: The Complete Second Season*. Writ. Matt Kiene and Joe Reinkemeyer. Dir. Ellen S. Pressman. Warner Brothers, 2017. DVD.

Invasion of the Body Snatchers. Writ. Daniel Mainwaring (based on a story by Jack Finney). Dir. Don Siegel. Republic Pictures, 1956. DVD.

Ireland, Brian. "'All I Saw Was Evil': *Supernatural*'s Reactionary Road Trip." *A History of Evil in Popular Culture: What Hannibal Lecter, Stephen King, and Vampires Reveal About America. V. 1, Evil in Film, Television and Music*, edited by Sharon Packer and Jody W. Pennington, Praeger, 2014, pp. 125–138.

Leow, Hui Min Annabeth. "Coloniality and the Chicana Gothic: Traveling Myths from the Pilot." *The Gothic Tradition in Supernatural*, edited by Melissa Edmundson, McFarland, 2016, pp. 91–102.

Rubin, Rachel, and Jeffrey Melnick. *Immigration and American Popular Culture*. New York University Press, 2007.

Stoker, Bram. *Dracula*. Archibald Constable and Company, 1897.

Dean's *Yellow Fever*

Acts of Forgery in Genre

CAMILLE DEBOSE

Horror, fantasy, and science fiction all contain narrative elements which diverge from what is possible in our everyday world. The rules of reality are broken in various ways in all three genres. They share the use of ontological rupture in their narrative, but they diverge in their core intent. Horror is produced to create fear in its audience (Butler 20). Science Fiction tends to explore ethical questions related to our use of, or reliance upon, technology. What we refer to as fantasy, David Butler argues, is more an impulse than a genre; citing Kathryn Hume, Butler discusses fantasy and mimesis as the two primary impulses of literature undertaken as a need to play or modify our realities (Butler 41). Based on his survey of fantasy films in *Empires of the Imagination*, Alec Worley has identified four categories of fantasy film: fantasy films, Earthbound fantasy, heroic fantasy, and epic fantasy. On the Worley scale, *Supernatural* qualifies as an Earthbound fantasy. The adventures and trials experienced by the brothers take place, for the most part (with occasional detours into unearthly realms such as Heaven, Hell, and Purgatory), in a world which closely resembles our own in look as well as socio-political context. Even when the episode narratives are post–Apocalyptic, that world is still ours transformed and traumatized. There are clear elements of horror in the narrative consistent with the "monster of the week" format of the show. The sub-genre of fantasy-horror into which we might fit the show creates the boundaries of narrative and performance expectations.

The scenery and setting of *Supernatural* is, in the Deleuzian sense, organic: "the setting described is presented as independent of the description which the camera gives it, and stands for a supposedly pre-existing reality" (Deleuze 126). While all episodes except the pilot episode of *Supernatural* have been filmed in Canada, the image presented each week is

"Anytown, USA." We may be shown a haunted house in Iowa, a revival-ist tent in Kentucky, seedy motels in Maine, and various locations in between. This organic presentation works to establish the sensory con-text of each scene. Many of the fantasy elements of each episode are transcribed upon the bodies of the characters as opposed to transform-ing the space.[1] The space within the frame is often dominated by Amer-icana. The mise-en-scène of *Supernatural* works to establish the show as a hyper-masculine, all–American, monster of the week narrative. Vast stretches of open road are occasionally interrupted by diners which seem pulled from the American '70s and service stations that require a trip inside to pay for your fuel. There are no credit card readers in these stations. Dean's beloved, black '67 Impala is the consistent means of travel from one adventure to the next, carrying them along our great American highways. The politics of the scenery is underscored by Dean's rejection of modernity. The Impala functions as a metallic embodiment of "true" American mascu-linity. It is a "muscle car" unsullied and untainted by the politically correct softening of the new millennium. Dean drives fast and only plays classic rock. In one episode he tears out an iPod dock which Sam has seen fit to install in the car. Dean tosses the iPod from the car in disgust as they travel down yet another dark road. The roads are the Euclidian space which corre-sponds to the hodological space the brothers traverse.

The more mundane aspects of the show imbue the fantastic narrative with a sense of plausibility. The brothers so often do what most of us do when traveling long distances on the highway. They stop for gas. They also stop for food and supplies. For *Supernatural*, like the image, the narration is also organic, consisting of "the development of sensory-motor schemata as a result of which the characters react to situations or act in such a way as to disclose the situations. This is a truthful narration in the sense that it claims to be true […]" (Deleuze 127). The way that *Supernatural* tells us what it is through genre, mise-en-scène, and organic narration allows for very particular representations of the false. "If one considers performance an affective and sensational force that disrupts, redirects, and indeed affects narrative form, it is difficult to consign the affective-performative to stable and well-defined generic paradigms" (Herzog 140). Herzog, referencing E. del Rio, complicates our considerations of genre by suggesting performance within the frame has the power to disrupt narrative convention. This dis-ruptive power destabilizes the generic identity of the narrative lending it a degree of elasticity (Herzog 140).

In this essay, let us consider genre as the source of generic identity. Genre not only tells the audience what the show is about, it also tells the audience who the show is about. In this case, *Supernatural* is about two brothers who hunt monsters on a seemingly endless American road trip (even when, in later seasons, they acquire the Bunker as a base of operations, the basic formula of constant travel to solve cases continues). Those two brothers, particularly Dean, are rendered as white, heterosexual, ruggedly masculine, emotionally conflicted, adult males. Herzog suggests we might "view genre as maintaining a certain productive function in films, creating patterns and expectations that provide the foundation for counter-rhythms and deviations" (Herzog 140). In "Yellow Fever" (4.06) Jensen Ackles's performance of Dean provides just such a counter-rhythm, working to disrupt the performative and narrative expectations of the show while simultaneously creating a Deleuzian forgery which supports, clarifies, and remakes the narrative, moving it from organic to crystalline and back again.

Performance and Narrative Flux

The episode opens with Dean running full out while dressed in a suit. Regular viewers understand the suit as a costume within a costume. The brothers dress in suits when they are posing as government agents. It is a performance within the performance, but such layering is expected in this particular show. As he runs, Dean has a look of abject terror on his face. The soundscape is dominated by his labored, terrified breathing, bombastic horror drums, and the sound of a large dog barking. This scene repeats later in the narrative (we begin in medias res), and it is crystalline in its description of the cinematic world of the show. For Deleuze, crystalline description "stands for its object, replaces it, both creates and erases it—and constantly gives way to other descriptions which contradict, displace, or modify the preceding ones" (Deleuze 126). The aggressive barking in particular seems to be a bit of aural trickery when placed at the beginning of the episode. As he runs, Dean shouts a warning—"Run. It'll kill you!"—at a vagrant who glances at Dean warily as his gaze, and the camera, shift down to a small Yorkshire terrier with a pink bow in its fur. It is not disruptive enough that Dean is afraid of and running from a small dog. The gender politics of this particular show make it notable that Dean is afraid of a very small dog with a relatively large, pink bow, which works in stark relief to Dean's expected machismo and confusing lack of aggression. As the scene transitions, text on the screen places us 43 hours earlier, lending some context (but not clarity) to the opening scene. The brothers, dressed in their "agent" suits, meet with a local sheriff, Al Britton, about a case they are working. During the conversation the sheriff mentions the local sports team name. Dean, in a sophomoric display, snickers.

SAM: We understand some of your men found his body.
SHERIFF: They did. Me and Frank—we were friends. Hell. We were Game Cocks.

Dean chuckles, then regains his composure at the Sheriff's serious expression.

SHERIFF: That's our softball team's name.
DEAN: Mmm.
SHERIFF: They're majestic animals.

Dean is left speechless. The scene plays beautifully in its absurdity, but it also firmly establishes the show within its genre context. Within the first five minutes of the episode we are given gross out humor (Sam gets squirted in the face with "spleen juice"), and juvenile sexual innuendo all playing against the backdrop of a mysterious, suspected supernatural, death. The image and narration are completely consistent with the expected codes of the show, thereby creating the conditions whereby forgery can take place. For Herzog, "forgery provides a productive model for thinking about films, and filmmakers, who mutate and exploit preexisting codes and expectations. We might locate acts of forgery on the registers of sound, decor, colour, framing, and dialogue" (Herzog 142). *Supernatural*, narratively and aesthetically, functions within familiar territory creating the conditions in which the show can be deterritorialized.

I would extend Herzog's thoughts by also including bodily performance as a possible site of forgery. The introductory scene with the Sheriff not only re-affirms our expectations of Sam and Dean but it also begins to build and contextualize masculinity in the narrative. Early in the episode Dean begins to exhibit what is, for him, strange behavior. He avoids walking near a group of kids saying that he doesn't like "the look of them," but his stance, stride, and demeanor are still quintessentially Dean as he side-eyes the children. Sam's reaction shot underscores the strangeness of Dean's behavior. In fact, Sam's responses and facial reactions to Dean's behavior throughout the episode work to highlight the "wrongness" of Dean's actions, as if Sam is the viewer's collaborator. His reactions are our reactions. This is the beginning of a bodily performance that is meant to be, not believable, but disruptive. Or, perhaps we could assert that the performance is meant to be believably disruptive. Ackles's performance does not strike the viewer as a failure whereby we are shaken from the narrative only to be reminded that Dean is not real and is simply a character played by an actor. Instead, here Ackles incrementally unmakes Dean while simultaneously creating him anew without causing a breach in our engagement with the narrative.

The scene transitions to the brothers interviewing the victim's neighbor, Mark Hutchins, who seems to be a collector of exotic reptiles. In a nod to American popular culture, Hutchins remarks upon Dean and Sam's fake agent names: "Tyler and Perry. Just like Aerosmith." Such references to American popular culture of a particular era recur throughout the series. Later, Hutchins reveals the name of the large snake he is holding as well as a second which slithers across Dean: "Don't be scared of Donny. He's a sweetheart. It's Marie you gotta look out for. She smells fear." The snakes are clearly named for Donny and Marie Osmond, stars of an eponymous American variety show from the late 70s (*Donny & Marie*, 1976–79). It is here that Ackles's performance of fear becomes boldly apparent. His embodiment of fear becomes so overwhelming he is barely the character *Dean* as he cringes in silent terror while Marie the snake slithers across his leg. The camera frames him in a medium shot so we can see the snake on his leg. Then we are shown a close-up of Dean's face as he becomes rigid with fear.

An even larger spotlight illuminating the wrongness of Dean's character occurs in the next scene wherein Dean is driving his iconic, black Impala, very slowly.

SAM: Dude. You're going 20.
DEAN: And?
SAM: That's the speed limit.
DEAN: What? Safety's a crime now?

Sam looks away, perplexed but resigned. Throughout the series Dean is presented as a character who is an aggressive mix of cautious and cavalier. His caution usually manifests in ensuring that he and his brother are well armed. Once armed, he rushes headlong into danger. In "Yellow Fever" we are presented with a Dean who is risk-averse in word and deed. As they continue on slowly, we are shown the sign for the hotel, their destination, but Dean drives past it:

SAM: Dude, where are you going? That was our hotel.
DEAN: Sam, I'm not gonna make a left-hand turn into oncoming traffic. I'm not suicidal.

Once again, Sam's reaction shot works to underscore the oddness of Dean's behavior. But in a strange moment of metacognitive luminance, Dean himself points it out as well: "Did I just say that? That was kind of weird." Then he laughs nervously, seeming unsure of himself. It is here that their "EMF" detector alerts them that there is something supernaturally wrong with Dean, as he screams, "Am I haunted?!," offering a second ontological break.[2] The show itself offers a primary ontological break by asserting witches, demons, angels, vampires, etc., as all *normal* parts of its narrative framework (Fowkes 5). This second ontological break occurs through Ackles's performance of a supernaturally plagued Dean. This now allows a particular openness to the narrative as well as the performance of Dean. Ackles is no longer bound by the expected performance of Dean. He is no longer required to deliver a "red-blooded, All–American," fearless, junk food eating carnivore. We are asked to believe the unbelievable, which is Dean, afraid. This is critical, because the humor and cohesiveness of the episode all rest upon the performance of, and forgery of, Dean.

The actor's role is to embody the character, and character is constructed through action. The actor must fulfill this role by creating truthful behaviors, as Uta Hagen has argued in *Respect for Acting*. "Yellow Fever" is the sixth episode of the fourth season. The dozens of episodes before this one have all worked to establish and entrench the character of Dean. We know that he eats burgers, bacon, and pie as he washes it all down with beer or whiskey. But that Dean is being disassembled in this episode. For instance, in one scene Sam finds Dean on his back, rocking out to "Eye of the Tiger"[3] as he reclines in the Impala. The song works as a touchstone, connecting us to the Dean we *know*. However, this new, frightened Dean is visibly startled when Sam tries to get his attention. It seems he has retreated to the Impala (the muscle car) as a safe space. Sam dutifully explains he and Bobby's findings on "ghost sickness," and we are treated to more phallic humor. The rival team of the Game Cocks is the Corn Jerkers. It is here that Sam explains that all those afflicted with "ghost sickness" are hyper-masculine fear mongers or "dicks." Dean, confused, asks Sam why he hasn't contracted the illness. This allows the viewer an interesting moment to reflect upon how different the brothers' gendered coding is. Sam is not coded as feminine per se, but on the continuum of gender performance he is *more* feminine than Dean. Sam eats salads, drinks smoothies, and exhibits much more angst and vulnerability throughout the series. Resigned, a moment later Dean rejects the box of donuts Sam has given him, an action our typical Dean would never take. There can be no doubt the narrative of this episode is making a statement on bullying. It is also clear that the lesson is specifically targeted toward aggressive, male bullies. As a "monster of the week" show, *Supernatural* is not often so decidedly allegorical. At this point in the episode there are two clearly defined narratives, one organic and one crystalline, hovering in preparation of fully subsuming the organic. At the 13:40 time mark, the soundscape and the image become wholly untrustworthy. Dean, as well as the viewer by proxy, begins hearing and seeing what cannot actually be. At 13:55 the camera zooms in sharply for an extreme close-up on Dean's eyes. His brow is deeply furrowed as he peers down at horrific images in a book. While the shot was most likely chosen to reveal, through intimacy, the depth of his fear, it works nicely at this moment when the sights, sounds and actions of the organic narration are fracturing toward crystalline. In fact, Deleuze states crystalline narration "implies a collapse of sensory-motor schemata. Sensory-motor situations have given way to pure optical and sound situations to which characters, who have become seers, cannot or will not react" (Deleuze 128). The frame trembles and blurs as Dean rubs at his eyes, becoming increasingly more afraid and more aware of the sound of the ticking clock.

After Dean coughs up a wood chip, the brothers decide to visit an old lumber mill. With an assessing look, Dean declares, "I'm not going in there." Sam convinces Dean he needs him as back-up, appealing to the strong protective instinct we have come to expect from Dean. The exchange below follows after the brothers head to the trunk of the car to get supplies:

> DEAN: It's a little spooky isn't it?
>
> *Sam frowns, and ignores him. Sam then picks up a gun and offers it to Dean.*
>
> DEAN: Oh, I'm not carrying that. It could go off. I'll man the flashlight.
>
> SAM: You do that.

The complementary performance of Dean's actions and Sam's reactions function to maintain the tension of the forgery. Padelecki's (Sam) body becomes more rigid and drawn, as Ackles's body seems to open and rise. In this scene Dean grips the flashlight with both hands, bringing his elbows up and away from his body, giving him the look of a frightened child. A few moments later Sam glances at Dean questioningly as Dean realizes he has his hand on his brother's arm for support or perhaps assurance. He quickly removes his hand. We are shown this in a close up which works to emphasize the action as well as more intimately connect the viewer. This shot is interesting in its questionable intent. Should we be afraid with Dean? Should we be annoyed with Sam? Perhaps we are simply meant to bear close witness to Dean's misery and fear. Both emotions are writ large upon his body and face.

At 18:27 we are given a full, falsetto scream by Dean. Part of the hilarity of the moment is how wrong it is to see and hear this particular character, embedded within this particular show, screaming in fear. Part of Dean's masculine coding is fearlessness. Therefore, the laugh is wrenched from us in part because it is something we could never anticipate. Herzog offers an illuminating point on the impact of disrupted codes and stereotypes: "The code or stereotype becomes a guise for another set of affects and meanings; and the resonance of such a moment […] is heightened by the dissonance and uncertainty created in the act of deterritorializing (versus merely rejecting) the code" (Herzog 141). The moment is created by a fairly simple jump scare involving a cat leaping out of an old locker. But Dean's response to the jump scare is wholly topsy-turvy. He follows the scream with "That was scary," while offering an extremely wide smile. The smile is as wrong as the scream was. He whimpers as Sam walks away. Soon thereafter, at minute 20:00, Dean runs away after seeing the ghost, leaving Sam to fend for himself. This is another action the "old" Dean would never take. The camera finds him a moment later cowering behind the Impala (again, his safe space) guzzling alcohol, which transitions to him swaying from inebriation in the next scene. Dean's drunkenness is remarkable in its blatant inconsistency with the character. Dean regularly consumes alcohol during the series, but he rarely exhibits any impairment. Dean is normally presented as "man enough" to handle his liquor. But frightened Dean is drunk and afraid and unsure of himself. He is Dean and not Dean. Our eyes and ears cannot be trusted as we observe him through our pre-coded expectations. No longer is the story being told the story being told.

At 21:43 there is a close-up shot of the sheriff scraping his skin with steel wool. Bright red blood coats his forearm as he savagely rubs back and forth. In Anna Powell's discussion of Deleuze and sensation we are reminded of the ways that cinema generally, and fantasy-horror in particular, works on the body. "Filmmakers maximize their medium's sensational impact by key tools of sight and sound that simulate the haptic response of the other senses. By watching characters touch objects and each other on screen, we 'touch' them ourselves, with consequent affective responses" (Powell 100).

As the Sheriff continues to abrade his skin, the soundscape fills with disembodied voices. The image trembles to the rhythm of a beating heart as the frame becomes blurred and distorted. This scene works chronologically with the organic narrative as it precedes the Sheriff's confrontation with Dean. The scene is also crystalline in the way that what is real and what is imagined becomes confused, shifting, untethered, and reworked.

Beyond the way fear transforms Dean's actions (body) as the episode continues, the sickness works to unravel fundamental tenets of the show. Dean becomes convinced their fake IDs are obvious, and he doesn't want to use them. Their agent drag is a fundamental part of the show's narrative progression. Dean's loss of confidence in their agent IDs signals a deeper structural inability. With this fear there can be no Dean. Within the frame he is both Dean and not Dean. At 22:45 the brothers interview Jack Garland, the brother of Luther, the ghost, who reports, "Everybody was scared of Luther. They called him a monster. He was too big, too mean looking. Just … too different. Didn't matter he was the kindest man I ever knew." The flashback images which accompany the interview show Luther, a very large, sad looking man, gently lifting kittens from a box. The image of a large, frightening man cuddling a fluffy kitten is just as striking a commentary on gender as Dean running from a small dog with a pink bow. However, Dean's coded masculinity is deconstructed in the process, while Luther's is re-made.

As the brothers begin to unravel the mystery there is an interesting metacognitive exchange as Dean becomes frustrated with their lack of a solution to his illness:

DEAN: You know what. Screw this.
SAM: Whoa, Whoa, Whoa. Dean. Come on.
DEAN: No, I mean, come on, Sam. What are we doing?!
SAM: We're hunting a ghost
DEAN: A ghost! Exactly! Who does that?!
SAM: Us.
DEAN: Us? Right. And that, Sam. That is exactly why our lives suck. I mean, come

on. We hunt monsters! What the hell?! I mean. Normal people ... they see a monster, and they run...

He continues on to describe the very actions and codes we've come to expect from the show weekly, including the diners, Dean's womanizing, and his affinity for "the same five albums." Then, he seems to quit not just their job, but their lives. This brings us back to the opening scene of the episode where Dean encounters the small dog. Here the narrative morphs into something new. What we see and hear do not mean what they usually mean. Visual and aural signification become untrustworthy as the organic narrative is eclipsed by the crystalline. What seemed like aural trickery as the episode opened is now an experience through Dean's untrustworthy senses. Is he hearing what we are hearing? Or are we hearing what he imagines he is hearing? Sound and image no longer accurately represent the expected reality, and yet we understand the story being told.

The remainder of the episode consists of Sam and Bobby resolving the issue of the ghost while Dean is "home sick." But there are a few notable moments. At the height of his fever the sickness reveals to Dean what his greatest fears are. He is terrified of returning to Hell. He is equally if not more horrified by the thought that Sam will become a demon. These are the fears of the *real* Dean and not his frightened forgery.

There are two resolutions at the end of "Yellow Fever." One is false and one is true. The first happens at 39:29 as the brothers and Bobby process the day's events:

> **DEAN:** On the upside. I'm still alive. So, uh ... go team.
> **SAM:** Yeah. How're you feeling, by the way?
> **DEAN:** Fine.
> **BOBBY:** You sure, Dean? 'Cause this line of work can get awful scary.
> **DEAN:** I'm fine. You wanna go hunting. I'll hunt. I'll kill anything.
> **SAM:** Awwwww.
> **BOBBY:** He's adorable.

Both Bobby and Sam laugh. This comical dialogue offers an effective release valve to the tension caused by Dean's inability to be *Dean*, and certainly pulls a laugh from the viewer. His swagger is back. He's standing next to his beloved black Impala, rather than cowering behind it, and his back is straight as he drinks a beer. He *looks* like the Dean we have come to know. The true resolution, however, happens just moments later. Once Bobby has driven away and the brothers are alone this exchange occurs:

> **SAM:** So uh. So what did you see? Near the end, I mean.
> **DEAN:** Oh, besides a cop beating my ass?
> **SAM:** Seriously.

As Dean looks into Sam's eyes he sees, or imagines he sees, them glow yellow for just a moment. Dean hesitates and looks away from his brother before answering:

DEAN: Howler monkeys. Whole room full of them. Those things creep the hell out of me.

SAM: Right…

DEAN: Nah … just the usual stuff, Sammy. Nothing I couldn't handle.

Here we watch as he quietly re-cloaks himself in the previously coded, stoic masculinity that has come to define this character and the manner in which he responds and relates to all other characters and objects within the narrative. Fundamentally, the mise-en-scène of the episode is consistent with our expectations of the series. It is mainly the bodily performance of Ackles which changes the narration from organic to crystalline. "Forgers work inside the codes, occupying and mutating them" (Herzog 141). And in the final minute the narrative returns itself to organic as the brothers prepare to return to the open road.

Conclusion

Supernatural, I would argue, often undertakes complex narrative labor just beneath the surface of genre expectations. The fact that *Supernatural* ran for 15 seasons is strong evidence the show is *doing* something, and doing it very well. The interesting ways in which *Supernatural* periodically subverts genre spotlights the limited utility of generic description. "One might justifiably view the concept of genre with cynicism … they code our expectations and colonise our interpretations. Generic classifications artificially impose unity upon diverse texts after the fact, obscuring our access to their full optical and sonic richness" (Herzog 153).

The shifting narrative of "Yellow Fever" works as a surprisingly poignant treatise on aggressive masculinity and the danger inherent in using fear as a weapon. The entire episode is made, unmade, and remade as its narrative moves from organic to crystalline and back again. Codes asserted by the mise-en-scène are quickly rendered unintelligible by the bodily performance of Jensen Ackles.

The episode is filled with very big, American men frightened of very small things as punishment for their oppression of others in the past. While the narrative implicitly suggests a cautionary tale on bullying, it is Ackles's forgery of Dean that lends the narrative cohesion and comedic thrust while simultaneously disrupting the generic expectations of the show. Here, genre provides the limits, or boundaries of the frame which Ackles can now deterritorialize. The performance shatters the codes in a spectacular and humorous display. With regard to that shattering, it's important to note that subversion, deterritorialization, and forgery are dynamics always in relation to pre-existing boundaries. Therefore, I do not suggest any attempt to abandon cinematic systems of classification. Instead we can work to recognize the limits of genre, narrative boundary, as a catalyst for narrative expansion made possible through transgression of the generic frame. Forgers cannot produce forgery without the pre-existing rigidity of our current cultural codes.

Contemporary television shows provide rich and varied opportunities for identifying and understanding our constructed social realities. *Supernatural* in particular offers a glimpse of the great American landscape viewed from the windshield of an American muscle car traveling along our highways and byways. That perspective is uniquely masculine and fairly aggressive in conformity with its "monster of the week" format. But, while the generic coding of the show offers cohesion and enjoyment, the show also makes clear how genre television can be much more than its expected elements. The narratives and performances within *Supernatural* work on and within the codes, smoothly disrupting what the show should be in favor of what the show could be.

NOTES

1. While the show relies heavily upon lore, magic, supernatural creatures, and various realms which can be traveled to, the supernatural elements of the show are usually expressed in and through physical metamorphoses. For example, a character will move from human to vampire by means of physical transformation. The overall spatial setting will remain Anytown, USA.

2. Fowkes sets forth the parameters for what constitutes fantasy, or a fantastic narrative: "the audience must at the very least perceive an 'ontological rupture'—a break between what the audience agrees is 'reality' and the fantastic phenomena that define the narrative world" (Fowkes 5). I would offer the *Scooby-Doo* episode from Season 13 as another example of a narrative which includes a second hard ontological break. This occurs when the brothers are sucked into an old TV and end up in an animated episode of *Scooby-Doo.*

3. Released in 1982, "Eye of the Tiger" is an American hard-rock song by the band Survivor. The use of the song in this particular episode seems tongue in cheek given that a main character is gripped with fear throughout. It's also perhaps best known from the movie *Rocky III* (1982) as the song Rocky uses to pump himself up for the big fight.

WORKS CITED

Butler, David. *Fantasy Cinema: Impossible Worlds on Screen.* Wallflower, 2009.
del Río, E. *Deleuze and the Cinemas of Performance: Powers of Affection.* Edinburgh University Press, 2008.
Deleuze, Gilles. *Cinema 2: The Time Image.* University of Minnesota Press, 1989.
Fowkes, Katherine A. *The Fantasy Film: Wizards, Wishes, and Wonders.* John Wiley & Sons, Incorporated, 2010.
Hagen, Uta. *Respect for Acting.* Macmillan, 1973.
Herzog, Amy. "Fictions of the Imagination: Habit, Genre and the Powers of the False." *Deleuze and Film,* edited by David Martin-Jones and William Brown. Edinburgh University Press, 2012. 137–154.
Parr, Adrian. "Deterritorialisation/Reterritorialisation." *The Deleuze Dictionary,* edited by Adrian Parr, Edinburgh University Press, 2005. 69–72.
Powell, Anna. *Deleuze: Altered States and Film.* Edinburgh University Press, 2007.
Worley, Alec. *Empires of the Imagination: A Critical Survey from Georges Méliès to Lord of the Rings.* McFarland, 2005.

"You guys getting hungry?"
On Leviathans, Consumption and American Politics in Supernatural

ANGÉLICA VARANDAS

Hell Is a Place on Earth

In the realm of fantastic fiction, many have been the books and films that have, in one way or another, leveled a harsh critique at contemporary society, drawing attention to the dangers of modernity and anticipating a dark and hopeless future for humankind, even, in some cases, the end of the world. Originally created by Eric Kripke and premiering on television on September 13, 2005, *Supernatural* deals with the end of the world theme and simultaneously exposes the perils of our times, building an interesting and in some cases highly original critique of today's state of affairs. In this essay I will focus on Season 7, which includes many of the themes explored both by fantasy and SF writers, such as the decline and fall of civilization, the dangers of scientific manipulation and political propaganda, the threat of the monster/alien, the menacing power of absolute control over society, the consequences of extreme greed, and the annihilation of human emotions and free will. The series underlines the idea that humanity continues to be blind, perpetuating the old and same mistakes that have led to the destruction of civilizations or political systems. As a result, it questions our age as one of extremity, since "we live under continual threat of two equally fearful, but seemingly opposed, destinies, unremitting banality and inconceivable terror" (Sontag 42).

From the end of the 19th century, particularly in England, many fictional works were beginning to express a huge distrust in progress and in the nature of man. If Darwin's evolutionary theory announced that man was evolving in a constant process implying perfection of the species, it soon became clear, by direct observation, that beings could also regress biologically. According to Kelly Hurley:

> Whereas the Darwinian narrative was a non-telic one, governed by natural processes that worked in no particular direction and towards no particular end, the nineteenth-century imagination was preoccupied with the prospect of the reversal of evolution, insofar as this was understood as a synonym for "progress" [10].

This assumption was quickly adapted to other areas of human knowledge and activity, such as psychology and the new-born psychoanalysis, or history, which claimed that all advanced and apparently perfect societies, such as the Roman Empire, would end up by declining and eventually falling. This emphasis on regression and degeneration also became visible in the art of the Decadent Movement which flourished at the same time. In literature, it is present in Gothic fiction, closely associated with the emergence of fantasy as a genre: Mary Shelley's *Frankenstein* (1818), Robert Louis Stevenson's *Dr. Jekyll and Mr. Hyde* (1885) or H.G. Wells's *The Island of Dr. Moreau* (1896), for example, demonstrate how the human being can become a monster or a monstrous being when science is misused, as Fred Botting underlines when he claims that 19th century literature, mainly after *Frankenstein*, begins to acknowledge science both as a menace and a promise. Therefore, science is at the core of man's anxieties, since it can bring about a ruined future, devastated by experiments in genetics and hybrid and mutant forms of life (279).

These works mirror the *fin de siècle* preoccupations and anxieties over the misappropriation of Darwinism, dealing with themes common among Gothic novels, such as the dangers of biological evolution and scientific experimentation in the social fabric and in self-identity. As Roger Luckhurst states, "the possibilities of biological and entropic decline mark the character of the British scientific romance" (23).

Also, from the 19th century onwards, fantasy emerged as a genre absorbing many of Romanticism's ideological and aesthetic values. The Romantics professed the use of the imagination and the exploration of the mythical, the visionary and the obscure on the one hand, and, on the other, the rejection of absolutist power and the defense of the French Revolution's ideals: liberty, equality, and fraternity. These convictions fueled the recovery and reinvention of the past, the Middle Ages in particular, as a golden time free from the stench and noise of the machines, closer to nature and to a more honest kind of life. In fact, after the enthusiasm around the progress brought about by the Industrial Revolution, people understood that that same progress could be damaging both to the social system and to the environment. Many of the 19th century artists, such as the Pre-Raphaelites, demonstrated a profound distaste for industrialization and proclaimed a return to nature and to simpler values.

Following on these footsteps, the first fantasy writers also felt the need to deeply denounce social, political, economic and even religious issues, as well as ethical and moral attitudes and beliefs. J.R.R. Tolkien and C.S. Lewis, the founding fathers of the fantasy genre as we know it today, firmly criticized technology, war, and the absolute use of power which leads inevitably to the destruction and ending of all that exists. It is true that, for both authors, fantasy was still envisaged as a literature of hope. Taking *The Lord of the Rings* (1954–55) as an example, we understand that, in spite of the pain, suffering and sorrow due to Sauron's will to take control over Middle Earth, the world does not collapse, and a new age begins, the Age of Man, which starts with several promises, in particular that of a true and loyal king governing over a renewed land. Hope was fundamental to Tolkien, an astonishing fact when we know that he lived through the two world wars, having been directly involved in World War I. He saw Europe being devastated and his friends being killed, and even so he still believed that humanity could do better. It is certainly this belief that allows *The Lord of the Rings* to open up to a hopeful future where death, although present, can be vanquished by love, thus denying "universal final defeat [...], giving a fleeting glimpse of Joy, Joy beyond the walls of the world, poignant as grief" (Tolkien 62). It is certain that most of today's fantasy still repeats many Tolkienian formulas, maintaining the eucatastrophic quality of the genre as a means of escaping from "hunger, thirst, poverty, pain, sorrow injustice, death" and from "ancient imitations from which fairy-stories offer a sort of escape, and old ambitions and desires [...] to which they offer a mind of satisfaction and consolation" (Tolkien 60). However, some fantasy authors have also begun to paint fantasy with colors grimmer, turning the genre into a somber place where escape is rarely achieved and consolation is hardly present. The paradigmatic example is, of course, George R.R. Martin's *A Song of Ice and Fire* (1996–) where hope is annihilated at birth in an unmerciful world where the lust for power generates hatred, violence, torture, and death, portraying and vividly denouncing contemporary society.

This means that moments of optimism about progress and evolution in the history of mankind have generally been accompanied or followed by feelings of anxiety and distress regarding their dire consequences. This fact became perhaps more conspicuous after World War II and the dropping of the two atomic bombs on Hiroshima and Nagasaki in 1945. The former decade, the 1930s, witnessed excitement with the development of atomic research. After the 1929 Wall Street Crash, technocracy appeared as a means of reacting against the paranoia and fear caused by the Great Depression. Many canonical science fiction (SF) authors writing at this time argued that only science could save society and lead to progress. In some of their works, Robert Heinlein, Isaac Asimov and A.E. Van Vogt, among others, claimed that technocrats and engineers were the ones who could pave the way into a better future. John W. Campbell in "Who Goes There?" (1938), a short story written under his pen name Don A. Stuart, revealed his trust and hope in nuclear power. However, the first movie adaptation of this tale in 1951, Howard Hawks and Christian Nyby's *The Thing from Another World*, withdraws from Campbell's opinion by depicting a monster who symbolizes the atomic bomb. At the same time, making the monster look like Boris Karloff in James Whale's *Frankenstein* (1931), this film warns against the dangers of scientific manipulation. Speaking about SF movies in "The Imagination of Disaster," Susan Sontag alludes to the trauma created by nuclear weapons which SF clearly addresses, saying that "the accidental wakening of the super destructive monster […] is, often, an obvious metaphor for the bomb" (46).

This concern with what humans can do to themselves and to the world for the sake of progress is becoming more and more evident in many fictional works, from literature to movies and TV series. In *The Thing* (1982), which is also an adaptation of Campbell's "Who Goes There?," John Carpenter reflects about the destructive nature of human kind, a motif explored by many other films, such as Ridley Scott's *Alien* (1979), Kevin Reynolds's *Waterworld* (1995), Roland Emmerich's *The Day After Tomorrow* (2004), Francis Lawrence's *I Am Legend* (2007) and Christian Alvart's *Pandorum* (2009), to name just a few. In drawing attention to the fact that humans can put in jeopardy their own lives and the life of the planet they live on, several works of fantastic fiction, whether fantasy, SF or horror, have dislocated this threat that has been slowly growing from within to the other, a monster, and outer entity or an alien being, eager to destroy humanity and take its place in the universe. This is why Sontag states, "Science fiction films are not about science. They are about disaster, which is one of the oldest subjects of art. […]. Thus, the science fiction film […] is concerned with the aesthetics of destruction" (44).

The obnoxious effects of human manipulation of science, of the most elementary laws of nature and of the undermining of justice and freedom is indeed a motif in several SF works since the very beginning of the genre, showing how it soon developed a dystopian vein. Two of the most canonical SF texts, *Brave New World*, by Aldous Huxley (1932), and *1984*, by George Orwell (1949), are dystopias in which humans are controlled by a totalitarian and highly industrialized society in which there is no space for free will or imagination. Although written in the first half of the 20th century, these books seem to target their denunciation of the social and political state of affairs at today's society in which the threats caused by scientific and political manipulation are bigger than ever, expanded by terrorism and global warming. Sales of both books have increased significantly since Donald Trump became President of the United States in 2016 (see, for instance, Tuttle).

Actually, both *Brave New World* and *1984* show how political control of the population turns the populace into a mass of unemotional and apathic people with no will of their own and thus set the standard for many other works, whether literary or filmic, that have dealt with this same aspect since then. One of the first to delve into this issue was *The Day of the Triffids*, a book by John Wyndham (1951) in which some botanical scientific experiments led to the development of a totally new species of plant: the triffid (a noun coined by Wyndham). The triffids, capable of walking and with a high degree of intelligence, soon find out that it is easy to dominate the human world by taking from humans their primary sense: sight. This idea that we move in blindness, incapable of seeing the danger that we ourselves can create, is one of the main themes of *They Live* (1988), a film by John Carpenter, in which aliens are controlling humans by TV and media in general. *The Matrix* (1999) would take this state of affairs to its ultimate conclusion. After Wyndham, the blindness theme was later adopted by the Portuguese writer José Saramago in *Ensaio sobre a Cegueira* (1995). Also in 1951, Heinlein's *The Puppet Masters* depicts an alien invasion of slug-like creatures which can control people's minds, transforming them into beings with no will of their own.

Both Wyndham's *The Day of the Triffids* and Heinlein's *Puppet Masters* have been seen as anti-communist manifestos since they were written at the peak of McCarthyism in the USA. Four years later, in 1955, another novel developed the same themes. Jack Finney's *The Body Snatchers* depicts the invading aliens as seeds coming from outer space, thus highlighting a vegetable nature that they share with the triffids, which grow to become huge pods. These pods replace people in their sleep with alien duplicates who are incapable of showing any kind of human emotions. Based on Finney's novel, Don Siegel's movie *Invasion of the Body Snatchers* (1956) portrays the invasion of America by these seed pods which symbolize Soviet communism, leading to the loss of autonomy, freedom, free will, self-identity and emotion. In her summary of the main characteristics of SF movies, Susan Sontag states that the alien or the supernatural creature, often referred to by the personal pronoun "it," embodies these ideas related to the impersonal, bringing about the lack of identity and emotion and thus causing "a crime which is worse than murder," because otherworldly beings "do not simply kill the person. They obliterate him" (47).

Supernatural as a whole inherits many of these topics developed by such fantasy and SF works, addressing today's state of affairs. We are, in fact, witnessing the failure of the economic and social systems, after the economic optimism of the end of the 20th century, as well as the expansion of terrorism, dramatic change in the world's climate, the threat of nuclear war, and the alarming rise of extreme right-wing parties not only in Europe but all over the world. At the same time, the development of mass media, the appearance of social networks, and their intrusion in our everyday lives have highly contributed to the banalization of these same problems. We have to take into account all these issues in order to fully understand the depth of *Supernatural*'s Season 7, in which a strong political message is hidden in the fight against the Leviathans. We have to bear in mind that Season 7 was released between the 23rd of September 2011 and the 18th of May 2012, less than six months before Barack Obama, the Democratic candidate, faced the Republican Mitt Romney in the November 2012 USA presidential elections.

Moreover, weaving all these themes into an original plot, this season of *Supernatural*, much as the whole series, pays tribute to all the fantasy and SF authors, books and movies mentioned above as well as many others, such as *The X-Files* (1992–2002; 2016–18), *Buffy, the Vampire Slayer* (1996–2003), *Angel* (1999–2004), *The Twilight Zone* (1958–64), *Star Wars* (1977), Romero's *Night of the Living Dead* (1968), *Poltergeist* (1982), and *The Shining* (1980), just to name a few, since it would be impossible to cite them all. Some of the well-known actors of these films and series actually participated in several episodes of *Supernatural*, not only reinforcing the connection between their films and the series but also acknowledging it as a fictional artifact—an idea developed in several episodes, namely the one in which Sam and Dean are thrown by the angel Balthazar into the real world where they cease to be fictional characters and instead become the real actors who play them: Jensen Ackles and Jared Padalecki ("The French Mistake," 6.15). This narrative strategy of deconstruction, which is also visible when Chuck Shurley, the author of the *Supernatural* fantasy novels, is introduced in the series as a character, reveals how much this show owes to postmodern literature. It also illustrates how the series reflects on narrative construction, its status as a work of art and the role of actors and their relationship with the characters they interpret in the series.

The Road So Far

Then, as now, Sam and Dean Winchester are hunters, pursuers of demons and all sorts of evil creatures, a task they inherited from their dead father, leading them to a transient lifestyle. Permanently on the road, the two brothers don't belong to a particular city or to a particular state. Crossing the United States in Dean's black '67 Chevy Impala, the car he prizes above all his other possessions (his "baby," as he calls it), they are both citizens of America as a whole. In this sense we could say that they personify the American Dream of constant mobility associated with the journey and with the road. One of the books that had an enormous impact on Eric Kripke was *On the Road*, by Jack Kerouac (1957). The brothers' names allude to the protagonists of the book: Salvatore "Sal" Paradise and Dean Moriarty.

Their depiction sometimes suggests the cowboy, one of the most charismatic figures of the USA. This is evident not only in the way they dress but also in the guns they carry. The Colt, the mythical revolver the two brothers use from Seasons 1 to 3, is the same handgun produced by Samuel Colt in the first half of the 19th century. Moreover, their family name is Winchester, one of the oldest rifle brands in the USA and associated with Hollywood westerns. This identification of the two brothers with the mythical figure of the cowboy claiming the territory of America against monsters is made explicit in "Frontierland" (6.18), in which Dean and Sam end up in the old west to collect the ashes of a phoenix, and Sam asks for Samuel Colt's help. Dean ends up in a *High Noon* duel to kill the phoenix. The credits of this episode actually imitate those of a typical western. Specifically, they emulate the title card of *Bonanza* (1959–73), one of the longest running and most beloved of the western television shows.

This liaison with American social and cinematic history is particularly visible in Dean, the older brother, who took the responsibility of looking after Sam, the younger, after the death of their mother. His name—Dean—and the relationship he maintains with his car—the Chevy Impala—turn him into a James Dean figure. The tendency of living on the edge also connects Dean to the famous American actor, who once incorporated the American ideal of youth, beauty and rebellious spirit. Sam, on the other hand, is the intellectual who went to University and received a scholarship to study at Stanford. While Dean, the rebel, represents the most emotional side of the human psyche, Sam, the intellectual, stands for its rational dimension. At the beginning of the series, Sam is the good guy, always able to see the possible hidden goodness in human nature. Both brothers personify these two faces of the American spirit. Moreover, both the 1967 Impala as well as the rock and roll music played in the car, mostly music from the 70s, help to evoke an important historical period mostly because, as Simon Brown argues, this decade was the "moment of primal assertion for contemporaneously set American horror" (Brown 60), and he quotes from "The American Nightmare: Horror in the 70's," an article published by Robin Wood in *Hollywood: From Vietnam to Reagan* (New York, 1986): "In 1970's American horror films the true subject of the horror genre is the struggle for recognition of all that our civilization represses or oppresses, its reemergence dramatized, as in our nightmares, as an object of horror, a matter for terror" (Brown 61). It may be interesting to recall that the 70s were considered the "Era of Emptiness" by the French sociologist Gilles Lipovetsky, who wrote a book with the same name in 1993. "Carry on Wayward Son," by the band Kansas, a 1976 song that can almost be considered the hymn of the series, as it plays at the beginning of the finales as the re-cap of the season is shown, also stresses the importance of John Winchester as the figure of the father, or rather the lost father, another fundamental motif of American tradition and iconography. The Impala establishes another link between Dean and his father, John Winchester, because John was a car mechanic. Moreover, the song's title and the name of the band also allude to the fact that both Sam and Dean are closely associated with the city of Lawrence, in Northeast Kansas, where they were born. Additionally, they make a home in Lebanon, Kansas, in spite of being continually on the road from the time of their mother's death until Season 10.

The series can, in fact, be conceived of as a mixture between horror and road movie, with more emphasis on horror. All the adventures result from the journey of Sam and Dean across America, the journey being a unifying element among all episodes in the series; the title of one of the episodes in Season 1 is "Route 666" (1.13), alluding to the mythic route 66 and to the number of the beast. But *Supernatural* is also a journey through horror, SF and fantasy both in TV and in cinema, containing innumerable references to so many paradigmatic series and films, as I have already pointed out.

However, at the same time, Sam and Dean seem also very far away from the American Dream because they do not stand for traditional American values. Their mission does not allow them to settle down and lead a normal life, with wives and children of their own. In spite of having somehow found a home in the Bunker (Dean does much to make his room "homey"), the name of this place makes it resemble a setting associated with war rather than an actual home. The mainstream quiet life of marriage remains forever unrealized because it is an impossible dream. Furthermore, by driving along peripheral roads, Sam and Dean are also the visitors of marginal spaces, such as motels, suburban cafes and roadside restaurants, that offer experiences much different from a life in a white and cozy American suburban house. In these peripheral spaces they face foes that come out of marginal culture: demons, monsters, ghosts, werewolves, witches, vampires or pagan gods. As a result, *Supernatural* is "a testament to how telefantasy can often push the boundaries of narrative, genre, and aesthetics," as Stacey Abbot affirms (xiv).

Although conceived by Eric Kripke as a five-season storyline, *Supernatural* eventually ran for 15 seasons. After fighting against the yellow-eyed demon, who is responsible for their mother and father's death (Seasons 1, 2 and 3), Lucifer, the devil (Seasons 4 and 5), and Eve, the Mother of All (Season 6), the two brothers face, in Season 7, a much more threatening menace: the coming of the Leviathans into the world. Leviathans become their most dangerous adversaries against which all conventional weapons are useless. Robert Singer, one of the producers of the show, explains: "We wanted them [Sam and Dean] to be the last cowboys out there and the modern world was closing in on them. We wanted them to be not so equipped to fight this battle as they were to fight others. It was them against the world at a certain point" ("'Supernatural': Season 7 Spoilers").

We learn that the Leviathans were created by God in the beginning of time even before the making of man and angels. Before disappearing from our planet and abandoning us, leaving us defenseless against all evil, God realized that the Leviathans could turn into exceedingly dangerous creatures because of their extreme hunger and almost undefeatable power, a power so huge that they could destroy all of His creation, including angels. This idea is in line with Jean-Paul Roenecker's description of the Leviathan in *Le Symbolisme Animal: Mythes, Croyances, Légendes, Archétypes, Folklore, Imaginaire*: "Bien que Léviathan fût considéré comme la création et le jouet de Yahvé, la croyance voulait qu'il échappât à son créateur et que, à l'approche de la fin du monde, il défiât même les anges" (195).

To prevent this cataclysm, God built Purgatory, where the Leviathans were locked with all the other monsters and tortured souls not sentenced to Hell. However, a dispute for God's place in the universe among two factions of angels, led respectively by Castiel and Raphael, causes a breach in the door of Purgatory. In fact, most angels loathe humans, being envious of God's creation. When God abandons man, Raphael wants to take over His place and intends to release Lucifer from Hell where the fallen angel is imprisoned, in order to bring about the Apocalypse and thus destroy the human race. Raphael wants loyalty from the other angels who must obey him and follow him as the new God. He is depicted as a highly successful businessman, perhaps as a means of criticizing the greed for power and money and the absolute need to control and be obeyed. Castiel, on the other hand, wants freedom and fights for humanity to have free will. It is he, however, who, after destroying Raphael, brings the Leviathans into the world, thereby almost causing the annihilation of the human race. He swallows all the beings that inhabited Purgatory in order to have the power conferred by the souls, and thus he unwillingly also swallows the Leviathans, who are too strong and powerful to be held inside his body. Incapable of containing them or making them go back to where they belong, he lets them loose in the world. As Crowley states, "It's the souls. It all comes down to the souls in the end" ("The Man Who Would Be King," 6.20).

Leviathans and Vampires

The Leviathan is a sea-monster coming from the Hebrew tradition where it is sometimes identified as a whale. It is mentioned in the Old Testament, where it stands for every monster of the sea, namely in the Book of Job (40: 25–32, 41: 1–26), in Isaiah (27:1) and in Psalms (104: 25–26). In the Bible, the Leviathan is also named as a serpent and a dragon, two creatures commonly associated with one another and which symbolize the devil, particularly because of the imagery in the Book of Revelation. The Leviathan is also mentioned in the apocryphal Book of Enoch, where it is considered a huge creature living in the abyss below the water fountains. In Isaiah and in Job the Leviathan stands for the powers of chaos, contrary to the creative action of God. In Satanism, the Leviathan is related to water and to the cardinal point west, being also one of the princes of Hell. It is thus conceived as a threatening force to humanity, and it is in this sense that it comes to represent the oppressors of the people of Israel (such as in Job 3:8). *Supernatural* certainly draws on this imagery when portraying the Leviathans as evil and destructive beings, willing to swallow the most perfect of God's creatures: humans. In the Middle Ages, the Leviathan, and the serpent/dragon, were major symbols of Hell or of Satan, the Leviathan being depicted in the iconography of the period as a sea monster, sometimes identified with Jonah's whale, or as a devouring maw that engulfs the souls of sinners, that are thus eaten up by Hell: the Hell-mouth. As David Williams observes, Hell-mouths portray humans as food "ingested and digested, disappearing forever down the throat of an insatiable and implacable power" (144); being consumed by demons and thus becoming part of them.

The paradox in the series is that it is the Leviathans themselves who are devoured, living inside the body of an angel for some time before being released. The metaphor of swallowing, devouring or eating is present throughout Season 7, in the episodes about the Leviathans, mainly in the lines spoken by Richard (Dick) Roman, as well as in the episodes not directly connected to the main plot.

In *Supernatural*, the Leviathans share many traits with the sea-monsters of biblical myth: Firstly, they are related to water, spreading first through this element by polluting the public water supply in the Municipal Reservoir. They are evil and foul creatures whose black blood taints the water as if it were contaminated by a black tide caused by an oil spill. This thick, black and infectious blood is also reminiscent of the symptoms of the Black Death which devastated Europe between 1347 and 1352. The most common symptom was the appearance of black buboes on the armpits, neck or groin; these were extremely contagious when they bled. This disease was also mainly propagated by water, since the contaminated corpses were generally thrown away into rivers and wells. The word "plague" is actually used when some characters refer to the Leviathans' contamination of food. Secondly, the Leviathans swallow their victims, for what they most want and need is to feed on human life, by eating the internal organs of human beings. Their mouth becomes their lethal weapon. Round and enormous, full of sharp teeth, with a long, slimy and bifurcated tongue, this mouth symbolizes our most inner fear of being devoured.

In its aspect and in its role, this mouth is very similar to the mouths of vampires, monsters with whom Leviathans appear to have much in common. In "There Will Be Blood" (7.22), we learn that vampires descended from Leviathans, and Sam calls them "monster cousins." They both feed on human life and kill through their teeth and mouths. It is no wonder that they at some point join together to prey on humans more easily, although at the end vampires help Sam and Dean defeat the Leviathans.

In the same episode, another race of monsters is brought into account: ghouls. Although we come to know that Leviathans loathe "those disgusting little things that eat corpses" ("There Will Be Blood"), a link is established among these three types of monsters: the mouth and the urge for human flesh being the elements that sustain that bond. For David Williams, the mouth allows the self to deal with the other in a dangerous encounter in which "a single misstep may cause the slide of the one toward the other and end in the absorption and annihilation of identity and individuality" (Williams 141). But the mouth is also related to the cardinal sin of gluttony, the urge to eat without control, the need to surround oneself with food—a sin of the western world?

In spite of their parentage of vampires, Leviathans are by far the more perilous creatures. The end of the world that they are about to bring about presupposes not only the annihilation of humanity but also the disappearance of all the other monsters we are more familiar with, such as werewolves, vampires, and ghouls; as Edgar, one of the Leviathans, points out, the additive they are putting in food "kills the [were]wolves too, [shape-]shifters and those disgusting little things that eat corpses, anything with a taste for human, except us" ("There Will Be Blood"). According to Williams, "The Leviathan is the marine representative of a group of monsters whose chief significance is in their devouring activity" (186). The world is theirs for the taking, for they will devour everything we know. And when they disappoint their leader, they are obliged to devour themselves in a self-cannibalistic act.

Finally, these *Supernatural* Leviathans are also shapeshifters. They take over the bodies of humans and, like the alien seed pods in *Invasion of the Body Snatchers* which imitate human beings or the creature in John Carpenter's *The Thing*, they assume their shape. Looking like humans and talking like humans, Leviathans are, in fact, a mirror of the human, namely of the human dominated by power and greed, by the dark side of human nature. In his essay, "Horror, Humanity and the Demon in the Mirror," Gregory Stevenson says,

> By keeping God in the shadows, *Supernatural* shifts the focus to the human struggle. […] By keeping both God and Satan at a distance, potentially there but always in the background, *Supernatural* becomes a show about how human beings conduct themselves in the shadows of good and evil [43].

He explains further, stating that even though Sam and Dean confront all sorts of evil creatures, these fall short of all the terrible actions human beings can cause, such as child abuse or terrorism. "That is the real horror show," he says: "By taking our society's horrors and reflecting them back to us as demons and monsters, what *Supernatural* does is remind us of humanity's potential to act in demonic or monstrous ways" (51).

Hamburgers and the End of the World

In their need to eat humans in order to survive, Leviathans decide to take over America and turn men and women into easily accessible food. To do that, they start by taking the shapes of famous influential men, such as Richard (Dick) Roman, whose body becomes the vessel of the head of the Leviathans. Dick Roman is a billionaire and one of the top 35 most powerful Americans. He controls the defense and aviation sectors and owns several *Fortune 500* companies by resorting to a corporate takeover warpath in an extremely aggressive type of policy: "I believe in the good old American rules, like unlimited growth. And as I always say: 'If you wanna win, then you gotta be the shark. And the shark's gotta eat'" ("How to Win Friends and Influence Monsters," 7.09). Rich and famous, Roman is indeed a shark in the business world, but in his case the metaphor is far too literal, for his ultimate goal consists of turning humans into tasty meat for his race without having to fight with them. The plan is simple but Machiavellian: by controlling what American people eat, Leviathans can control America.

There are various steps to achieve this goal, the first consisting of buying and merging companies in order to transform them into fast food shops all over America. This procedure allows the Leviathans not only to infect fast food with additives, but also to manipulate food genetically, creating transgenic meat, such as the New Pepperjack Turducken Slammer, a hamburger made of a genetic combination of turkey, duck and chicken, sold in Biggerson's Sizzlin' Grill & Bar. Yet, this first experiment has some unexpected drawbacks, causing adverse reactions, such as behavioral disturbances and a gluttonous appetite, so gluttonous indeed that the person who eats the hamburger regularly also starts to crave for human flesh, turning into a monstrous creature. In spite of these side effects, the manipulated substances inside the Turducken hamburger fulfill the Leviathans' main objective: when ingested, they start to work in one's DNA, slowing the metabolism, causing obesity and narrowing the emotional range so that people become perfectly complacent. In the ironically titled "How to Win Friends and Influence Monsters," a family eats the transgenic food and sips soft drinks with eyes fixed on a TV screen, watching an eye surgery impassively, without noticing that one of their members, grandma, is already dead in the seat next to them. As Bobby Singer sums up, "A bunch of birds shoved up inside each other.... You shouldn't play God like that!"

Using his enormous influence, Roman moves on to extend his empire, which becomes so powerful and strong that it is significantly called the Roman empire. Roman himself writes a bestseller book. *When in Rome*, consisting of a series of motivational seminars. His title refers obviously to the well-known proverb, "When in Rome, do as the Romans do," meaning that he is in fact just taking the acts of the humans to their utmost consequences. In order to improve his experiments, he buys Sucrocorp, a leading manufacturer specializing in food additives made of fructose corn syrup, injected into almost every kind of food and drink, served in restaurants, pubs, grocery stores, supermarkets, and Gas and Sips. These additives allow for the pumping of sweetness into the human system, generating a sweeter, tastier meat that must also be free of all sorts of illnesses and major diseases. The eradication of cancer, AIDS and heart diseases becomes then one of the major issues of the Leviathan monopoly of the American world. In health research centers, a cure for several types of cancer is found so that human meat can measure up to the demanding standards of Leviathan consumers. A TV interview includes this exchange:

> **ROMAN:** And we need you just as healthy as you can be. Which is why we are diving whole hog into what keeps Americans living longer and tasting better.
> **INTERVIEWER:** You do of course mean to say the food will be tasting better?
> **ROMAN** (*smiling ironically*): That is exactly what I mean ["There Will Be Blood"].

These investigations lead to the building of a supposed biotech laboratory which is in fact "a state of the art slaughterhouse," as Bobby points out in the episode "The Girl with the Dungeons and Dragons Tattoo" (7.20). And he goes on, "We are the beef. [...] They're not hunting anymore. They are engineering the perfect herd."

The ultimate idea consists, then, of turning America into an enormous meat market by dividing the country into three main areas according to a Slaughterhouse Programme introduced in the last episode of the season, "Survival of the Fittest" (7.23): the first would be Ohio (the Labor Area), where Beta tests would be developed; the second Wisconsin (the Testing Area) where meat would be processed, and the third Florida (the Livestock area) where a Breeding Program would be created, consisting of several fertilization clinics to prevent the risk of human meat running out of stock. The idea then is to serve humans as food. "To Serve Man" is the title of a classic episode of *The Twilight Zone* (1959–64), a series combining horror, fantasy and SF, created by Rod Serling in 1959. In this episode (original air-date March 2, 1962), based in its turn on the short story "To Serve Man" (1950), written by Damon Knight, an American SF author, the Kanamits land on earth claiming that they intend to serve man: they share their knowledge in technology, cure diseases, and put an end to hunger. A cryptographer deciphers the title of one of their books as *To Serve Man* but finds out, in the end, that this book is actually a cookbook. Playing with the two meanings of "serve" in English—"to help others" or "to serve as food"—this episode is referred to in *Supernatural* when Sam and Dean find on a shelf a book having the same title ("There Will Be Blood")—a tribute to *The Twilight Zone*.

The critique of Americans' consuming habits is thus evident: fast food and the urge to eat it, which causes obesity in people until they are no longer able to move or think, will ultimately be the cause of the death of American society. In their craving for human flesh, Leviathans choose to dominate America first by accelerating this process. Moreover, they can be satisfied with America only, as Dick Roman makes clear when negotiating dominion over the world with Crowley, the new leader of Hell after Lucifer's imprisonment. Roman doesn't mind if Crowley stays within Canada as long as he can keep the USA: "We need America. They are so fat!" he claims ("Survival of the Fittest").

America is thus depicted as a society of excess in which eager consumers take profit from living in a land of plenty in order to satisfy all their utmost desires, from sex and drugs to food and money. These unstoppable characteristics of greed and hunger were earlier incarnated in Season 5 in the character of Famine, one of the Four Horsemen of the Apocalypse (The Black Horseman), who "wields power over people's self-control" (Engstrom and Valenzano 88). After being released from the cage where he was imprisoned, Lucifer starts to take care of Famine, sending him souls so that he can digest them to restore his health. In losing self-control and succumbing to greed and hunger, people are unable to stop fulfilling their carnal desires and end up by killing themselves or one another, thus feeding Famine's insatiable craving for human souls.

Season 7 is certainly implying that it is essential to change this state of affairs and stop American consumerism, by privileging healthier food, namely the ingestion of vegetables, as Sam and Dean themselves try to do after realizing that the problem is "in the meat!" ("How to Win Friends and Influence Monsters"), as they say. But the series is also calling attention to the dangers of genetically manipulated food and its consequences to public health, and to the dangers of urging unnecessary consumption when one is not hungry. In this sense, it likewise denounces the consumer society of the Western world as a whole, and its most significant representative, the United States. Morally, it seems to condemn the sin of gluttony and its consequences on the human body and the human soul. Leviathans are gluttonous, but so are humans, especially Americans, who grow fatter and fatter, seeming to be ignorant of or indifferent to food waste and to hunger, a calamity that affects still too many countries around the globe. It further suggests that Americans never appear to satisfy their needs although they live in the land where everything is at their disposal. In "My Bloody Valentine" (5.14), Castiel points out that Famine can be described as the lack of something or starvation for something beyond just food:

> CASTIEL: This town (…) is suffering from hunger. Starvation, to be exact. Specifically, Famine.
> SAM: As in the Horseman? I thought Famine meant starvation, like, as in, you know, food.
> CASTIEL: Yes, absolutely. But not just food. Everyone seems to be starving for something: sex, attention, drugs, love….

This association between Famine and starvation, coming from an angelic figure, acquires a spiritual meaning: the utmost need to consume becomes an "intense desire that we all have […] to fill an emptiness in our being" (Engstrom and Valenzano 89). Those who succumb to this desire end up by destroying life and soul. Therefore, Famine will ultimately bring about the end of the world, much the same as in the Book of Revelation when it appears with its brothers, Pestilence, War, and Death, as signs of the Apocalypse (Revelation 6: 1–8). In the same episode, Castiel, speaking in a quasi-scriptural style, says, "And then will come Famine, riding on a black steed. He will ride into the land of plenty and great will be the Horseman's hunger for he is Hunger. His hunger will seep out and poison the air."

The land of plenty is an obvious reference to the United States symbolized in the episode by the all-you-can-eat restaurant. Famine himself highlights this association and, at the same time, establishes the intimate connection between insatiable consumerism and lack of spirituality, considering them one of the major problems of American society:

> Oh, America—all-you-can-eat, all the time. Consume, consume. A swarm of locusts in stretch pants. And yet, you're all still starving because hunger doesn't just come from the body, it also comes from the soul.

Consequently, this season also directs a moral lesson to the United States where people try to fill in their spiritual emptiness, "created by selfishness and moral relativism" (Engstrom and Valenzano 90), in an ever-growing capitalist society. In comparing Americans to locusts, Famine is referring to the biblical episode of the ten plagues which affected Egypt after the refusal of the Pharaoh in freeing the Israelites. The plague of the locusts, the 8th plague, caused a huge devastation in Egypt, since the insects devoured everything in their reach (Exodus 10: 4–6, 14). Like insatiable locusts, Americans are, on the one hand, spreading obesity as a social plague, and, on the other, showing severe signs of a disease of the soul caused by their excesses: even if they devour everything they want they will always starve since they suffer from lack of spirituality and of self-control, and, as Engstrom and Valenzano remark, "only through self-control and spiritual realization can people combat the emptiness within; without such control, their own end times will fast approach" (90).

According to Tony and Trisha Kemerly, Season 7 also opposes the fat body to the thin one, implying the superiority of the latter over the former. The fat body signals a state of both physical and mental weakness which needs to be healed. It is associated with three of the Seven Deadly Sins, namely gluttony (because fat people not only eat too much, they have poor eating habits), sloth (since fat people rarely exercise), and greed (fat people reject the accepted social ideals related to the body). Thus, it "becomes a manifestation of self-indulgence and spiritual imperfection" (59) in a society marked by a discourse which others the fat body and is symbolized in this season by the Leviathans.

Finally, Season 7 constitutes a profound condemnation and a strong critique of political propaganda and demagogy: addicted to poor-quality food and eating transgenics, people become obese, indifferent and apathetic, as if blind to what is around them, and thus are more easily controllable by political power. Without opinion, without free will, these people constitute easy prey for political parties and men of power who do not care about health or environmental issues but are only interested in making money. And the big target of this fierce critique seems to be the Republican Party.

We come to know that Dick Roman's aggressive merger and acquisition policy attracts the attention of the conservative party, and that at one time he was considered to be the strongest candidate for its leadership. In many of the photos we see in his office, Roman is shaking hands with influential and famous people, such as Prince Harry, but also with George W. Bush. Moreover, when talking to Dean about Roman's acquisition of a parcel of land, Frank Devereaux compares one of the billionaire's female workers to Sarah Palin, the well-known candidate for the vice presidency of the

USA as running mate of John McCain, who became famous due to her extremely conservative ideas:

> FRANK: Check out Sarah Palin.
> DEAN: Who is she?
> FRANK: Amanda Willer. Surprise, surprise! She works for Richard Roman.
> DEAN: What was she doing?
> FRANK: Being a naughty bossy little girl ["Adventures in Babysitting," 7.11].

Dick Roman's name itself may allude to Obama's Republican adversary, Mitt Romney, and to Dick Cheney, Vice-President of the USA under George W. Bush.

Still, a Happy Ending ... or Not?

By using Leviathans to criticize political power in America, *Supernatural* is not only drawing on biblical myth, it is also referring to Thomas Hobbes's *Leviathan. Leviathan or the Matter, Forme and Power of a Common Wealth Ecclesiastical and Civil* was published in 1651, during the English Civil War (1642–1651), in which Parliamentarians (Roundheads) opposed Royalists (Cavaliers). The frontispiece of the book, created by the French artist Abraham Bosse (1602/4–1676), shows a crowned figure containing the bodies of hundreds of persons, which immediately reminds us of the Leviathans inside Castiel's body. This monstrous and gigantic figure carries a sword, which is the symbol of earthly power, and a crosier, the symbol of the power of the Church, suggesting that both powers should be united under the head of civil law. Above this huge character is written a verse from the Book of Job: "*Non est potestas Super Terram quae Comparetur ei. Iob. 41. 24*" ("There is no power of earth to be compared to him"). This quotation suggests that we are facing the Leviathan mentioned in Job, here understood by Hobbes as the perfect form of government: a government that links the spiritual and earthly power, thus being undivided, that is to say, absolute. This is for Hobbes the most legitimate form of government that comprehends all and incorporates all, ruling over the whole society.

If humans want peace, they must submit to this absolute authority (a theory that would be called the social contract theory) thus surrendering their love of liberty and dominion over others. Humans must live in the Commonwealth and surrender their rights and wishes to this form of government; only by doing so can humanity live in peace and avoid civil war, anarchy or chaos. That is why, in the frontispiece, inside the Leviathan's body, the individuals are portrayed as an indistinct mass of people who turn their backs on the viewer, since they are facing their sovereign, empowered by their mutual consent. The sovereign of the Commonwealth in question cannot be dismissed, accused of injustice or put to death. He must be obeyed at all levels. The Commonwealth itself can be a monarchy, an aristocracy or a democracy, monarchy being, for Hobbes, the best model.

Is *Supernatural* conveying the same message or telling us otherwise—that contemporary America should not submit to the absolute rule of the Leviathan, this form of strong and authoritative government? It seems that the answer is no, we should not submit to these particular types of government, which in the United States of America have been associated with the ideals defended by American conservatism and the Republican party, mainly the maintenance of tradition, anti-communism, absolutist morals, individualism and Christian orthodoxy. In *Supernatural*, there is a tendency to favor more liberal ideas, such as equality, liberalism as well as consumer and environmental protection. In fact, throughout the run of the series there is a call for free will and for the right to choose, as the two brothers keep teaching us when, for example, they deny being the vessels of Michael and Lucifer in Season 5:

> MICHAEL: And you think you know better than my father? One unimportant little man…. What makes you think you get to choose?
> DEAN: Because I got to believe that I can choose what I do with my … unimportant little life.

Later, Dean says to Sam: "This is it. […] Team free will." ("The Song Remains the Same," 5.13)

The fight against the Leviathans is another example of freedom of choice. Refusing to accept what apparently was a dogma—Leviathans cannot be killed—Sam and Dean find out that these apparently indestructible monsters can be eliminated after all. As happened with the Roman Empire, Roman's rule was also bound to decline and fall. With the help of the Word of God, deciphered by Kevin Tran, a vegan Asian boy, who is thus not contaminated by meat, they manage to destroy these monstrous creatures when Dick Roman is finally killed by Dean. The two brothers are still able to save America. If we were to establish a comparison between *Supernatural*'s Season 7 and Tolkien's *legendarium*, we could almost say that this is the season of hope. There are very particular reasons behind this which surpass the expected happy ending. First, as I have underlined previously, *Supernatural* constantly calls attention to itself as a cinematic art form and as a narrative construction. In this sense, Season 7 is also recalling its status as a cultural artifact, reclaiming for art, and in this case, for popular culture, a space of questioning and inquiring, a space of freedom. Second, as I have pointed out, the 23 episodes of Season 7 were shown on public television between the 23rd of September 2011 and the 18th of May 2012. In six months' time, the USA would be electing its 44th President. Barack Obama was competing for his second term as American President against the Republican candidate Mitt Romney, who may be depicted in the season by Dick Roman, as I have suggested. Choosing the Leviathans as the monsters to be fought by the two cowboy-like heroes, Sam and Dean, Season 7 is expressing the fears surrounding the possible victory of the Republicans and their conservative and authoritarian ideals and, simultaneously, embracing the hope that Americans can choose better. By comparing Republicans to the biblical devouring monster and Hobbes's absolute form of government, this season explores the moral as well as the social and political consequences of their eventual rise to power and making an argument for freedom and free will. At the same time, this season also condemns the consumer habits of the American population (particularly eating too much meat and fast food), associated with gluttony, fatness and self-apathy, as well as the pollution of the environment and of food. In fact, there is a clear critique of genetic experimentation, specifically of the genetic manipulation of food, and of the dangers of this kind of scientific progress. But Season 7 also offers a denunciation of political propaganda and demagogy as a means of conveniently maneuvering people. Let us not forget that apart from being the leader of the Leviathans, Dick Roman is also "a CEO [...] giant in the motivational speaking world" ("There Will Be Blood"), easily controlling people's minds and behaviors. Finally, this season also focuses on the consequences of extreme greed and of the menacing power of absolute control over society. Following the example of most of the authors and works I mentioned at the beginning of this essay, *Supernatural*, Season 7, asks us to stop being blind, and therefore can eventually be understood as "a diagnosis, a warning, a call to understanding and action, and—most important—a mapping of possible alternatives" (Suvin 378). If Americans are alert, they can fight political manipulation and refuse to be de-humanized, transformed into obese and unemotional puppets. To choose is to be able to think and, therefore, to act.

This emphasis on these issues, and on free thinking in particular, is also what makes the political message of this season much more than an exhortation to 2012 audiences. It addresses political and ideological regimes of all times around the world. That is why we are tempted to regard it as a foreshadowing of what was to befall America and the world only four years later, in 2016. In fact, we are impelled to ask: if it were made today, in this American administration, would Season 7 still contain a sign of hope? Or, instead, would the greedy monsters finally be the death of Sam and Dean, leaving us defenseless to fight against the end of the world?

Acknowledgment

This essay is dedicated to my daughter, Inês, a huge fan of *Supernatural* who convinced me that it would be worthwhile to watch the series.

Works Cited

Abbot, Stacey and David Lavery, eds. *TV Goes to Hell: An Unofficial Road Map of* Supernatural. ECW Press, 2011.

The Bible. Authorized King James version. www.kingjamesbibleonline.org/.

Botting, Fred. "Aftergothic: Consumption, Machines, and Black Holes." *The Cambridge Companion to Gothic Fiction*, edited by Jerrold E. Hogle, Cambridge University Press, 2002, pp. 277–300.

Brown, Simon. "Renegades and Wayward Sons: *Supernatural* and the 70's." In Abbot and Lavery, 60–75.

Engstrom, Erika and Joseph M. Valenzano III. *Television, Religion, and Supernatural*. Maryland, Lexington Books, 2014.

Hobbes, Thomas. *Leviathan, or the Matter, Forme and Power of a Common Wealth Ecclesiastical and Civil*. 1651. Penguin, 1985.

Hurley, Kelly. *The Gothic Body: Sexuality, Materialism, and Degeneration at the* fin de siècle. Cambridge University Press, 2004.

Kemerly, Tony and Trisha Kemerly. "A Supernatural Tale of Agency, Othering and Oppression: The Road So Far." In *Popular Culture Review*, vol. 29, no. 1, 2018, pp. 51–63.

Luckhurst, Roger. *Science Fiction*. Polity Press, 2005.

Roenecker, Jean-Paul. *Le Symbolisme Animal: Mythes, Croyances, Légendes, Archétypes, Folklore, Imaginaire*. Éditions Dangles, 1994.

Sontag, Susan. "The Imagination of Disaster." *Commentary*, vol. 40, no. 4, 1965, pp. 42–48.

Stevenson, Gregory. "Horror, Humanity, and the Demon in the Mirror." *In the Hunt: Unauthorized Essays on* Supernatural, edited by Supernatural.tv with Leah Wilson, BenBella, 2009, pp. 39–52.

"'Supernatural' Season 7 Spoilers: Robert Singer Talks Leviathan Payoff." *Spoilersguide*, 17 March 2012. www.spoilersguide.com/supernatural/season-7-spoilers-robert-singer-talks-leviathan-payoff/. Accessed 3 Dec. 2019.

Suvin, Darko, "On the Poetics of the Science Fiction Genre." *College English*. vol. 34, no. 3, 1972, pp. 372–82.

Tolkien, J. R. R. "On Fairy-Stories." *Tree and Leaf, Including the Poem* Mythopoeia, by J. R. R. Tolkien, Unwin, 1988, pp. 9–73.

Tuttle, Brad. "Sales of Dystopian Novels Have Been Spiking on Amazon Since the Election." *Money*, 25 Jan. 2017, http://money.com/money/4648774/trump-1984-dystopian-novel-sales-brave-new-world/. Accessed 2 December 2019.

Williams, David. *Deformed Discourse. the Function of the Monster in Medieval Thought and Literature*. Exeter: Exeter University Press, 1996.

PART TWO

Text and Context

Re-Constructing Monstrosity

Faces of Evil, from Mary Shelley's Frankenstein
to the TV Show Supernatural

TATIANA PROROKOVA-KONRAD

Introduction

The confrontation between good and bad, or heroes and villains, is frequently explored on film and TV, including the TV show *Supernatural*. Film and television offer numerous portrayals of evil; yet, as this essay argues, the Creature from Mary Shelley's novel *Frankenstein*, written exactly two centuries ago, remains one of the most complex, terrifying, and fascinating monsters of all time. Its image has exercised a considerable influence on literature and film and found multiple reflections in various narratives and cultural texts. *Supernatural* has devoted three episodes—"Book of the Damned" (10.18), "Dark Dynasty" (10.21), and "The Prisoner" (10.22)—to the story that evokes the characters from Shelley's *Frankenstein*, too. The latter two episodes, especially, tease out the connections, and will be the focus of this discussion. Coming from Eastern Europe, the Styne family (later known to the viewer as the Frankenstein family) are powerful supernatural creatures who, by means of skillful surgical manipulations, take various body parts of their victims to enhance their own power. Being blamed for most of the wars and terrorist attacks that took place throughout the 20th and 21st centuries, the Stynes become Sam and Dean's arch-enemies after they murder the brothers' friend and arguably surrogate sister, Charlie. The Winchesters ultimately execute the Stynes who live in the United States, yet other members of the Styne family continue to commit their evil deeds throughout the world. This essay will focus on the elements of intertextuality used in *Supernatural*, with a particular reference to Shelley's novel *Frankenstein*. Paying close attention to the (re-)construction of monstrosity both in *Frankenstein* and *Supernatural*, the essay will examine how the image of the Creature from *Frankenstein*, being an embodiment of evil, has been transformed in the 21st century with the help of *Supernatural*, now personifying multiple evil groups—from the Nazis to terrorists and beyond. Such a portrayal certainly reinforces the evil nature of terrorism, but it also foregrounds the inevitable transformation that monstrosity as such undergoes over time, being an effective tool to communicate various problems, fears, and anxieties that strike countries, nations, and societies on political and cultural levels.

The Monster After 9/11

The episodes in which *Supernatural* makes reference to *Franken-stein* were released in 2015, i.e., almost one and a half decades after the terrorist attacks on September 11, 2001. By 2015, cinema and TV had already been largely transformed by 9/11. Terrorism was and still is recognized as one of the most evil forces responsible for unjust violence and killing that take place throughout the world. It is thus unsurprising that film and television frequently use the image of terrorism to intensify the evil nature of the villain. *Supernatural* is, in this regard, not an exception, as the series frequently refers to terrorism in either explicit or implicit ways. The Frankenstein episodes are one of the vivid manifestations of that. Through the references to *Frankenstein*, *Supernatural* tackles the complex meaning of terrorism as "the monster," from both political and cultural perspectives. But is terrorism an entirely new monster on film and TV?

It is not. Prior to 9/11, terrorism was reflected on screen, too. However, one might detect the evolution of terrorism in American film from the 1970s to the present. Thomas Riegler observes:

> When reviewing Hollywood's output on terrorism, it is obvious that it correlates with the waves and historical development of political violence: previously sporadic encounters with terrorism in Hollywood cinema, like Alfred Hitchcock's *Saboteur* (1942), became more frequent in the 1970s, at a time when international terrorism and especially hijacking of jetliners orchestrated by Palestinian groups made headlines and featured in newsreels (35).

In the 1980s, film continued to attract audience attention to the "terrorist threat" (38). A decade later, in the 1990s, the action movie genre was largely transformed by the persistent terrorism-trope (38). Finally, terrorism becomes one of the most painful yet frequently recurring story elements after 9/11, although Riegler accentuates that "[i]t took more than five years for the entertainment industry to tackle 9/11 directly" in Paul Green-grass's *United 93* (2006) (41).

Riegler elucidates the evolution of terrorism on screen through the discussion of the changing role of terrorism in real life: "In 1970s cinema terrorism was escapist entertainment with little basis in reality. [...] This mode of representation changed during the 1980s—greatly influenced by the engagement of the US in the Middle East and the experience of devastating attacks like those in Beirut in 1983" (42). The 1980s was the decade when the terrorist became "a sworn public enemy of everything America stands for" (42). With the end of the Cold War, "the former stereotypical villains lost much of their symbolic value" (42). Yet in the 1990s, "cinema envisioned a crumbling world order with failing state power, the emergence of asymmetric threats, and new players in the form of transnational networks" (42). Finally, 9/11 was *the* tragedy that has forever transformed terrorism from the chief source of cinematic entertainment to the real threat that is no longer perceived as improbable or hard-to-imagine. To borrow from Riegler, "More recent movies deliberately aim to capture the phenomenon even more realistically" (42).

Terrorism is, indeed, one of the larger factors that contributed to the construction of today's monsters. Yet scholars tend to foreground the general turmoil in social, political, and economic spheres that surrounds the U.S. since 9/11. Marylou Naumoff, for example, offers the following observation:

> The United States is confronted by a great deal of uncertainty. Factors such as the 9–11 (*sic*) attacks, war, accusations and proof of torture, the failing economy, the appointment of our first black president, the uprising of the Tea Party, mass shootings, continued terrorist threats or attacks, and the persistence of multiculturalism all coalesce, leaving Americans anxious about the U.S. and its future. This uncertainty produces competing and contradictory rhetorical texts that seek to speak for or represent the country [2].

Through the re-creation of these events, the violence that characterizes the post–9/11 world has been swiftly transferred onto screen, filling it with images of war, murder, and fear. The violence that we face in real life not only nourishes the genre of horror but it irrevocably transforms it, making the monsters on-screen more recognizable than ever.

The recent scholarship on horror after the terrorist attacks on 9/11 reveals that 9/11 itself and the events that followed it became the most popular subject matters to deal with in horror films. We, as film critics and cultural studies scholars, are thus left to discuss the metaphorical representations of concrete events like the destruction of the World Trade Center, the Iraq War, and the tortures perpetuated at Abu Ghraib and other detention centers; the rise of new subgenres such as "torture porn"; big-budget remakes of classic horror films, as well as the reinvention of traditional monsters (e.g., vampires, B-movie creatures, and zombies); and the new awareness of visual technologies as sites of horror in themselves (Briefel and Miller 1–2).

One should focus on the concept of "the horror film as an allegorical genre," the one that "transfigures the 'real' into the representational" (2). *Supernatural* has adopted these new rules and created monsters such as the Frankenstein family, who today open to its audience new perspectives on violence that Shelley's *Frankenstein* simply could not do in 1818.

Supernatural is deservedly labeled as a gothic series, the show that from its very beginning "has included storylines based on popular Gothic legends and mythology" (Edmundson 3). In doing so, *Supernatural* not only succeeds in making violence tangible and terrifying, but it also transforms the characters from legends and myths into the objects that are real and around us, bringing the problem of terror and the murder of the innocent closer to the viewer. In this respect, Melissa Edmundson makes a crucial observation: "Taking the supernatural out of the castle and into average, ordinary homes taps into a whole new set of fears, especially contemporary anxieties about the average, ordinary home being invaded by unpredictable violent forces and bad things happening to seemingly good people (the first five minutes of almost every *Supernatural* episode)" (1–2). Erasing the boundary between public/private and safe/unsafe spaces, *Supernatural* most explicitly emphasizes the influence that 9/11 has exercised on our minds and bodies, making the state of psychological collapse and body mutilation integral parts of our everyday reality. On screen, displaying terrorists or acts of terror as monsters is not only inevitable today, but is helpful in establishing a more complex relationship between the hero and the villain.

Even the image that the protagonists Sam and Dean embody in the series is equivocal in many ways. Aaron C. Burnell provides an interesting reading of the two characters as being neither heroes nor villains but rather something "in between": "By being grifters(/hunters), the Winchesters […] can neither fully align themselves against the capitalistic work force nor the imagined community of suburbia. They can exist neither as complete monsters nor as total heroes. Instead, they are something in between, they are 'white trash'" (47). Their actions, in turn, help re-establish the so-called "hegemonic American identity": "Through their actions, which we see as operating at personal and societal levels, the religious and secular-based tenets of American Exceptionalism and the Frontier Myth become folded into a larger story of the hegemony of Christianity, and the perpetuation of the Judeo-Christian tradition" (Engstrom and Valenzano 100). While these actions can be questioned throughout the run of the show, in this essay I suggest classifying Sam and Dean as American post–9/11 heroes. That is, while I agree with Alexandra Lykissas that the Winchesters are "the representatives of the man who pulls up his bootstraps, returns to normalcy, and continues to fight our enemies, which seemed to be the resounding rhetoric after 9/11" (20), their heroism is compromised by the means whereby they fight evil and by their own character-transformation that they experience during this war. The monstrous heroism of the Winchesters reveals the difficulty of dividing the characters in *Supernatural* into purely good and bad ones, despite the fact that the main monster of today is, as both real life and film/TV overly articulate, terrorism. This largely corroborates two arguments: first, that "fifteen years of media production after 9/11 have neither allayed fears about international terrorism nor brought viewers much closer to understanding the preconditions and prognoses for it" (Froula 118), and, second, that after 9/11 the monster is not only among the villains but is also among the heroes.

Creating the Monster: Mary Shelley's Frankenstein

My reading of the Frankenstein family from *Supernatural* as terrorists results from an analysis of their monstrosity and the way it is portrayed in the series. To understand the reason behind using the Frankenstein figure for such a purpose in *Supernatural*, it is, however, important to go back to the original characters created by Mary Shelley in 1818—the Creature and Victor Frankenstein.

The ambivalent nature of the Creature from Shelley's novel has generated multiple readings of what it could stand for. Shelley's descriptions of the Creature change constantly, from a pure monster to a rejected being, thus making the reader both fear and sympathize with him. While both the good and evil characteristics of the Creature are equally important in constructing its image, I will primarily focus on the evil ones to demonstrate how the creative scientist Frankenstein and his creation evolved into terrorists.

In the novel, Victor Frankenstein is portrayed as an individual with the mindset unique to his time: "The world was to me a secret which I desired to divine. Curiosity, earnest research to learn the hidden laws of nature, gladness akin to rapture, as they were unfolded to me, are among the earliest sensations I can remember" (Shelley 35). The creation of something unusual is thus foreshadowed already in the early descriptions of the young scientist. The Creature that he gives life to turns out to be one of the darkest beings that humanity has ever faced. The novel extensively accentuates the monstrosity of the Creature through its horrifying appearance as well as the depressive settings in which the reader usually encounters it. The multiple descriptions of the Creature that the novel showers the reader with insist on the Creature being a monster. For example, it is usually referred to as "the wretch, the filthy daemon" (73). The Creature's actions are classified as evil, for Victor thinks that he "had turned loose into the world a depraved wretch whose delight was in carnage and misery" (74). Finally, the Creature's physical appearance is described as mutilated to such an extent that it provokes fear in every human: "its gigantic stature, and the deformity of its aspect, more hideous than belongs to humanity" (73), are consistently terrifying to anyone who sees it, since "his countenance bespoke bitter anguish, combined with disdain and malignity, while its unearthly ugliness rendered it almost too horrible for human eyes" (94–95).

The novel, hence, establishes a clear difference between humans and the Creature, or, as Josh Bernatchez puts it, "[t]he human versus monster binary" (207). Yet, while the characteristic of the Creature as a *monster* can be interpreted in multiple ways, from a metaphoric reference to the duality of human nature to intolerant, discriminating, and ableist view, I am interested in what way the "monster" from 1818 contributes to the creation of the terrorist-monster (associated with Victor Frankenstein and the Creature) in the post–9/11 era.

There are, indeed, several aspects that help one draw parallels between the Creature and modern-day terrorists. First, it is, of course, the visual image of the Creature that renders terrorism as ugly, monstrous, and revolting to every nonterrorist. This horrifying appearance also helps intensify the power of terrorism to inspire humanity with fear and panic. Second, the Creature's bodily constitution deserves special attention. While Bernatchez claims that "[t]he creature is initially composed out of other human beings; as a created object, he is a metaphor for the dependence of the individual on a community, for he is an individual composed of many other individuals" (212), I propose expanding this interpretation, and argue that the body of the Creature stands for the terrorist net that is powerful *because* it includes a large number of members who are located in/can easily move to different parts of the world.

Yet it is not only the visual but also the verbal aspect that allows one to view the Creature as a terrorist. In the case of 9/11 and the War on Terror, the terrorists' Otherness has been frequently intensified through their national belonging, helping oppose the U.S. and the Middle East. In the 9/11 plots, terrorists are foreigners who speak another language. The idea of linguistic Otherness is thoroughly developed in Shelley's *Frankenstein*, too, for the Creature is at first unable to speak the language of the people who surround him. In her essay "Autistic Voice and Literary Architecture in Mary Shelley's *Frankenstein*," Julia Miele Rodas provides a fresh discussion of the Creature from a disability studies perspective, zeroing in "on autistic language, and exploration of the semiotic and rhetorical qualities of *Frankenstein* that foreground the novel's articulation of autistic voice" (171). Yet while Rodas explores the ways in which the Creature's inability to communicate stands for a form of disability, I look at the problem from a different perspective and argue that the failure to take part in a conversation might be the result of the Creature's foreignness. The Creature shares his first experiences with communication with Victor Frankenstein: "I found that these people possessed a method of communicating their experience and feelings to one another by articulate sounds. [...] This was indeed a godlike science, and I ardently desired to become acquainted with it" (Shelley 107–8). It is significant that the novel provides longer descriptions of the way that the Creature learns the language just as any other individual would learn a foreign language, word by word, listening to the speakers, paying attention to the objects they use or point at to understand how each is called in the language that is foreign to the Creature. The idea of multiplicity of languages is additionally corroborated through the inclusion of such characters as the "sweet Arabian"—the Turkish girl Safie who "uttered articulate sounds and appeared to have a language of her own" and who "was neither understood by, nor herself understood, the cottagers" (113). In her earlier encounter with one of the cottagers, Felix, the communication between the two is described as follows: "They conversed with one another through the means of an interpreter, and sometimes with the interpretation of looks; and Safie sang to him the divine airs of her native country" (120). The linguistic foreignness that the novel so prominently speaks of is, hence, another aspect that unites the image of the Creature and that of terrorists, constructing the so-called verbal monstrosity/Otherness in the two.

Finally, the mobility of the Creature allows a comparison between himself and terrorists, too. The ability of the Creature to move with "superhuman speed" (Shelley 94) parallels the elusiveness of terrorists who, as reality reveals, are very hard to catch. Yet the interest of the Creature to come closer to humanity, instead of living in seclusion, stands for something even more complex, when comparing the Creature to terrorists. To borrow from Bernatchez, "The Creature, continuing his progression of expanding self-extension [...], moves outward toward successively larger emblems of civilization, from a hut of one room to a town of many houses" (206). One might speculate that this expansion and the move closer to civilization, in a way, mirrors the attacks of 9/11, when terrorists came to New York City, which is densely populated and, indeed, offers more privileges and comforts of civilization compared to the dwellings of terrorists.

Shelley's *Frankenstein* is thus helpful when trying to understand not only the issue of monstrosity in general but also the development of the monster and its evolution after 9/11. As the analysis of the novel reveals, the phenomenon of the monster is, in principle, not entirely new, and the modern monster, indeed, can borrow certain elements even from the monster from the beginning of the 19th century.

Supernatural *and the Metaphor of Frankenstein*

"Is it possible to make a Hollywood blockbuster without evoking 9/11?" (Buchanan qtd. in McSweeney 136). It is rather hard to do so. Indeed, it is almost impossible to provide cultural interpretations of American current issues without making an explicit or implicit reference to 9/11. The terrorist attacks on September 11, 2001, represent a landmark in U.S. political and cultural history that enforced a filter of fear on post–9/11 representations. It is through the prism of fear that cultural texts discuss current problems, thus proving that "fear is not a timeless and universal experience, but a socially structured discourse that conditions behavior and belief in certain ways" (Takacs 1).

As a post–9/11 text, *Supernatural* also skillfully uses fear, discussing not only our personal anxieties but also those of the U.S. and the world in general. In their pursuit of "the 'family' business of 'saving people, hunting things'" (Edmundson 1), the Winchesters face some of the most important political, social, and religious concerns that really exist in the United States. Among them are 9/11, the War on Terror, and the military interventions in the Middle East—all are discussed in the two episodes that focus on the Frankenstein family, namely "Dark Dynasty" and "The Prisoner."

Post-9/11 cinematic production has provided multiple "challenging 'remakes' of September 11th 2001" (McSweeney 136), and *Supernatural* has contributed to this, too. While the two episodes are not an adaptation of Shelley's novel, they borrow elements from the original and use them to explain 9/11 and the problem of terrorism. The success and complexity of Shelley's *Frankenstein* is recognized by the multiple cinematic adaptations of the novel that approximate to "nearly two hundred films" (Heffernan 136). James A.W. Heffernan wonders "What then can film versions of *Frankenstein* offer to academic critics of the novel? Can they be anything more than vulgarizations or travesties of the original?" (136); whereas I am more interested in which way the use of the monster from the beginning of the 19th century helps one understand the terrorist from the post–9/11 era.

The Styne family, as the audience first learns to know it, consists of numerous members, the majority of whom are males. The head of the family, Monroe Styne, is a direct embodiment of Victor Frankenstein from the novel: he is the one who operates on the members of his family, transplanting various inner organs and body parts, to make the men physically stronger and thus practically invincible. Monroe is the father to Eldon and the uncle to Eli, who are directly involved in the search for the Book of the Damned that is at that moment in the possession of Sam. The Stynes are described as being responsible for most of the misfortunes that took place in the past thousand years, including more recent ones. For example, when trying to find any information on the Stynes, Dean tells Sam, "Well, that's pretty much what we do know, that they screwed with financial markets, they helped Hitler get started, along with God knows what else … probably disco. But you go back to the 1800s, and the trail goes dead. There's nothing in the research, there's nothing online. It's like the family just popped up one day" ("Dark Dynasty"). The reference to the 1800s is arguably made to connect Shelley's novel, which was written in 1818, to the episode's plot. The viewer is reminded about the novel again later, when Eldon says that "Mary Shelley … spent a few nights in castle Frankenstein and stumbled upon our secrets, and forced us to change our names and go underground" ("Dark Dynasty"). Mary Shelley is thus the one who, indeed, "wrote a book" about the Frankenstein family, yet "no one believed it to be true" ("Dark Dynasty"). Later in the episode, Eldon shares with the Winchesters, "Let me tell you about my family business.[1] You're in way over your heads. The family is vast. Spread over the world. And that power that you mentioned doesn't come from the Book. It comes from intelligence and will. The Book facilitates. Stock market dive, recession, 9/11…. Any of them ring a bell? Arab Spring? Didn't even break a sweat." Towards the end of the episode, Sam adds more to the list: "I mean, one thousand years of nasty. They made a ton mopping up the Black Plague. They started the Hundred Years War." The Stynes are thus the family that, in a way, personifies a terrorist net that through "secrecy" and "discipline" succeeds in spreading chaos and causing death for many years.

Along with the Stynes' terrorist actions, their appearance also helps construct their image as monsters. Discussing cinematic adaptations of the novel, Heffernan pays close attention to how monstrosity is created visually: "By forcing us to face the monster's physical repulsiveness, which he can never deny or escape and which aborts his every hope of gaining sympathy, film versions of *Frankenstein* prompt us to rethink his monstrosity in terms of visualization: how do we see the monster, what does he see, and how does he want to be seen?" (136). *Supernatural*, in principle, does the same in the scenes that foreground the physical/bodily appearance of the Stynes. "Dark Dynasty," for example, starts with a scene where Eldon cuts out the eyes of an innocent victim who has excellent eyesight (the audience assumes that the eyes will be later transplanted to one of the Stynes). In a later scene, Eldon boasts of the new method that the Stynes use to make themselves more powerful: "It's a family specialty. Bioengineering. Surgical enhancement. And I'm not talking about nose jobs. [*Shows the large scar on his chest.*] See? Two hearts in here. Bunch of extra muscles, especially in the legs. Every man in the family's had a little something. Pretty much what you'd expect though, given the family tree" ("Dark Dynasty").

While the visible physical mutilation and the actions of the Stynes that are aimed to terrorize people worldwide construct them as monsters, overtly labeling terrorism as *the* monster of the post–9/11 era, *Supernatural* develops the issue of monstrosity further in the next episode, "The Prisoner." Here, the series seems to complicate the problem of "[the post–9/11-] cinema simplicity" when characters are plainly divided into "heroes and villains" articulated by John Markert (1). *Supernatural* invites the viewer to question the Stynes' "sole" monstrosity by compromising the images of Sam and Dean. Going back again to the previous episode, "Dark Dynasty," the interrogation scene is noteworthy. When Sam and Dean, as they try to find out more information on the Frankenstein family from chained Eldon, both leave the room for a moment, Eldon escapes, tearing off his arm and leaving it chained. While this was done by the prisoner himself, such a violent action accentuates the fact that Dean and Sam, indeed, pose a danger to Eldon and the Stynes in general, making the Winchesters superior and capable of committing more violence. Indeed, earlier episodes of *Supernatural* have repeatedly made clear that the Winchesters are more than capable of inflicting torture; Dean has even been trained in torture techniques by a demon.

In "The Prisoner," the issue of torture is raised again, when Monroe Frankenstein forces his youngest son, Cyrus Styne, to operate on his schoolmate who bullied him earlier. A similar scene takes place later, when Dean is captured by the Stynes who attempt (but eventually fail) to perform a similar operation on him. The two episodes thus resurrect the scenes of torture that in a post–9/11 context one immediately connects to the real tortures conducted by some American soldiers in detention camps, including Abu Ghraib. Discussing the ambivalent nature of torture porn—a prominent horror sub-genre of the post–9/11 cinema—Catherine Zimmer claims:

> The phenomenon of torture porn is widely considered the lowest common denominator in the global reinvestment in horror in the new millennium. The ultra-graphic violence of these films, in combination with narratives that seem predominantly invested in providing the basis for incredibly drawn-out scenes of torture—rather than the rhythmic suspense of a more "traditional" slasher film or the eerie uncanniness of the contemporary Asian or Spanish ghost films—situates them as somehow both the pinnacle and the gutter of contemporary horror. (84)

And although these two episodes of *Supernatural* hardly attempt to turn into torture porn (though the show does so in "Keep Calm and

Carry On" [12.01], when Sam is interrogated and tortured by Lady Toni Bevell and Ms. Watt from the British Men of Letters), the scenes of torture revive the pain of 9/11 and the atrocity that became part of the War on Terror. Yet because the torture is exercised by both the Stynes and the Winchesters, Sam and Dean also embody the monster of the post–9/11 era.

This is, however, not a terrorist-monster but rather a transformed American who avenges the deaths of his loved ones and protects the innocent. The death of their friend Charlie at the hands of Eldon is thus a metaphorical 9/11 in the two episodes, and it triggers the monstrous reaction in Dean. He first promises to Sam, "Oh I'm gonna find whoever did this. And I'm gonna rip apart everything and everyone that they ever loved. And then I'm gonna tear out their heart" ("The Prisoner"). The revenge turns Dean into a monster similar to the Creature from *Frankenstein*, who threatens Victor in literally the same way. Dean's monstrosity is particularly visible toward the end of "The Prisoner," when he shoots down Cyrus Styne, despite Styne's pleading with him not to do so, and his attempt to prove that he is different from the rest of his family and does not support what his family does. The murder of the innocent might figuratively stand for the civilian deaths that were caused during the interventions in Afghanistan and Iraq as a response to 9/11.

The monstrosity that *Supernatural* constructs in the two episodes, borrowing various elements from Shelley's novel, is intricate in many respects. Yet when read in light of 9/11, the monster of today is not an "isolated" form of evil; it is rather a *characteristic* that becomes inherent in the post–9/11 world and that erases the boundary between the hero and the villain. Jessica George notices similarities between some monsters and the Winchesters: "The existence of these sympathetic, more-or-less human monsters makes Sam and Dean themselves appear more or less monsters" (205). Yet it is not only "sympathetic" monsters that allow one to associate the Winchesters with monsters, but generally every monster that reminds one of a human being, such as, for example, the Stynes. The metaphor of Frankenstein only reinforces the idea of monstrosity being part of every human being, especially in the post–9/11 era.

Conclusion

The cultural imagining of the monster has undergone considerable changes since the 19th century. The monster has always been a response to societal fears and anxieties, and is thus greatly shaped by the time that it emerges. It is, however, particularly interesting to observe that the monster that was created by Mary Shelley in *Frankenstein* in 1818 remains relevant even today, and numerous current narratives borrow specific elements from the novel to construct the monster of today. The violence generated by the Creature in *Frankenstein* as well as Victor Frankenstein's selfish obsession to satisfy his own ambitions without thinking of the dreadful ramifications that this might entail draw the interest of writers and directors who attempt to re-create "evil" of a specific time. Reviving the well-known images from Shelley's novel perhaps ensures that the monster will be noticed right away, and its deadly deeds will be recognized as such. It is thus understandable why *Supernatural* borrows certain elements from the novel trying to re-create today's most horrible monster—terrorism. Through physical violence and psychological tension, *Supernatural* re-constructs the real-life situation that the world in general and the United States in particular find themselves in after 9/11. While *Supernatural* is only one of many cultural texts that offer their views on the problem, its version of post–9/11 confusion and the state of permanent war against terrorists is not only legitimate but is, indeed, convincing. The choice to refer to the classical text and, in a way, the classical monster only reinforces the idea of terrorism as a great menace that humanity faces in the post–9/11 world.

NOTES

1. The reference to a "family business" allows one to draw a parallel between the Stynes and the Winchesters. Yet while the Stynes work against humanity, trying to destroy it, the Winchesters work for it, saving human beings from such monsters as the Stynes and many other ones. Moreover, the Stynes' Book can be linked to John Winchester's—Sam and Dean's father—journal, which itself is a patchwork of entries, sources, and illustrations. In a sense, the "power" that the Stynes get from the book can be figuratively compared to the power that the Winchesters get from the journal, finding out more information about various monsters and creatures and the ways of how to kill them.

WORKS CITED

Bernatchez, Josh. "Monstrosity, Suffering, and Sympathetic Community in *Frankenstein* and 'The Structure of Torture.'" *Science Fiction Studies*, vol. 36, no. 2, 2009, pp. 205–16. *JSTOR*, http://www.jstor.org/stable/40649956. Accessed 1 May 2018.

Briefel, Aviva, and Sam J. Miller. "Introduction." *Horror After 9/11: World of Fear, Cinema of Terror*, edited by Aviva Briefel and Sam J. Miller, U of Texas P, 2011, pp. 1–12.

Burnell, Aaron C. "Rebels, Rogues, and Sworn Brothers: *Supernatural* and the Shift in 'White Trash' from Monster to Hero." *TV Goes to Hell: An Unofficial Road Map of* Supernatural, edited by Stacey Abbott and David Lavery, ECW P, 2011, pp. 47–59.

Edmundson, Melissa. "Introduction." *The Gothic Tradition in* Supernatural: *Essays on the Television Series*, edited by Melissa Edmundson, McFarland, 2016, pp. 1–12.

Engstrom, Erika, and Joseph M. Valenzano III. *Television, Religion, and* Supernatural: *Hunting Monsters, Finding Gods*. Lexington Books, 2014.

Froula, Anna. "What Keeps Me Up at Night: Media Studies Fifteen Years After 9/11." *Cinema*

Journal, vol. 56, no. 1, 2016, pp. 111–18. *Project Muse*, https://doi.org/10.1353/cj.2016.0056. Accessed 1 May 2018.

George, Jessica. "'The Monster at the End of This Book': Authorship and Monstrosity in *Supernatural.*" *Monsters & Monstrosity in the 21st-Century Film and Television*, edited by Cristina Artenie and Ashley Szanter, Universitas P, 2017, pp. 199–221.

Heffernan, James A. W. "Looking at the Monster: 'Frankenstein' and Film." *Critical Inquiry*, vol. 24, no. 1, 1997, pp. 133–58. *JSTOR*, http://www.jstor.org/stable/1344161. Accessed 1 May 2018.

Lykissas, Alexandra. "Gothic Anxieties—Then and Now: A Post-9/11 Examination of the Gothic." *The Gothic Tradition in* Supernatural: *Essays on the Television Series*, edited by Melissa Edmundson, McFarland, 2016, pp. 15–24.

Markert, John. *Post-9/11 Cinema: Through a Lens Darkly*. Scarecrow P, 2011.

McSweeney, Terence. *The 'War on Terror' and American Film: Frames Per Second*. Edinburgh UP, 2014.

Naumoff, Marylou. "Loving Monsters: Understanding Horror Fiction Consumption as a Response to the Uncertainty of American Identity." *Monsters & Monstrosity in the 21st-Century Film and Television*, edited by Cristina Artenie and Ashley Szanter, Universitas P, 2017, pp. 1–21.

Riegler, Thomas. "Through the Lenses of Hollywood: Depictions of Terrorism in American Movies." *Perspectives on Terrorism*, vol. 4, no. 2, 2010, pp. 35–45. *JSTOR*, http://www.jstor.org/stable/26298447. Accessed 1 May 2018.

Rodas, Julia Miele. "Autistic Voice and Literary Architecture in Mary Shelley's *Frankenstein.*" *Disabling Romanticism*, edited by Michael Bradshaw, Palgrave, 2016, pp. 169–90.

Shelley, Mary. 1818. *Frankenstein; or the Modern Prometheus*. Penguin Books, 1994.

Takacs, Stacey. "Monsters, Monsters Everywhere: Spooky TV and the Politics of Fear in Post-9/11 America." *Science Fiction Studies*, vol. 36, no. 1, 2009, pp. 1–20. *JSTOR*, http://www.jstor.org/stable/25475205. Accessed 1 May 2018.

Zimmer, Catherine. "Caught on Tape? the Politics of Video in the New Torture Film." *Horror After 9/11: World of Fear, Cinema of Terror*, edited by Aviva Briefel and Sam J. Miller, U of Texas P, 2011, pp. 83–104.

Knowledge Is Power

Information Literacy in Supernatural

PAULA S. KISER

Supernatural has pushed the limits of television show self-awareness. The meta-elements woven into the show strengthen the storyline by providing additional layers of meaning and context while entertaining the audience by allowing them to share in the cultural inside jokes. The show exists in a world that mirrors elements of the viewer's world, and it uses that level of realism to allow viewers to recognize their own issues in the problems the Winchesters face. One element in the *Supernatural* universe that grounds their struggles is the realism of the well-honed research skills the Winchester brothers utilize to further the story. The depiction of research in shows with supernatural themes is common, yet realistic representations of the entire research process with information literacy skills are rare. Characters such as Buffy and her Scooby Gang from *Buffy the Vampire Slayer*, Raquel and Amy in *Crazyhead*, and Quintin Coldwater and Alice Quinn in *The Magicians* all gather information to solve problems. However, these shows portray a version of research that only involves leafing through random books or occasionally searching online.

The Winchesters show evidence of being highly information literate, and the showrunners depict research in a realistic way. In the first five seasons with Eric Kripke's tenure as showrunner, the show's approach to research aligns perfectly with the Association of College and Research Library (ACRL) Information Literacy Competency Standards of Higher Education (2000). The first five seasons of *Supernatural* show the viewer the Winchesters' entire research process: identifying their information need, determining which resource to use, experimenting with a variety of search terms, and evaluating the information to determine its reliability and appropriateness for their need. Viewers are treated to scenes of the Winchesters performing research to learn the origins of ghosts, the way to kill a newly encountered monster, or what kind of enemy they're fighting. Hunters use a variety of print and digital primary, secondary, and tertiary sources to gather information. They consult material culture information sources and rely on first- and second-hand accounts derived from the experience of other hunters. The brothers also think critically to determine the reliability and relevance of the information they gather. These are information literacy skills that were identified as essential standards by ACRL during the early 2000s. Sam and Dean Winchester are fantastic at their job, not because of brute strength or mastery of weapons, but because they can do research to understand their enemy and know its exact weaknesses.

From 2000 to 2016, librarians used the ACRL Information Literacy Competency Standards as a guideline for teaching students how to do research. The Standards were a prescriptive list of skills students needed to be successful in seeking, finding, and using information appropriately and well. In institutes of higher education, the concept of information literacy was a familiar one by the early 2000s (Sonntag 2001). The Standards have since been retired and the Framework for Information Literacy for Higher Education (2015), which focuses on threshold concepts for understanding and using information, has been adopted. However, the functional skills needed to apply what the threshold concepts explain in theory are still those that had been enumerated in the Standards. During the time that Kripke led the show, Kripke created realistic research expectations for Sam and Dean as presented by the Standards, as they worked within the parameters of real information formats and dealt with the limitations of information retrieval. The creatures Sam and Dean defeated were fantastical, but the brothers' ability to find information to defeat them was based in real life research skills. The show's depiction of the importance of research skills adds real-world veracity to the characters' ability to defeat their supernatural foes.

Information literacy skills as described in the Standards consist of recognizing an information need or a knowledge gap and actively seeking to fill it (Standard One); knowing where to go for that information and understanding what types of sources will be most valuable (Standard Two); evaluating the reliability of the sources by recognizing biases and agendas from the source while determining if the information is not only reliable but relevant (Standard Three); and processing the information to be able to draw connections between information sources that offer valuable meaning (Standard Four). The fifth information standard is related to using information responsibly and ethically.

The first information literacy standard is to recognize that an information gap exists, and to have a plan of action to fill it. Do you realize that you don't know something, and do you know where to go to try to find the answer to your question? Throughout the series, Dean and Sam are very cognizant of the need to find information. Their function as hunters is to eliminate any threat posed by monsters and supernatural creatures, and in order to accomplish this they first need to know what type of evil they are fighting. It's not uncommon for the opening scenes of an episode to depict either Dean or Sam perusing online or print newspapers, scanning carefully for articles that report extraordinary events ("Bugs," 1.08; "Shadow," 1.16; "Provenance," 1.19; "The Usual Suspects," 2.07; "The Kids Are Alright," 3.02; "Mystery Spot," 3.11). In "Bugs," Sam refers to this as looking for a "new gig." In the cases of "Home" (1.09), "Nightmare" (1.14), and "Croatoan" (2.09), the job presents in the form of Sam's visions. Occasionally other hunters, such as their father John or their surrogate father Bobby, send the brothers on jobs ("Wendigo," 1.02; "Asylum," 1.10; "Long-Distance Call," 3.14; "Death Takes a Holiday," 4.15), and they provide the boys with information about the job. Different seasons follow the brothers' attempts to solve mysteries or to fill diverse overarching information gaps. The first five seasons follow a strong mystery arc: locating the Winchesters' missing father, learning more about the yellow-eyed demon that killed their mother, searching for the infamous Colt revolver that can kill almost anything, or discovering and protecting the Seals that imprison the Devil. Within each season, different cases (i.e., "monster-of-the-week" episodes) present varying information needs. With every case, the information need leads to research. Upon researching one element of a case, new information gaps appear, and as a result Sam and Dean must pursue a new avenue of investigation, an accurate depiction of the information research cycle. This need for further exploration informs the Winchesters' actions. The episode "Bloody Mary" (1.05) commences when the Winchesters discover a strange death in an obituary. Upon interviewing the victim's daughter, the brothers determine the girl said "Bloody Mary" in the bathroom of her home, and this takes them down a new rabbit hole: they need to learn the lore of Bloody Mary. In "Hook Man" (1.07), Dean encounters a newspaper article in the *Plains Courier* entitled "Mysterious Death of a Fraternity Brother" that leads them to a case. The brothers know from firsthand experience that salting and burning the bones of an angry spirit will often (though not always) stop it in its tracks. They salt and burn the bones of Preacher Jacob Karns, a specter that had been killing those he deemed sinners or sexual deviants. But Karns reappears, indicating that something else tethers his spirit to the physical world. The Winchesters have to return to the proverbial drawing board and perform further research to find out what they'd missed; in this case it was the hook with which he had killed 13 prostitutes in 1862. The need for further research after their tried and true method of disposal fails is also seen in "Route 666" (1.13) with Cyrus Dorian's truck continuing to attack them after they burned Dorian's bones.

Standard One also calls for familiarity with the types of data various sources provide and an understanding of which types are appropriate to supply the relevant information. The mastery of this skill allows people to go to the right types of places to get the information they need efficiently and with a greater chance of getting the right kind of information. This may take the form of a textual source, but it can also be going to an expert. The Winchesters' dual father figures trained the brothers from childhood to grasp which experts are most appropriate for various information needs. In the area of medicine, the brothers rely on the expertise of doctors and coroners for their initial queries. When a dead body is brought to a morgue, they inquire whether the coroner can determine cause of death, and whether there are any odd aspects to the corpse. In the episode "Bedtime Stories" (3.05), Dean talks to the local doctor and reads the coroner's report in order to determine if the body had been attacked by a werewolf. In "Something Wicked" (1.18), the brothers gather information about sick children from the local doctor treating the children. From here they keep pushing; they personally examine bodies and crime scenes for anything out of the ordinary, searching for details that might have eluded the expert, since training in medicine does not often overlap with expertise in the supernatural. The medical community is frequently puzzled by strange deaths but willing to accept them at face value. In the episode "I Believe the Children Are Our Future" (5.06), Dean and Sam examine the body of a young woman who appears to have scratched through her own skull. In the next episode, "The Curious Case of Dean Winchester" (5.07), they see the body of a man who died of old age but was only 24. In these instances, the medical experts can explain the nature of the death but are incapable of discerning the supernatural causes. Sam and Dean know the limitations of medical experts as information sources; they understand when to start with them, and when they need to seek other resources to dig deeper.

Aside from the medical community, academics also provide the Winchesters with plenty of basic knowledge. The brothers often use this information as a springboard for their own research. Professors in colleges and universities help them gain access to a great deal of information quickly, but are limited in the same way as medical experts. In "Scarecrow" (1.11), Dean asks a community college history professor for background information about the location of a mysterious death and the local folklore. From this initial inquiry, Dean learns that the townsfolk descended from Northern European immigrants whose religious texts mentioned the Norse Vanir. The professor reveals a historical text to Dean, who in turn reads: "The Vanir were Norse gods of protection and prosperity, keeping the local settlements safe from harm. Some … villages practiced human sacrifice, one male and one female. This particular Vanir's energy sprung from a sacred tree."

The information provided by the professor suggests to Dean that the Scarecrow is the creature responsible for killing couples; however, based on the professor's input regarding the town's worship of the Vanir, Dean deduces that the townspeople control the Scarecrow. Dean then uses his own knowledge of magic to make a logical leap: the citizens are sacrificing these outsiders, and he needs to locate and destroy the sacred tree upon whose energy the Vanir feeds. In "What Is and What Should Never Be" (2.20), Dean finds himself in an alternate world as he is drugged by a Djinn. He approaches a college professor and learns more information about the creature than he had known before, despite the academic's skepticism about the topic, such as the Djinn's godlike power and ability to alter the perception of reality. The Winchesters innately understand that laypeople can provide certain types of knowledge, but that they can't be relied upon as the only source. Since most collegiate lecturers are unaware of or highly skeptical toward supernatural elements, the academics' utility is limited. While realizing this limit and working around it, the Winchesters skillfully engage expert laypeople to fill gaps in information.

When dealing with supernatural information fissures, Dean and Sam know to turn to supernatural experts, such as their mentor and friend Bobby Singer, for dealings with monsters. While Bobby doesn't have a Ph.D. to validate his expertise, his knowledge is immensely valuable. This appreciation of the value of non-traditional experts will be outlined later in the Framework Threshold Concept "Authority is Constructed and Contextual." Bobby keeps an extensive library of supernatural-related secondary and primary sources, and he is a polyglot, able to translate obscure texts quickly and accurately. Bobby is a recurring character, and as a surrogate father figure to the brothers, his veracity and reliability is time-tested; the Winchesters trust no one more than Bobby. The showrunners introduced Bobby at the end of Season 1 in "Devil's Trap" (1.22). He introduces the brothers to the devil's trap, a large symbol usually drawn on a floor or ceiling that immobilizes demons inside of it, caging them within a vertical column. He can quickly recognize spells based on their ingredients ("In My Time of Dying," 2.01). If the Winchesters are stumped by a situation, can't identify a big bad, or are ill-informed after identification and their initial research attempts aren't fruitful, Bobby is their next resource. It was Bobby who realized that the demon that possessed Sam in "Born Under a Bad Sign" (2.14) had sealed himself in Sam's body with a brand that they had to remove before he and Dean could perform an effective exorcism. In "Tall Tales" (2.15), the Winchesters are completely stumped by the nature of the incidents in the college town, but Bobby immediately knows that it must be a Trickster based on the modus operandi of the creature, creating chaos and mischief. While the Trickster is later revealed to be the archangel Gabriel, he had indeed played himself off as the trickster god Loki for hundreds of years. The Winchesters know they can call Bobby with small pieces of information and he'll be able to use that information to do further research and find out more.

As well as using the medical, academic, and hunter communities, the Winchesters exhibit a strong understanding of which textual resources can help meet specific types of information needs. They frequently use court records, blueprints of buildings, newspapers, and oral interviews to fill information gaps, knowing inherently which sources are best for which types of information. In "Route 666," while Dean searches through the digitized archives of the local newspaper for information connecting the murders in the 1960s to current events, Sam scours courthouse records and deeds to find any relevant information about a local family. Together, the brothers' extensive research uncovers a dark supernatural history in mundane documents: the mayor purchased the Dorian family land with plans to bulldoze an old house, which in turn triggered the angry spirit. When they need to find information about the spirit responsible for the murders in "Hook Man," the brothers' first stop is the college library. With a librarian's assistance, the two comb through two boxes of archival material that contain arrest records going back as far as 1851, removing neatly labeled folders until they stumble upon something relevant. While the precise details of the entity they seek are nebulous, they understand what type of information they need, and more importantly, that historical arrest records can provide that. The archival arrest record in this case also includes a drawing of the hook the preacher used for a hand, leading the Winchesters to the correct conclusion that this is the origin of the angry spirit.

In "Asylum," Dean uses the Internet to determine that the longitude and latitude coordinates John assigned them were for Rockford, Illinois. Afterward, he zeroes in on the local newspaper, *The Rockford Metro News Online*, to scrutinize the publication's digitized archive. He knows that searching within a smaller collection (*The News Online*) will reveal more relevant results than a broad inquiry across the entire Web. There he discovers an article titled "Local Officer Murder-Suicide," which in turn triggers a memory of an entry in John's journal about the Rockford Asylum. In the second season, the Winchesters suspect a shape-shifter is behind a series of robberies based on common circumstances at each crime scene ("Nightshifter," 2.12). One piece of information immediately kicks off a chain of realization; when a witness shows the brothers a street map marking each location, the Winchesters suddenly realize that shifters inhabit and use sewer systems to travel secretly. With this information along with what they had learned about shifters preferring to move underground in

"Skin" (1.06), they move on to blueprints of the sewer system to determine where the next target might be.

The Winchesters often turn to historical newspapers to find contextual information about the history of a certain location, event, or person. As with medical and academic resources, the brothers know the limitations of these sources, but use them to provide a broad sketch of history while reading between the lines to gather details on supernatural elements to which the journalist might have been oblivious. The following episodes represent a short list of examples including scenes of newspapers use for information gathering: "Pilot" (1.01), "Dead in the Water" (1.03), "No Exit" (2.06), "Hollywood Babylon" (2.18), "Yellow Fever" (4.06), and "Heaven and Hell" (4.10). In the *Supernatural* universe, recognizing where to find information is an essential hunter skill. Dean quizzes Jo Harvelle, Ellen's daughter, on this knowledge when she goes off on her own hunt in Philadelphia ("No Exit"):

> **DEAN:** So, have you checked the police reports? County death records?
> **Jo:** Obituaries, mortuary reports, and seven other sources. I know what I'm doing.

Another piece of Standard One is weighing the pros and cons of how to acquire information such as deciding whether or not to learn a new language in order to "gather needed information and to understand its content." Sam and Dean made the decision to become comfortable and familiar with Latin, to add to their arsenal of skills in gathering information and defeating monsters, as shown through their ability to read through and identify Latin-language spells necessary to summon and/or exorcize demons, with Sam showing greater levels of knowledge of the language. Sam memorized the demon exorcism spell and didn't rely on a book as of the middle of Season 3 ("Jus in Bello," 3.12) while Dean still relied on a written copy of the spell and had not memorized it earlier in the season ("Sin City," 3.04). Luckily, neither Sam nor Dean run into problems like Ash in *Army of Darkness* (1992), causing catastrophic consequences from mispronounced words. In "Red Sky at Morning" (3.06), Sam uses a spell in Latin found in John's diary to help Bela Talbot, a dealer in magical items often procured through underhanded means, after she sold the one magical item that could have saved her life after seeing a ghost ship. The Winchesters do not learn the language of every spell they encounter, though. In "The Kids Are Alright," for instance, Sam and Bobby use a translation program for a spell in Sanskrit.

When the type of information they are seeking is specifically supernatural, the Winchesters examine sources precisely suited to those information needs, whether they be John's journal, books from Bobby's or another hunter's collection, or websites such as *Welcome to The Witching*

Corner ("Something Wicked"). They have also shown that they are willing to learn new skills to gather information such as learning a new language. In nearly every episode that depicts research, the Winchesters show that they are fully comfortable with the first Standard.

The second information literacy standard is the ability to search within sources to access "needed information effectively and efficiently." As illustrated, not only do the Winchesters innately know which sources are most appropriate to fill information gaps, but they also competently locate and then search within those sources for relevant information. Finding information as quickly as possible without sacrificing accuracy is an important skill for all researchers, and in the world of the Winchesters, it may have life and death consequences. The Winchesters illustrate their familiarity with the various methods of searching primary, secondary, and tertiary sources. After determining which source of data is suitable to meet the information need, they also decide on the appropriate method of investigation. They effectively search through print and digital collections, archives, and court documents, and perform verbal searches by questioning and interviewing individuals. The Winchesters, who understand the limitations of each resource, search the Internet when appropriate and constantly reevaluate their search strategies depending on the quantity, quality, and relevance of their results. This skill is introduced in the pilot as Dean and Sam use a digital newspaper archive to search for information about the Woman in White. Dean begins by using a keyword search for "Female Murder Hitchhiking" with the AND Boolean operator, connecting the terms and not limiting by date ranges. When these terms do not achieve helpful results, he changes the term "Hitchhiking" to "Centennial Highway." When no results appear, Sam suggests that they might not be looking at a murder. Sam then changes the keyword terms to "Female Suicide Centennial Highway" and a result pops up: the Winchesters' search skills lead them to the conclusion that Constance Welch, who committed suicide in 1981, is the origin of the vengeful spirit.

Sam and Dean utilize a search engine called Search the Web, a generic search engine that likely stands in for Google or Bing or any other search engine. In "It's a Terrible Life" (4.17), Dean and Sam are trapped in an alternate universe the angel Zachariah created. Sam, who remembers nothing of his past life, begins to dream about hunting creatures with Dean. His dreams trouble him, and to alleviate his disquiet he uses Search the Web to search for "vampires." He starts with a general keyword search to gather broad information. In "Swap Meat" (5.12), Sam searches for local lore online and finds the *Bay State Witchcraft* site, which provides a starting point for his investigation into an angry spirit.

Dean and Sam also seem to be proficient hackers and frequently use federal and state law enforcement databases to search for information about missing people, knowing that this is the most straightforward way of getting to information about specific people. In "Bloody Mary," Dean searches the National Crime Information Center and the FBI database until he pulls up police photographs of a woman who died in front of a mirror. As Sam struggles to find a missing girl who has psychic powers similar in origin to his own, he mentions to his fellow hunter Ellen Harvelle that he searched federal, state, and local databases to find information ("Playthings," 2.11). In "Something Wicked," Sam uses Lexis Nexis, a proprietary database, to search for information about unusual events.

The Winchesters also conduct research through print and microfilmed sources as well as digital sources. In "Bloody Mary" the brothers search for a deceased woman beginning with local records at the Central Public Library, and illustrate their familiarity with (and frustration with) older methods of research such as microfilm readers:

> **DEAN:** This will be annoying.
> **SAM:** It won't be so bad.
>> *They see that the computers are out of order.*
> **SAM:** I take it back. This will be very annoying.

While they don't enjoy searching old newspaper files the antiquated way, they are still capable. In "Something Wicked," Sam combs through old microfilms of newspapers to find that there had been a rash of sick children every 15 to 20 years in a variety of towns going back as far as the 1890s. The microfilm includes a timeworn photograph that depicts an impossibly youthful figure. As it turns out, the pediatrician in the town they are currently investigating had been alive and killing children for hundreds of years, and is indeed the monster the Winchesters seek. Sam exhibits this skill again in "Roadkill" (2.16) when he uses a microfiche reader to view the article "Tragic Accident Kills 2 on Highway 41" from February 22, 1992, along with 15 other articles about crashes along that stretch of road. Despite his proficiency at using microfilmed newspapers, Sam prefers digital research, as exemplified again in his irritated interaction with Dean in "Tall Tales":

> **DEAN:** How's the research going?
> **SAM:** You know how it's going? Slow. You know how it would go a heck of a lot faster? If I had my computer.

The Winchester brothers often use their father's personal journal as a source of information, both as a primary source and as a reference source. Their father's journal is a reliable source of information that guides them through the first few seasons of the series; they fundamentally trust John's research and its representation. Dean has read John's journal so many times that he can call up by memory a creature or a place from its pages. In the second episode of the series, "Wendigo," he remarks to Sam, "This is Dad's single most valuable possession. Everything he knows about every evil thing is in here. He's passed it on to us. I think he wants us to pick up where he left off. You know, saving people, hunting things: the family business." The writers use this line, which is indicative of so much in the characters' and the show's arc, in the beginning recap of almost every episode throughout the entire first eight seasons of the show. The journal is often Dean's first resource, a kind of talisman; he utilizes it religiously to find information about a creature. However, since the entries are chronological, to be a functional resource John's journal must be read in its entirety. Sam and Dean refer to John's journal for information in "Phantom Traveler" (1.04), "Skin," "Croatoan," "Houses of the Holy" (2.13), "Time Is on My Side" (3.15), and "Jump the Shark" (4.19). The Winchesters are familiar with their information sources and how to search them efficiently and effectively, the hallmark of the second Standard.

Standard Three is the ability to evaluate the prepared sources and the validity of their information, adding into a "knowledge base and value system." Researchers need to be able to determine how accurate information might be, recognize when something isn't reliable, and be able to add the relevant information into their understanding of the topic. The Winchesters often reiterate to each other information that is relevant to their search, synthesizing it with what they already know. They also illustrate information assessment frequently enough for the viewer to grasp its importance. The brothers question the reliability of the websites they visit. They remain highly skeptical of sensational or biased sites such as *HellHoundsLair.com*. In "Hell House" (1.17), Sam seems mortified to be using such an unreliable and unvetted resource:

> **DEAN:** Let me guess, streaming live out of Mom's basement.
> **SAM:** Yeah, probably.
> **DEAN:** Most of those websites wouldn't know a ghost if it bit 'em in the persqueater.

Viewers also get a glimpse of the characters' healthy skepticism in "Mystery Spot." Dean frequently relies on his own experience to help determine the reliability of information sources. While searching for the missing Professor Hasselback, Dean mentions that these mystery spots are often completely fabricated, and doubts the veracity of the case. As it turns out, the Trickster, later revealed to be the archangel Gabriel, is responsible for the mystery spots.

The brothers also exercise skepticism toward verbal interviews. The Winchesters do not take someone's word at face value, but evaluate the source of that information. If Crowley, the Crossroads Demon turned

King of Hell, offers them information, they naturally question his motives ("Abandon All Hope…," 5.10; "The Devil You Know," 5.20). Likewise, when the demon Ruby appears to help Sam throughout seasons 3 and 4, Dean questions her veracity at every turn ("Malleus Maleficarum," 3.09; "Jus in Bello"; "No Rest for the Wicked," 3.16; "I Know What You Did Last Summer," 4.09; "When the Levee Breaks," 4.21). Just as the Winchesters know the limits of experts, they also know to doubt certain information sources.

Sometimes the information the Winchesters uncover appears initially to be relevant, but the addition of other sources clarifies that the original lead is a dead end or that the primary information is only peripherally germane. Part of the research cycle is knowing when to be flexible in searching and not to stop all lines of inquiry. There is a flexibility in the Winchesters' research process that illustrates that they remain skeptical of information until information can be verified. In "A Very Supernatural Christmas" (3.08), Sam initially believes that the creature who was killing people and dragging their bodies up chimneys is Krampus, Santa's evil brother. He pulls up a variety of lore about this creature, convincing himself and his brother that this has to be the answer. Even so, they know to ask Bobby about the case, to locate another source of information, and Bobby negates the initial theory. Each victim possessed a wreath of meadowsweet, and since meadowsweet was used in pagan lore for human sacrifices, Bobby's experience tells him the culprit is more likely a pagan god. The Winchesters show that they know not all information is accurate as they evaluate the veracity and relevance of what they find out.

The fourth information Standard is the capacity to incorporate information into a bank of knowledge, take action based on that information, and be able to effectively communicate the information to others. Reading pieces of information without doing anything with it or understanding it is meaningless. For the Winchesters this equates to taking information and successfully using it to defeat supernatural creatures. Every time they research and use newly absorbed information to find the weak spot of a monster, they exhibit a mastery of this information Standard. The characters further exemplify this Standard by requesting information from an expert. In "Yellow Fever," they contact Bobby, who explains the modus operandi and weakness of the Buru Buru, an Edo-era Japanese spirit, and Sam uses that information to plan how to scare the ghost to death. In "The Kids Are Alright," Dean and Sam suspect changelings are responsible for kidnapping children in a small subdivision, based on a number of information points: blood found on scene, the apparently accidental deaths of the patriarchs, and strange marks on the backs of the matriarchs' necks. Sam searches online for information and finds both websites and e-book chapters, *Changelings: Fact or Fictions*, "Identifying a Changeling," and "The

Changelings Lore Part 3." Using this information, the brothers determine that they'll find the living children in a house under construction, and then they kill the changeling with fire.

The writers also showcase the characters' mastery of the fourth information literacy Standard when the Winchesters find holes in current research or current principles of their profession, but through observation they make decisions and act on them. When the traditional means of abolishing an angry spirit are not possible, the Winchesters improvise as best they can with the information at hand. This is the case in the pilot episode. As previously mentioned, an angry spirit can often be destroyed by salting and burning the ghost's physical bones, but the Winchesters frequently encounter situations in which the case is not so simple. The Woman in White was cremated, leaving no bones to salt and burn. The Winchesters instead use their knowledge of the case, understanding of specters, and new research to determine the best course of action. They realize they can pit apparition against apparition: Sam drives Dean's precious Impala through the front door of the ghost's prior home, forcing her to confront the phantoms of the children she had drowned, whose spirits destroy her connection to the physical world.

The showrunners illustrate this again in "No Exit" when the brothers find it impossible to locate and excavate the bones of Herman Webster Mudgett, a.k.a. H.H. Holmes, since his was one of many unmarked graves. Instead, the Winchesters and Jo trap the ghost in a box using salt and iron, and then lay cement over it for good measure. In "Roadkill," the brothers convince the spirit of the lost woman, Molly McNamara, that she is actually dead, and help her let go and pass out of the physical realm. In "Bedtime Stories," the apparition is not of someone dead but the spirit of a woman in a coma, and the Winchesters put her spirit to rest by convincing her grieving father that her stepmother had poisoned her. In this case, the spirit only needed her father to know the truth. The Winchesters build upon their prior knowledge of ghosts and combine it with newly acquired information to discern how to dispose of an angry spirit, exemplifying the fourth Standard.

The fifth information literacy Standard is the ability to understand the legal and ethical issues of information use and to act accordingly, using information legally and ethically. This Standard has the least traditional bearing in the world of the Winchesters. They care little about the legal means of acquiring information, but they use that information in an effort to save lives. They often hack citizens' personal computers ("The Usual Suspects"; "Crossroad Blues," 2.08; "Houses of the Holy"; "It's a Terrible Life") and impersonate law enforcement or government officials in order to obtain access to crime scenes, interview witnesses, and look through police files ("A Very Supernatural Christmas"; "Yellow Fever"; "Sex and Violence," 4.14; "Free to Be You and Me," 5.03; "The Curious Case of Dean Winchester"). They do whatever they need to do to find information; their largest information priority is gathering it.

The illegality of the brothers' research techniques is overshadowed by their need to protect the populace. They use even improperly acquired information in an ethical manner, with each often acting as the other's conscience. The Winchesters strive to protect the world from things that are often beyond the purview of the legal system and the capability of law enforcement. Because the *Supernatural* universe isn't our own, because it is brimming with monsters, it is impossible to claim that regular laws and ethics apply to information-gathering. As an example, the Winchesters respect human life and will never torture a person; however, they have no problem brutalizing demons in the name of getting information ("Time Is on My Side"; "On the Head of a Pin," 4.16).

Regardless of how they collect information, the Winchesters always try to act ethically, and if that seems impossible, they act as foils for one another, voicing disapproval and skepticism about unscrupulous behavior. This is apparent in situations where the Winchesters and another party possess the same information but arrive at different conclusions about the appropriate plan of action. In "Metamorphosis" (4.04), Dean and Sam rendezvous with another hunter, Travis, to hunt down and kill a Rugarou, a cannibalistic creature that appears human until it reaches maturity and turns into a monster. Travis, who previously fought and killed a Rugarou, requests Dean's and Sam's assistance to eradicate its offspring. Sam performs his own research and finds evidence that not all Rugarous turn; if the creature never eats human flesh, it won't become a monster. Though aware of this important detail, Travis cynically insists the creature doesn't have the willpower to withstand the hunger. Sam and Travis have the same information, but Sam wishes to spare as many lives as possible, to act as ethically as he can. Sam wants to tell the victim about his affliction so he can fight it, while Travis simply wants to kill the creature. In "It's the Great Pumpkin, Sam Winchester" (4.07), the brothers learn that they must stop a demon from rising to avoid breaking another seal and weakening the Devil's prison. The Winchesters try to locate the witch who wishes to raise the demon Samhain and stop him/her. The angels Castiel and Uriel are privy to the same information, but they plan to destroy the entire town to keep the witch from summoning the demon and breaking the seal. In "Jus in Bello," Ruby possesses knowledge of an exorcism that could get rid of all demons in a one-mile radius, allowing the Winchesters to avoid Lilith and save the people with them in the police station. However, said exorcism requires a virgin sacrifice. This is acceptable for the demon Ruby, but Dean is adamant that they find a way that doesn't require a human sacrifice. The Winchesters consistently illustrate that whenever possible, they use illegally gathered information in the most ethical manner possible.

In 2016, ACRL adopted the Framework for Information Literacy for Higher Education after initially filing the document in 2015, and these replaced the Standards. The new Framework helps to emphasize a philosophical understanding of information and an understanding of social and political issues related to information along with the functional aspects of finding and using it (Foasberg 2015). The skills within each Standard are now "knowledge practices" and "dispositions" within each Frame that show how a student exhibits their understanding of the following concepts: Authority is Constructed and Contextual, Information Creation as a Process, Information as Value, Research as Inquiry, Scholarship as Conversation, and Searching as Strategic Exploration (ACRL 2015). Despite the Standards' retirement, the skills shown by the Winchesters can still be mapped within the Framework. Instructors of information literacy could use this series to help illustrate knowledge practices and dispositions such as "design and refine needs and search strategies as necessary" and "use different types of searching language" from the Searching as Strategic Exploration frame or "synthesize ideas gathered from multiple sources" from the Research as Inquiry frame. Students with an understanding of information literacy should be able to watch episodes cited in this essay and map the Winchester's research abilities to the Framework, despite the depictions not fitting as perfectly into the Framework as they do into the Standards.

From the very first episode, the writers depict Dean and Sam Winchester as experts in hunting and performing research. It is their research ability and their information literacy that grants them the necessary knowledge to complete their hunts and eliminate supernatural threats. Dean and Sam illustrate time and time again that they realize when they need to gather information; they know where to go for that information; they evaluate its relevancy and reliability; they act based on it; finally, they use that information to make reasonable ethical decisions. It is these information literacy skills that make them talented hunters, far beyond their birthright, brute strength, and fighting skill. As shown clearly in every season, the Winchesters are skilled researchers who are familiar with using a wide variety of source materials. Their highly honed critical thinking skills allow them to use the information they gather in the best possible and effective manner. Their use of information and capability for synthesizing it into vast knowledge is their greatest asset. For the Winchesters, knowledge is power.

Works Cited

Association of College and Research Libraries. "Information Literacy Competency Standards for Higher Education," *American Library Association*, 2000, http://www.ala.org/Template.cfm?Section=Home&template=/ContentManagement/ContentDisplay.cfm&ContentID=33553.

Association of College and Research Libraries. "Framework for Information Literacy for Higher Education," *American Library Association,* 2015, http://www.ala.org/acrl/standards/ilframework.

Foasberg, Nancy M. "From Standards to Frameworks for IL: How the ACRL Framework Addresses Critiques of the Standards." portal: Libraries and the Academy, vol. 15 no. 4, 2015, p. 699–717. Project MUSE, doi:10.1353/pla.2015.0045.

Sonntag, Gabriela. "Report on the National Information Literacy Survey: Documenting Progress Through the United States." Association of College and Research Libraries News, vol. 62, no. 10, 2001, https://crln.acrl.org/index.php/crlnews/article/view/23088/30015.

"There is no singing in *Supernatural!*"

Fan/Producer Relationships, Metanarrative and Supernatural's 200th Episode Special

K ESHIA M CCLANTOC

In September 1975, *The Rocky Horror Picture Show* premiered in the USA, after first opening in England, and brought with it a fan frenzy to the horror genre unlike any before. Although rampant participation in fandom began nearly a decade earlier with fans of *Star Trek, Rocky Horror* was able to bridge the gap between science-fiction and horror, cultivating a new audience of enthusiastic fans. Fans of *Rocky Horror* shadowed characters on stage, performed prop-based rituals, and came back to see the film again and again. Though television shows and films had followings before, none seemed to have the fervent energy of *Rocky Horror* fans, a trademark that contributed to the musical's acclaim for its cult-like following. Over 40 years later, fans of *Rocky Horror Picture Show* are still celebrating its success (Moylan). *Rocky Horror's* fan following is a primary example of participatory culture, which Henry Jenkins states is a form of mediated interaction, that "makes it possible for consumers to archive, annotate, appropriate, and recirculate media content in powerful new ways" (Jenkins 8). In the age of Web 2.0, participatory culture most often refers to the production of fan works as well as the fan/producer relationships surrounding books, films, television shows, and more. Here, producers can refer to the actors, writers, directors, editors, actual producers, or any other entities involved with the creation of a form of media. Though the original *Rocky Horror* fans did not use Web 2.0, their simultaneous practices as consumer and fan cultivated an early form of participatory culture. Fans are now active participants who write fan fiction, create fan art, plan and attend fan conventions, interact with entities involved in production, and disseminate and navigate plot via fan discussions. The boundaries that once made consumption of media a passive event are increasingly shrinking, forcing producers to reckon with an audience whose ability to participate affects popularity. Media that actively reject participation may struggle to survive while those which allow participation without complete disintegration of fan/producer boundaries will thrive. While this is not always the case, the CW hit, *Supernatural,* which has its own cult-like following, serves as a prime example of a show that mediates participation in a way that invites and celebrates fans while still maintaining balanced consumer boundaries.

Much like *Rocky Horror, Supernatural* started with a small crowd of fervent fans. The show follows the Winchester Brothers, Sam and Dean, who hunt, chase, and wage wars with monsters, angels, and demons. *Supernatural* is known for breaking the boundaries between fan/producer relationships, inviting the fans to participate in a way that few other shows have attempted. The show excels in creating self-reflexive metanarrative, seemingly striking a balance between playing with meta and maintaining fan relationships. Here, metacommentary refers to moments where fan commentary is addressed or acknowledged within the narrative of the show. According to *Supernatural* aca-fans Katherine Larsen and Lynn Zubernis, metacommentary is an "intellectual discussion centering on larger ideas and issues raised by the fanned series/book/film" (243). The metacommentary within the show serves the dual purpose of commenting both on fans and the show itself, positioning fans as interpreters of the narrative while reinforcing the producers as the actual narrators. It does this by inserting the fans as characters within the narrative itself, often positioning Sam and Dean as reflections of the producers. *Supernatural* relies so heavily on this form of metacommentary that it is an incorporated part of the in-universe mythos, consistently mediating the boundaries of fan/producer relationships.

Though *Supernatural* contains many of these meta moments, none are as prominent as those in the 200th episode special, aptly named "Fan Fiction" (10.05). This episode pays attention to fan jargon and practices, produces self-referential and reflective commentary, and validates fans in a way the series had not done before. It represents the changing nature of the show's attitude toward fandom and the way in which fans are now part of a mediated relationship between audience and media. Fans are not passive consumers; instead, fans are tweeting, posting, sharing, and discussing media in real-time, determining what works or does not work from the moment of the release. Cultivating relationships during these moments and allowing fans to be active consumers is a part of participatory culture that *Supernatural* excels at. As more shows and movies begin to do this, the boundaries between fan/producer relationships will become spaces that are flexible rather than fixed, allowing fan interpretation to spur reflexive metacommentary. However, the navigation of these fan/producer relationships is a strenuous task. Although *Supernatural* has long-practiced such a relationship with its fans, that relationship has not always been positive. Early instances of reflective metanarrative commented negatively on fangirl culture, purposely subverted fan expectations, and made the fans, as characters, into humorous jokes. Though this metacommentary within the show began relatively early, it took some time to reach a fan/producer relationship that validated the fans. This essay maps fan/producer relationships across three of the series' most meta episodes—"The Real Ghostbusters" (5.09), "Season 7, Time for a Wedding!" (7.08), and "Fan Fiction." In some of these episodes, the commentary is scathing; in others it is validating and complimentary. Analysis of these episodes provides a map of the relationship between *Supernatural* fans and producers over the years, with "Fan Fiction" as the episode that finally strikes the balance of positively mediated fan/producer relationships.

Web 2.0 now positions producers, writers, actors, and any other persons involved in the production of a film or television show in platforms where fan interaction is both possible and often needed for success. Fan/producer relationships are now an integral part of marketing, as interaction with fans no longer has to pass through the filters of management, media outlets, or gatekeepers. When fans tweet, post, or share news related to a television show and someone involved in the making of that show responds, their actions create a line of communication between the media and the fan. Though these accounts are typically run by assistants and communication guidelines are still in place, social media provides a seemingly direct line from fan to producer. If these forms of communication are cultivated, television shows have the potential to create a strong fanbase built on fan/producer relationships. In "The Few, The Fervent: Fans of *Supernatural* Redefine TV Success," Neda Ulaby comments that "the metrics of success determine whether a television show lives or dies." As audience members, fans provide the numbers and demographics of these metrics. As participatory culture becomes the norm, cultivation of fan/producer relationships will be an essential part of show success, as "fan engagement gives color and volume to dry data, such as ratings" (Ulaby). In the past, these relationships were cultivated through activities like fan letters, attendance of fan conventions, and production of fanzines, but social media gives a form of real-time engagement between fan and producer. Though metrics and ratings still determine the ability of network shows to live or die, fan participation via Web 2.0 has the benefit of producing continual discussion about a show, therefore increasing continued fan interest. Many films and television shows are now embracing this form of cultivating fan/producer relationships, but *Supernatural* has gone above and beyond to break these boundaries.

In part, these boundaries are broken by cultivating the SPN Family. As a story based around the relationship between two brothers, a recurring theme in *Supernatural* is the importance of family. As a result, the fandom that grew around *Supernatural* has developed a familial bond as a community. Often, that connection crosses paths with the fan/producer relationships. In her essay "Family Don't End with Blood: Building the *Supernatural* Family," Mary Frances Casper says that "[f]amilies develop their own languages based on shared experiences and storytelling […] in a similar fashion, *Supernatural* fans enact their membership in the *Supernatural* Family through quoted dialogue, story extension and fantasy chain scenarios using a myriad of formats" (77). This idea of fandom as family results in the fans' tendency to cultivate identity, meaning, and narratives around the series. When producers acknowledge these within the show itself, they are cultivating fan/producer relationships through metacommentary. This relationship is unique because they cultivate a familial community based on the underlying theme of the show. As Kristin Noone says, "[t]he heart of the show […] lies in *Supernatural's* advocacy of family and familial bonds as a refuge against the monsters of the darkness, a refuge that has been eagerly welcomed by the viewers in the large and active fan community" (para. 1). With the SPN Family as the driving force behind fan/producer relationships in *Supernatural*, metacommentary within the narrative is deeply personal, as it is a reflection of fans and the familial relationship and community cultivated by the fandom.

Looking carefully at the moments of metacommentary within these episodes maps the way that fan/producer relationships have grown over the years; this analysis begins with "The Real Ghostbusters." In this episode, Sam and Dean receive a text message from Chuck to come to a hotel; they soon learn the text was really from fangirl Becky Rosen, who tricks them into attending a "Supernatural" Fan Convention. In "The Real Ghostbusters," the show picks up an in-universe meta mythos that began in the episode "The Monster at the End of This Book" (4.18). In this previous episode, Sam and Dean learn about a book series called "Supernatural" which follows their lives, written and published by Carver Edlund, aka Chuck Shurley. This moment introduces an in-universe mythos into *Supernatural* that continues to be referenced in the show and delight real-life fans. One season later, in "The Real Ghostbusters," the metacommentary via this mythos is strong, as Sam and Dean visit the "Supernatural" Fan Convention, a slanted reflection of real-life *Supernatural* fan conventions.

In "The Real Ghostbusters," Sam and Dean respond to the "Supernatural" Convention with a sense of shock and fascination, looking over cosplayers and merchandise sales as the opening credits roll. The next scene takes them to the main stage, where a slew of panels is announced, like "Frightened Little Boy: The Secret Life of Dean," and "Homoerotic Subtexts in 'Supernatural.'" When Chuck comes on stage, the fans greet him with just as much enthusiasm as real-life *Supernatural* fans show when they greet the people involved with the show (almost invariably actors, rather than writers or other participants) at actual conventions. The episode is filled with a myriad of fan references and metacommentary, but the real tension begins when Sam and Dean pair up with two cosplayers to stop a haunting that takes place during the convention. Though the haunting initially begins as a scavenger hunt set up by the convention organizers, the episode reveals that the hotel is actually haunted when one attendee complains of a ghost not included in the game. Sam and Dean become suspicious when they overhear the attendee complaining. They then begin an investigation, bumping into fans, Demian and Barnes, who have stumbled upon clues not set up by convention organizers. This begins this episode's metacommentary, in which Demian and Barnes serve as reflections of real-life *Supernatural* fans and Sam and Dean serve as reflections of the producers.

In the first moment of metacommentary, Dean asks, "What the hell is wrong with you, why would you choose to be these guys?" to which Barnes answers, "because we're fans, like you." Dean then goes into a rant, talking about the horrors that he and his brother have faced, and most notably saying, "their pain is not for your amusement." Demian then tries to assure Dean that fictional characters do not care about the ways that fans find joy in their story. This implication is complex, as fictional characters are just that—fiction. However, the in-universe mythos of this episode presents fictional characters as real via Sam and Dean, and they care that Demian and Barnes find amusement in their pain. Soon after this conversation, Sam and Dean find and defeat the ghost, only to release a trio of new ghosts. These ghosts trap everyone in the hotel, including Sam and Dean. When one wandering fan is killed, Sam and Dean convince Chuck to distract the fans while they stop the ghosts. Demian and Barnes join them, despite Sam and Dean's protests and their own fear, because "that's what Sam and Dean would do." As Sam and Dean fight the ghosts, Demian and Barnes burn the bones of their original bodies, ridding the hotel of the spirits. Everyone leaves the convention unscathed, and Sam and Dean have one last conversation with Demian and Barnes, who tell them that they do not understand the real meaning of "Supernatural." Demian tells Dean, "In real life, he sells stereo equipment. I fix copiers. Our lives suck. But Sam and Dean. To wake up every morning and save the world. To have a brother who would die for you. Well, who wouldn't want that." In this potent moment, fans speak about how much the show means to them while the producers simultaneously reinforce the overarching theme of *Supernatural* to real-life fans.

Outside of this moment, the episode is overflowing with moments that both stimulate and negate fan/producer relationships. Most significant is the concept of the convention itself, which the episode cites as the first-ever "Supernatural" Convention. In real life, the first-ever *Supernatural* convention happened three years before "The Real Ghostbusters" was broadcast (*Supernatural Wiki*). With the inclusion of panels and LARPing events, rampant cosplay and merchandise sales, this in-episode "Supernatural" Convention attempts to echo many of the first *Supernatural* conventions that were held. Though the "Supernatural" Convention in this episode varies largely in both demographics and activities from real fan conventions, by placing this type of convention within the episode itself, the producers make a significant nod to the fans. In "It's a Bird, It's a Plane! No, Wait, It's a *Supernatural* Fan," Jessica Jackson says, "the show runners took the time to genuinely acknowledge the fans, they dedicated an episode to them that also revolved around them, which rarely happens in showbiz" (90). Inclusion of fans as characters in an episode, via a meta mythos, positions *Supernatural* as a show that uniquely validates its fans. It also validates their efforts in creating and cultivating these conventions, and presents them as a place where fans, like the characters Barnes and Demian, can find happiness and community. Despite this, the in-episodes fans, and the conversations Sam and Dean have with and about them, are not entirely positive. Instead, the episode presents a complex message of fan acknowledgment, where the fan/producer relationships are mediated through fictional characters without losing the integrity and authenticity of the characters themselves. Though the overall message is one of fan acknowledgment, the episode works to reveal how hard it is to balance fan/producer relationships via metacommentary.

The *Supernatural* fandom is made up primarily of female fans. In "The Real Ghostbusters," however, most of the fans that attend the convention are male, with Becky Rosen serving as the only example of female fan representation. Though Becky delivers key information to Sam and Dean within this episode, her role is largely sidelined by the male fans Demian and Barnes. Though there are certainly male *Supernatural* fans, by misrepresenting the gender demographics within the fandom, the episode becomes dismissive of the most significant part of the fan base. In turn, rather than serving as a validating and accurate portrayal of *Supernatural* fan conventions, it ignores much of the fan base, giving them representation only through a lone figure. Early in the episode, Sam and Dean have a conversation with Chuck that seems like a commentary on fan fiction, one in which both men are upset with the production of more books within Chuck's series. Dean asks Chuck, "who gave you the rights to our life story?" while Sam says, "our lives are not for public consumption." As Sam and Dean act as reflections of *Supernatural* producers within this episode, their comments read as a subtle commentary about who can claim ownership over characters and who cannot; whether the fans are given that right in this moment is complicated. In the context of this mythos, Chuck is a professional writer making money off of a very real Sam and Dean, who express rightful displeasure at the use of their story. When fans write fan fiction, they are co-opting fictional characters, who, as Demian implies previously, do not have the ability to care how fans use their story. As reflections of *Supernatural* producers in this moment, Sam and Dean represent the tumultuous nature of fan/producer relationships, with moments that simultaneously cultivate and negate that relationship.

This relationship becomes considerably more complicated when Becky, whose role was minimal in "The Real Ghostbusters," gets her own episode, one that portrays fans in a wholly unappealing light. Becky was first introduced in the episode "Sympathy for the Devil" (5.01), as the self-proclaimed number one fan of the "Supernatural" book series. Almost immediately, Becky's character is a negative and stereotypical portrayal of fans. She is awkward, dresses horribly, and is seemingly reclusive. She writes Wincest fanfic, but considers herself a "Sam Girl," an obsession that leads to her individual episode, "Season 7, Time for a Wedding!" From her introduction, Becky appears sporadically through seasons 5 through 7, with nods to her character in Season 9.[1] Though Becky's character serves practical purposes throughout the series, fan reception is conflicted. While some fans found her portrayal as an erratic fangirl amusing, many found it disappointing, putting fans in a light they never wanted to be seen in. In *Fangasm,* Katherine Larsen and Lynn Zubernis discuss a sense of shame that often accompanies active participation in fandom, saying, "Fans— especially female fans—are so accustomed to accusations of insanity and prohibitions against being out of control that we become hypervigilant for any evidence of those sorts of behaviors" (31). When Becky is introduced, she exhibits many of the absurd behaviors that those in fandom are shamed for. In turn, Becky as fan representation shamed the fans, with the meta-commentary in "Season 7, Time for a Wedding!" dealing a hard blow to fan/producer relationships.

In this episode, Becky uses a love potion on Sam and tricks him into marrying her. The episode opens with Dean meeting Sam at a wedding chapel in Las Vegas, where he tells Dean, "I'm in love and I'm getting married," to a bride who turns out to be Becky. Dean is aghast, and yells at Sam, saying, "Really, super fan 99?" showing clear disdain for both Becky and the situation. This disdain continues throughout the episode, coupled by suspicions of Becky's motives. Later, as the now-married Becky and Sam stop by her high school reunion, Becky retrieves a potion from a wiccan, which she forces Sam to take as the initial love potion weakens. When this secondary potion wears off, Becky knocks Sam out and ties him up. When he awakes, he guesses that Becky used a potion on him, but she defends herself, saying, "it wouldn't even work unless you already love me deep-down, it just activates it." When attempting to get more potion, Becky learns that the wiccan is a crossroads demon, who offers her 25 years of Sam's love in exchange for her soul. At first, it seems that Becky takes the deal, but she tricks the demon, who is soon disposed of. Becky and Sam sign an annulment, with Sam telling her that he will not see her again but to "just do your thing, whatever that is."

Becky is clearly presented as a possessive, obsessive, and delusional character. Working as fan representation in this episode, Becky is the epitome of the crazy fangirl stereotype, literally drugging the subject of her affections. The episode paints Becky as naive to the consequences of her own actions, with her answering, "but we had a great time, you were happy," when Sam accuses her of having roofied him. This conversation is particularly jarring because it demonstrates just how far Becky was willing to go to have Sam. Although she claims that they had not consummated their marriage, there are heavy implications of sexual assault. In the end, Becky's shame is what changes her mind, telling Sam, "I know you don't love me, I know what I am, okay, I'm a loser … honestly the only place people ever understood me was the message boards." These lines are powerful because they echo the common feelings of those within fandom, not only the sense of internalized shame that *Fangasm* discusses, but also the sense of community found on message boards as a place "to vent, to share, to find comfort and friendship and offer the same" (Larsen and Zubernis 24). With such a telling line, it is hard to separate Becky from the real-life *Supernatural* fans who often find solace in the SPN Family.

Overall, the episode feels like an admonishment to fans, undercutting the fan/producer relationships that effective metacommentary had been building for years. Although Becky is a fictional fan, this does not separate her from the in-universe mythos that the show had been building since the introduction of Chuck's "Supernatural" series. Episodes like "The Real Ghostbusters" worked with that mythos to acknowledge real-life *Supernatural* fans and cultivate fan/producer relationships. "Season 7, Time for a Wedding!" did just the opposite, demeaning fans by portraying Becky as taking criminal actions in her plot to earn Sam's affections. From the start, Becky's characterization is difficult for real-life fans to consume, but this episode makes this incarnation of fans barely tolerable. In part, the struggle of fan/producer relationships in this episode is due to the changing producers within *Supernatural.* Season 5's finale marked the end of Eric Kripke's run as showrunner and the introduction of Sera Gamble as showrunner (*Supernatural Wiki*). Gamble lasted only two seasons, with Season 7 being ill-received by many fans, who blamed Gamble for poor writing (*Supernatural Wiki*). In "I See What You Did There: SPN and the Fourth Wall," Lisa Macklem says that Becky's ending speech "paint[s] a more sympathetic view of what fandom can offer: a place where fans can feel they can belong. However, it also intimates that that sense of belonging is fleeting and will prove to be unsatisfying" (41–2). Becky's sense of shame and dissatisfaction with her life insinuates that fandom is not enough, effectively dismissing the community that can be found there. Additionally, Macklem adds that "[t]his curiously bitter version of fandom comes at a time when Gamble was under siege from fans [...]. Fan reaction to this version of Becky saw this as a negative comment from the show about fans which did not seem consistent" (42). This now unsteady fan/producer relationship made many fans nervous about further inclusion of this type of metacommentary, which is why many were not sure what to expect when *Supernatural* announced its 200th episode special.

"Fan Fiction" opens with two girls, dressed as Sam and Dean, appearing in a staged production of Chuck's "Supernatural" series. Another girl pauses the production and reprimands the actors. This leads to a brief argument that a frazzled teacher breaks up. Later, the teacher is attacked by a scarecrow-like creature, with a quick cut to an unusual *Supernatural* opening, filled with a plethora of pop culture references via title splash cards. Meanwhile, Sam and Dean read about the missing teacher and decide to investigate, walking in on a musical rendition of their early lives and their mother's death. The musical is a fan fiction, based on the in-universe mythos of the book series. Immediately, the pair are surprised, with Dean telling Marie, the writer/director of the show, "There is no singing in 'Supernatural,'" to which the stage manager, Mae, answers "well this is Marie's interpretation." Within these first few moments, this episode establishes itself as a more validating narrative than other incarnations of fan metacommentary. This pattern only continues as the episode goes on. While Sam and Dean investigate, their interactions with Marie and Mae are filled with fan jargon and inside jokes, like "the boy melodrama scene," "a single man tear," "transformative fiction," and ship names like "Destiel." Claiming he has copies of Chuck's unpublished manuscripts, Dean tells Marie what really happened to him and Sam over the past few years, to which she says, "that is some of the worst fan fiction I have ever heard." In the in-universe mythos of *Supernatural,* Chuck's book series follows Sam and Dean's lives through Season 5 of the show, with Chuck disappearing soon afterward. When Dean tells Marie what happened after Season 5, she sees it only as fan fiction of Chuck's "Supernatural," series, much like her musical.

As they continue to investigate, Dean becomes increasingly annoyed by the production while Sam finds it amusing. After a cast member is taken by the same scarecrow-like monster as the teacher, Sam and Dean reveal their true identities to Mae and Marie. Both girls laugh, with Marie saying, "I'm willing to accept that monsters are real, but those books are works of fiction." As opening night comes around, Marie steps in to play Sam for the missing cast member and the brothers learn that the scarecrow-like monster is a product of Calliope, a muse whose goal is to eat Marie after Marie's vision is fulfilled. Deciding that the show must go on, Sam and Dean plan to defeat Calliope while Marie's vision is fulfilled. Before the show, Sam asks about who is playing Chuck, to which Marie replies, "The whole author inserting himself into the narrative thing, just not my favorite, I kind of hate the meta-stories." Sam and Dean both aptly reply, "me too." Throughout the musical, Marie and other cast members perform a series of songs riddled with fan jargon and inside jokes. While Dean fights the scarecrow-like monster backstage, Sam finds Calliope in the basement with a student and teacher prisoner. She tells him "'Supernatural' has everything; life, death, resurrection, redemption, but above all, family … it isn't some meandering piece of genre drek, it's epic." Despite her speech, Sam and the others manage to slay Calliope easily and the monster explodes on stage, which the audience takes as a special effect. Before taking off, Dean tells Marie, "you know, this has been educational, seeing the story from your perspective." When Marie asks him "even if it doesn't match how you see it," he replies, "I have my version and you have yours." After the show, Marie is greeted by Chuck, who had been absent since Season 5, and tells her the production was "not bad."

"Fan Fiction" works as a moment of metacommentary that wholly solidifies fan/producer relationships, because unlike all the other times that the producers inserted fans within the show, this episode succeeds in validating that relationship. It does this by employing the language of the actual fans throughout the episode, taking fan jargon and introducing it to the characters Sam and Dean, without allowing those characters to demean it. According to Art Herbig and Andrew Herrmann, "'Fan Fiction' presents both celebrations and critiques of the show's history," done primarily by working with the language of actual *Supernatural* fans (757). In this episode, this jargon works as a nod to the fans as well as using Sam and Dean as producer to validate these practices. While Dean expresses frustration at some moments, at no point do the brothers demean the girls for being fans. In turn, actual *Supernatural* fans do not see these in-episode incarnations of themselves as something being debased, like Becky in previous episodes, but rather as playful nods and acknowledgments of fan participation over the years.

Other moments within the show represent this too, as when a girl playing Adam, Dean and Sam's brother, appears in Marie's interpretation. Adam's disappearance from the show[2] has long been a frustration of many real-life *Supernatural* fans, and this reference to him was what Herbig and Hermman posit as "a metatextual recognition by the writers of the show that a subsection of *Supernatural's* fan base finds this unanswered dilemma problematic" (757). When Sam, Dean, and Marie have the conversation about the author inserting himself into the narrative, they are lightly poking fun at Eric Kripke, who many believed used Chuck to insert himself into the *Supernatural* narrative. This is also present when Dean tells Marie what happens to the brothers after Season 5 and she tells him that is "the worst fan fiction I have ever heard." In many ways, Marie's attitude toward Dean represents the feelings of many *Supernatural* fans after Kripke left the show. Marie's commentary on the actual *Supernatural* story may have been a moment of metacommentary about fan upset at Gamble's storylines. By employing fan jargon to make commentary not only on fans but also the show itself, this episode works with meta to simultaneously validate fans by employing their language and using that language to address the problems that fans have had with the show.

As with the other episodes, the show also uses Sam and Dean as characters to reflect producer feelings. These nods are seen throughout the episode, such as when Dean tells Marie it was interesting to see her interpretation and that everyone can have their own version of a story. This is far cry from the Dean who, five seasons earlier, complained to Chuck about continuing production of the book series. In part, this attitude change could be because Chuck, acting as a professional writer, was profiting off of Dean's actual story, while Marie is passionately performing a fan fiction. Acting as producer in this moment, Dean validates *Supernatural* fans' position as interpreters of the narrative while reinforcing the idea of producers as narrators. Another of these moments comes in Calliope's speech about why she was drawn to this fan fiction of "Supernatural." Like Sam and Dean, Calliope is acting as a reflection of *Supernatural* producers. When she tells Sam "Supernatural" has everything, including "family," she is referencing not just the in-universe familial relations between Sam and Dean but the real-life SPN family itself. In many ways, Calliope's manifestation is a validation of both the in-universe fandom and the real-life fandom, because as a muse, she only appears when someone is passionately engaged with a piece of art. Her appearance within the episode and her role as producer of metacommentary within the episode function to validate the passion that fans have consistently put into the *Supernatural* fandom.

Additionally, Chuck's appearance at the end of the episode plays a significant role. Chuck is reintroduced in this episode not just to begin the God storyline that would happen a few seasons later but also as another representation of the show's initial creator, Eric Kripke. When this incarnation of an actual *Supernatural* producer tells Marie her production is "not bad," he is telling fans they are not bad, a validation that was needed after the disaster of Becky. Though this praise is not high, it is certainly not belittling, and therefore represents a well-balanced fan/producer relationship.

Unlike Becky, the fangirls in this episode are confident and proud to be fans. This pride is what made "Fan Fiction" such an excellent example of fan/producer relationships. Though "The Real Ghostbusters" included fans who were proud, these fans were adult males, while much of the *Supernatural* fandom is made up of female fans, much like what is represented by the teenage girls in this episode. The only female fan representation present before was Becky, who epitomized the crazy fangirl stereotype. With Marie and Mae, the producers finally show perhaps the most accurate representation of real-life *Supernatural* fans. When Dean and Sam try to question the musical and the nature of their fan fiction, the girls do not back down, with Mae defending Marie's "interpretation" of the books. As Aja Ramono says, "It took five seasons for us to finally get a counterpoint to delusional, lost-in-fantasy Becky as the show's resident fangirl, but now we've got a whole ensemble of counterpoints, and they're great." Throughout the episode, it is Marie who tells Dean to relax over the subtext of Wincest and Destiel, the girls laugh when Sam and Dean try to reveal who they really are, and Marie and Mae make tongue-in-cheek snarky comments. For the first time, fans are given positive representation, one that takes the time to poke fun at the show itself through metacommentary that subverts all previous incarnations of producers exclusively poking fun at fans.

This episode went over so well because it was meant, as Season 10 showrunner (and one of the figures from whose name Chuck's pseudonym—Carver Edlund—is derived) Jeremy Carver said, "as a love letter to the fans" (Herbig and Herrmann 754). As the 200th episode special, it was meant to be an especially significant episode, and though not monumental to the greater storyline itself, it was monumental for the fans and their continual support that had led *Supernatural* to that point. Carver adds, "Many aspects of the fandom are going to see themselves represented and in many different ways and in the most loving way possible" (Herbig and Herrmann 754). In more ways than one, this episode's purpose was to use metacommentary to acknowledge and validate the fans of *Supernatural,* thanking them for the passion they put into following the show over the years. This intended love letter is seen most prominently in the episode's embrace of Marie. As Ramono says, "Marie, is informed that her belief in the world of her fan fiction is a literal life-saver. Moreover, the show's explicit embrace of Marie and her narratives is the long-missing link between the canon and its fans." As fan representation, Marie is the character who finally becomes the missing piece between fan and producer, solidifying relationships that had been in an up and down battle for years. The significance of "Fan Fiction" cannot be overstated; it stands not only as a testament of the way *Supernatural* fandom's fan/producer relationships have evolved over the years, but also as testament to the potential of fan/producer relationships to keep a show going.

Supernatural is the longest running show on the CW Network (Ingham). In part, the reason the show is so successful is the strong fan/producer relationships it has cultivated throughout the years, both through real life interactions and through validating moments of metacommentary like "Fan Fiction." The producers of *Supernatural* consistently use metacommentary to make nods to fans, with "Fan Fiction" effectively thanking the fans for the show's growth over the years. This essay documents only three prime examples, but the series as whole is ripe with metacommentary, which demonstrates the continuous relationships between fan/producers leading up to "Fan Fiction." Although several seasons have passed since this episode and there are other moments where fan/producer relationships have struggled, metacommentary on fans within the show remains consistently positive since "Fan Fiction." The show's success is a product of this metacommentary, and even after the series ends, it is likely to have a cult following like *The Rocky Horror Picture Show*, with fans who continually come back to the show and participate. If anything, *Supernatural* serves as a leader in the way media is changing. Fans and producers now interact more than ever before; smart producers take note of that and let fans participate, perhaps through metacommentary, perhaps through real-world interactions via Web 2.0. Regardless, the hallmark of a successful show is no longer something defined by the cold numbers of ratings but by the fan/producer relationships cultivated around the show. Not many shows make it as far or last as long as *Supernatural* has, but thanks to fans, it has the privilege of doing so.

NOTES

1. This book was in press prior to Becky's and Adam's reappearances late in Season 15.
2. *Ibid.*

WORKS CITED

Bennet, Lucy, and Bertha Chin. "Exploring Fandom, Social Media, and Producer/Fan Interactions: An Interview with *Sleepy Hollow*'s Orlando Jones." *Transformative Works and Cultures*, Transformative Works and Cultures, journal.transformativeworks.org/index.php/twc/article/view/601/436.

Carlson, Adam. "The Poet Laureate of Fan Fiction." *The Awl*, The Awl, 19 June 2015, www.theawl.com/2015/06/the-poet-laureate-of-fan-fiction/.

Casper, Frances Mary. "Family Don't End with Blood: Building the *Supernatural* Family." *Fan Phenomena: Supernatural*, edited by Lynn S. Zubernis and Katherine Larsen, Intellect Books, 2014, pp. 76–87.

Garrison, Stephanie. "How *Supernatural* Blurs the Lines Between 'Fan-Fiction'" *Black & Gold Review*, 13 Mar. 2015, www.blackandgoldreview.com/2014/12/15/supernatural-blurs-lines-fan-fiction.

Herbig, Adam and Andrew Herrmann. "Polymediated Narrative: The Case of the *Supernatural* Episode 'Fan Fiction.'" *International Journal of Communication.* vol. 10, 2016, pp. 748–765.

Hughes, Jason. "'Supernatural' 200th Episode Meta-Musical Is Pure Fan Service." *TheWrap*, The Wrap, 12 Nov. 2014, www.thewrap.com/supernatural-200th-episode-meta-musical-is-pure-fan-service/.

Ingham, Alexandria. "How 'Supernatural' Became the Longest-Running CW Show (and Won the Hearts of Fans)." *Hidden Remote*, FanSided, 4 Apr. 2017, hiddenremote.com/2017/04/04/how-supernatural-became-the-longest-running-cw-show-and-won-the-hearts-of-fans/.

Jackson, Jessica P. "It's a Bird, It's a Plane! No, Wait, It's a *Supernatural* Fan!" *Film Matters*, vol. 8, no. 1, 2017, pp. 89–91.

Jenkins, Henry, and Ravi Purushotma. *Confronting the Challenges of Participatory Culture: Media Education for the 21st Century.* MIT Press, 2009.

Larsen, Katherine, and Lynn S. Zubernis. *Fangasm:* Supernatural *Fangirls.* University of Iowa Press, 2013.

Macklem, Lisa. "I See What You Did There: SPN and the Fourth Wall." *Fan Phenomena: Supernatural*, edited by Lynn S. Zubernis and Katherine Larsen, Intellect Books, 2014, pp. 34–45.

Moylan, Brian. "The Fan Rituals That Made *Rocky Horror Picture Show* a Cult Classic." *The Guardian*, Guardian News and Media, 19 Oct. 2016, www.theguardian.com/culture/2016/oct/19/rocky-horror-picture-show-fan-rituals-fox-remake.

Noone, Kristin. "What Are Little Ghouls Made Of? the *Supernatural* Family, Fandom, and the Problem of Adam." *Transformative Works and Cultures*, vol. 4, 2010, 15 pars. doi.org/10.3983/tw.2010.0136. Accessed 18 Dec. 2018.

Romano, Aja. "After 200 Episodes, *Supernatural* Finally Gets Its Fangirls Right." *The Daily Dot*, Daily Dot, 24 Feb. 2017, www.dailydot.com/parsec/supernatural-episode-200-fan-fiction-takes-on-fangirls/

"Sera Gamble." *Supernatural Wiki,* Last updated April 10, 2018. http://www.supernaturalwiki.com/index.php?title=Sera_Gamble

Ulaby, Neda. "The Few, the Fervent: Fans of 'Supernatural' Redefine TV Success." *NPR*, NPR, 15 Jan. 2014, www.npr.org/2014/01/15/262092791/the-few-the-fervent-fans-of-supernatural-redefine-tv-success.

"WinchesterCon." *Supernatural Wiki*, Last updated November 4, 2014. http://www.supernaturalwiki.com/index.php?title=WinchesterCon

PART THREE

The Politics of Fandom

Slash Fiction

Homoerotics and the Metatextual Fangirl

Emily E. Roach

Supernatural is consciously metatextual, with allusions to everything from popular culture to classic mythology, together with tongue-in-cheek nods to genre specific influences and its status as a television show. Over the course of its run, *Supernatural* demonstrated a preoccupation with narratology and has frequently employed metafictive devices to explore the creative art of storytelling. Like many horror franchises it draws on stories from the past, working with legend, folklore, fairy tales, fantasy and biblical narratives, many of which are steeped in the tradition of scribes and oral story-telling, stories whose precise authorship is often ambiguous or in dispute or stories with multiple authors focusing on different perspectives. A large online fandom has developed around the *Supernatural* series, with the first fan fiction posted only 24 hours after the pilot aired. Together with metatextual commentary on its own diegetic strategies, the series also comments on the stories other people tell, explicitly referencing the practice of writing homoerotic slash fiction within the show. Jules Wilkinson suggests that "*Supernatural* is concerned with exploring the stories people construct and tell about themselves and their relationships" (6.1) and at the heart of the story are two brothers, protagonists Sam and Dean Winchester.

On the surface the story is one of masculine coded heroism. The brothers are isolated and on the outskirts of society, with no significant female influence left in their lives, an unsurprising state of affairs given that women in general fare badly on the show. Their job is initially framed as being a continuation of their father's work, a task that is rooted in patriarchal lineage (though it is eventually revealed that their mother also came from a family of hunters). The horror genre holds masculine associations. However, there are strategies at play which disrupt the heteronormative hero arc and enable a more complex and queer reading of *Supernatural*.

Melissa Bruce observes "strong melodramatic conventions, offering a glimpse into a genre typically read as feminine" (1.1). Catherine Tosenberger notes that "*Supernatural* frequently calls attention to its own homoerotic energy" ("'The Epic Love Story'" 1.5) and suggests that slash fiction that imagines erotic, incestuous possibilities between brothers Sam and Dean ("Wincest") is not an example of a subversive, resistant interpretation of a hetero-masculine text, but is instead an expansion on homoerotic elements that can be read into the narrative subtext. Tosenberger acknowledges the dominant presence of masculine conventions, but also observes that "as brothers, [Sam and Dean] are given a pass for displays of emotion that masculinity in our culture usually forbids, which intensifies the potential for queer readings" ("'The Epic Love Story'" 1.2). Through metatextual devices, the series has woven slash fiction into the show itself, and by analyzing how the characters respond to being made aware of the existence of slash fiction and the people writing it, it is possible to gain some insight into the views those in creative control hold about transformative works and their place within the creator-sanctioned story.

In engaging explicitly, if not always thoughtfully, with slashing and shipping, *Supernatural* has exposed itself to queerbaiting challenges. Eve Ng observes that "the norm used to be not to acknowledge, let alone encourage, queer interpretations of canonically heterosexual characters and narratives" (3.3). The position now seems to be the other extreme. Fans have more access to creators, and creators have greater access to increasingly public fan activity. As a result, multiple recent television shows have been accused of queerbaiting when they flirt with the possibility of a same-sex union, with no real intention of ever making the character(s) in question canonically queer. This approach tends to be accompanied by jokes at the expense of queer people and a robust, and in some cases narratively inconsistent, confirmation of heterosexuality, colloquially called a "no homo" moment. Queerbaiting encourages LGBT investment in a series but doesn't offer any meaningful representation. *Supernatural* is still running, and some suggest the question of whether or not it has been queerbaiting its fans depends on how the series concludes. That particular debate is beyond the scope of this analysis, but the show's handling of the relationship between Dean Winchester and the angel Castiel (shipped in fandom under the name "Destiel") continues to be raised in connection with the topic, by fans, pop culture writers (see, for instance, Eliel Cruise, "Fans Take *Supernatural* to Task for 'Queer Baiting'"; Sadie Gennis, "*Supernatural* Has a Queerbaiting Problem That Needs to Stop"; Anna Campbell, "Queerbaited: Homoeroticism & Homophobia in *Supernatural* in the Age of the Internet"; Emily E. Roach, "How Queerbaiting Discussions Show Heteronormativity is Alive and Well"; Sima Shakeri, "Television Has a 'Bury Your Gays,' Queerbaiting, and LGBTQ Representation Problem"), and in scholarship (Cassandra M. Collier, "The Love that Refuses to Speak its Name: Examining Queerbaiting and Fan Producer Interactions in Fan Cultures"; Emma Nordin, "From Queer Reading to Queerbaiting: The Battle over the Polysemic Text and the Power of Hermeneutics"; Eve Ng, "Between Text, Paratext, and Context: Queerbaiting and the Contemporary Media Landscape").

With its metatextual episodes which make fandom part of the narrative, *Supernatural* has now explicitly referenced both Wincest and Destiel, allowing the brothers onscreen time to react to the knowledge that those ships exist and that fans write erotic fiction inspired by them. The show has offered various interpretations of the fangirl and her pursuits, and the validity of her pursuits has been commented upon either explicitly or in the way her narrative arc ultimately concludes. By analyzing the narrative function of fangirls Becky, Marie and Charlie, and comparing and contrasting modes of female fannishness with fanboy Dean, I suggest that *Supernatural* has provided metatextual comment on fans and their pursuits in an unorthodox manner, whilst still ultimately perpetuating stereotypes of female dominated fan activities and demonstrating a gendered bias towards certain modes of fannish engagement. By explaining how *Supernatural* operates as a metatextual exploration of narratology, authorship and ownership of text, and exploring the way the fangirl functions within the broader diegesis, I suggest that the show simultaneously invites and shuts down queer readings, just as invitations to participate in transformational fandom practices are counterbalanced with a reassertion of the dominance of creator-sanctioned authorship. I conclude by suggesting that the way the series has incorporated its slash fiction writing fangirls into the text is not divorced from a queerbaiting analysis and explain how the two connect.

Meta Fiction: Supernatural *as a Meta Text*

In the pilot episode of *Supernatural* the familiar image of the woman in white is one of the first images the viewer encounters. Sam and Dean's mother, Mary Winchester, is dressed in a white nightgown when she is murdered by the demon Azazel. When Sam's girlfriend Jessica Moore is murdered by the same demon 22 years later, she too is in a white nightgown, the image of the woman in white bookending the narrative arc of the episode. The episode's primary antagonist is Constance Welch, also referred to as a Woman in White. Although Constance's story most closely aligns with the Mexican La Llorona legend of the weeping woman, the image has universal relevance within many cultures that have formed their own myths and legends around the specter of the woman in white. The name of the spirit immediately evokes the Wilkie Collins novel of the same name, a novel which was in popular consciousness just a year prior to the airing of the first episode of *Supernatural*, thanks to Andrew Lloyd Webber's musical which opened in London's West End in 2004 and on Broadway in 2005. The novel is deeply concerned with narratology and uses epistolary techniques to offer differing perspectives, with autonomous narrator Walter Hartright ultimately controlling the way the other narrative voices are employed. It contains many elements of queerness and the Victorian Gothic, including an intense, sapphic sibling bond (see for example Ardel). With the pilot episode of *Supernatural* it is possible to argue that these intertextual elements foreshadow a series invested in exploring narrative function and the homoerotics of Gothic convention. As critics such as Catherine Tosenberger have comprehensively articulated, *Supernatural* demonstrates a clear familiarity with the Gothic, in "the formal study of the folklore Sam and Dean track, a fascination with the otherworldly, and, most importantly, persistent discourses of both queerness and sympathetic sibling incest" ("'The Epic Love Story'" 4.1). Even if the Collins connection feels like too much of a stretch, at the very least *Supernatural* demonstrated a clear interest in intertextuality from the outset with the choice of a figure which has a transnational folkloric relevance as its pilot episode's antagonist.

Together with intertextuality, the series began engaging with its own status as mediated fictional narrative early on. For example, in Season 2's "Hollywood Babylon" (2.18), written by Ben Edlund, the show deployed a number of metatextual strategies. The primary action takes place on the set of a horror film and marks the first appearance of fanboy Dean, the horror film buff within a horror-based television franchise. This positioning of Dean as conversant with geek trivia enables the show to engage intertextually with other iconic horror franchises, such as Dean's reference to the curse that befell the *Poltergeist* (1982) film. Metatextually the episode pokes fun at *Supernatural*'s status as a work of mediated fiction, through a number of in-jokes about the show's creators, the appearance of several people who work on *Supernatural* as onscreen crew members and the episode's final shot of the brothers walking into the L.A. sunset, only for the "sunset" to be revealed as a prop, replaced by pine trees which are more reminiscent of the landscape in British Columbia, where a significant amount of *Supernatural* is filmed. The episode is also an early indication of the show's preoccupation with the question of authorial control over the narrative, through a plot which focuses on a writer's anger at his story not being told the way he wants it to be. This episode foreshadows the show's interest in exploring its own fiction, a strategy it employs far more explicitly in Season 4's "The Monster at the End of This Book" (4.18) by introducing the "Supernatural" book series into the series narrative. The books are penned by author Carver Edlund, an amalgam of *Supernatural* writers Jeremy Carver and Ben Edlund, a pseudonym for the writer Chuck Shurley, and an avatar for *Supernatural* creator Eric Kripke. These texts within the text which follow the narrative arc of the series itself allowed the show to revisit its interest in exploring the status of the author and the relationship between the author and text, and the episode is discussed in more depth below.

In Season 9, the episode aptly titled "Meta Fiction" (9.18) opens with angel and Scribe of God, Metatron, on a typewriter, telling a story of his own with copies of the "Supernatural" books on the desk. Metatron looks up from his typewriter and takes off his glasses, staring into the camera, addressing the audience as he talks about storytelling: "What makes a story work? Is it the plot, the characters, the text? The subtext? Who gives the story meaning? Is it the writer, or you?" The camera zooms in on Metatron's face as he asks the question to the audience, the "you" he appears to be addressing. The usual opening sequence with the title "Supernatural" appears only briefly to be replaced with the word "Metatron," indicating the viewer is being told the story from an alternative narrative perspective.

Towards the end of the episode Metatron asks a bound and gagged Castiel what makes a story work. The silencing of Castiel renders the character voiceless, a curious scene which invites several possible readings. It could be that Metatron takes on the role of fan fiction writer, bending Castiel's character to his will in a similar fashion to the way authors can do whatever they wish with their characters. The silencing of Castiel might also represent the way the viewers feel in connection with the stories they are being told, unable to alter the direction the author decides to take with the narrative. Eventually Metatron allows Castiel to speak and comments that "well drawn characters […] may surprise you." Ultimately, however, the author, Metatron, reasserts control once more with his omniscient understanding of the narrative: "I know something they don't know. The ending." This positioning of the author as the ultimate power is reinforced yet again in Season 11, when Chuck Shurley, the author of the "Supernatural" books, is revealed to be a god-like prophet in "Swan Song" (5.22), his status as God finally made explicit in "Don't Call Me Shurley" (11.20). The introduction of the "Supernatural" books has enabled the show to make extensive comment on the narratology of storytelling, playing with the idea of multiple authors (with Metatron's function as Scribe), the relationship between author and text and the fiction of the show itself.

Introducing the "Supernatural" books allowed the show to engage directly with its own fandom by building a cult fandom into the diegesis. It afforded the creators an opportunity to comment on storytelling and the hierarchy between canon creators and fans, by writing fans into the narrative. Broadly speaking these fans can be observed engaging in different modes of fan activity, transformational on the one hand and affirmational on the other. The terms transformational and affirmational are attributed to Dreamwidth user obsession_inc (2009) and they have been adopted by scholarship which seeks to distinguish the fan practices which involve "bending and stretching the text beyond the boundaries established by the original author" (Polesak 1.1), from "affirmational" fandom, which obsession_inc defined as practices such as cosplay and convention attendance. Crucially, those affirmational practices are "creator sanctioned," ones which demonstrate an adherence to the creator-centric view of the universe, affirming, rather than transforming, the canon.

Ashley Polesak's article on Sherlock fandom, and obsession_inc themselves, acknowledge there is not a clear line between "transformational" and "affirmational," with obsession_inc suggesting that the lines frequently blur, and Polesak going further to deconstruct the distinction, suggesting that fans can "share the urge to identify as members of that community through affirmational discourse, and also the desire to see themselves and their understandings of their world reflected in the texts they love through transformational discourse" (6.1). In many fandoms the lines between affirmational and transformational motivations and discourse frequently overlap, and the critical scope of analysis around transformative works and fan practices associated with them, such as shipping and writing fan fiction, is now far more expansive and generally positive, with "transformative works" a legal term of art in and of itself, designed to protect works which fall within "fair use" definitions for copyright purposes. However, the "transformational" and "affirmational" distinction between types of fannish practice remains a useful one for the purposes of this essay, if only to categorize different types of fannish practice, to engage with how they are presented within *Supernatural* and to explore certain gendered assumptions made in connection with them.

In her article on gender and geek hierarchies, Kristina Busse comments that although obsession_inc doesn't reference gender, the assumption that transformational fan practices are female dominated activities and that affirmational fan practices are male dominated activities "tends to be accepted as a truism" ("Geek hierarchies" 82). In reality, of course, the gendered nature of the different modes of fan engagement is far more complex. Cosplay, for example, is just one of the modes of affirmational fan practice that is much more queerly diverse than reductive assumptions might suggest, as fans deconstruct gender binaries through gender-bending cosplay, and contemporary drag artists find a place for artistic expression in geek culture. Some queer fans gravitate towards cosplay as a safe exploration of their own gender identity, a topic I explored in my article "Cosplay, Drag and the Transformative Nature of Living Out Your Fandom." However, it is the *assumption* of gender bias inherent within the distinction between affirmational and transformational fan practice that is important in the case of *Supernatural*, where the creators appear to make gendered assumptions about modes of fan activity. Indeed, although the gender demographic of affirmational fandom certainly requires some interrogation, a census conducted in 2014 across 10,005 users of multi-fandom fanfic archive site Archive of Our Own, where a significant amount of *Supernatural* fan fiction is hosted, identified 85.2 percent of users as female identified, with a higher number of users identifying as non-binary (11.6 percent) than male (3.0 percent) ("AO3 Census"). The same survey also highlighted that the majority of surveyed users identify as LGBT, with only 38 percent of surveyed respondents identifying as heterosexual. The queerness of these spaces is also an important factor when engaging with the way the show depicts the "typical" fangirl.

Supernatural does not limit itself to exploring metatextuality through self-referential strategies or the breaking of the fourth wall enabled by bringing Carver Edlund's cult fandom into the narrative. It also adopts metafictive strategies in the blurring of the lines between the real world and the fictional world, most notably in Season 6 episode "The French Mistake" (6.15). In the episode, three of the key characters within the show, Sam and Dean Winchester and Castiel, become the actors who play them, Jensen Ackles, Jared Padalecki and Misha Collins, respectively. Within the episode the actors make jokes about their own acting—with Ackles who, like Collins, deliberately deepens his voice for the role of Dean, putting on an exaggeratedly gruff tone. The real lives of the actors become part of the diegesis, with Padalecki's wife Genevieve Cortese, who played Ruby, the demon who partners with Sam in the fourth season of the series, appearing as "Padalecki's" wife in "The French Mistake." A picture of Padalecki's and Cortese's real life wedding day is displayed in the home they share in the episode. The real lives of the actors are further referenced when Sam makes fun of Dean for the soap opera past he discovers when he Googles "Jensen Ackles." He unearths a real clip of Ackles when he appeared in the popular American soap *Days of Our Lives* (1965–), and plays the clip for a moment, to the horror of Dean.

Wilkinson has observed that "Twitter has been responsible for redefining the relationships between fans and celebrities, as the application allows a new immediacy and intimacy in interactions" (5.5). In "The French Mistake" the show flips the access fans have to creators on social media around, bringing the text into the sphere of actor/fan social media interaction, heightening the level of intimacy between the fan and the narrative. In "The French Mistake" Misha Collins is shown tweeting about

"J2," the fandom name coined for Jared and Jensen, and makes reference to his fanbase as "mishamigos," a term used by Collins in the episode but not one that the real-life Collins uses in interactions with his fans (6.15). These tweets were posted by Collins himself in real time as the show aired, something Collins later tweeted was a result of his phone being stolen and ending up in an alternate universe. This blurring of the lines between fact and fiction is something *Supernatural* has played around with in a multitude of creative ways, positioning itself as a show which consciously uses metatext to explore its own function, fanbase and story. In doing so, it offers both light-hearted judgment of where the story sits in a broader literary context, with Metatron describing the "Supernatural" books as "pulp" ("Meta Fiction"), and the tongue-in-cheek depiction of the author as God, playing with literary critical theories on authorship and narrative function. It is important to understand how *Supernatural* employs meta fictive strategies more broadly, in order to consider the role of the fangirl within the series, and where the producers see themselves in relation to the fangirl.

"Sam Girls, Dean Girls and what's a slash fan?"

One of the first episodes of *Supernatural* to substantially engage with the transformative side of fan activity was Season 4's "The Monster at the End of This Book" (4.18). In the episode, Sam and Dean discover the series of books which tell the story of their lives. The brothers learn that there is a cult fandom based around the books when the owner of the shop in which they see the books assumes that they are live-action role-players (LARPers), role-playing as Sam and Dean from Edlund's series. The episode brings its own fandom into the text through this reference to real life fan practices. When the camera zooms in to offer the viewer a close-up of the cover of the book, the viewer is provided with a visual which has a distinctly homoerotic tone. Although Sam resembles model Fabio Lanzoni, who appeared on the cover of a number of heterosexual romances in the 1990s, those covers frequently depicted Fabio by himself, or with women. The character of Sam is shirtless, and Dean wears a white muscle-vest. With the hyper-masculine depiction of semi-naked men, the cover shares more similarities with original male/male erotic fiction than with the horror genre, or the heterosexual romance genre. The coupling of Sam and Dean on the cover offers self-referential commentary on the homoerotic subtext which is part of the brothers' relationship and a foreshadowing of the role transformational fandom, and slash fiction writers in particular, play in the cult fandom which has formed around the books.

It is worth briefly noting that Hollywood and authors in general have been cautious about engaging with fan fiction based on their own works, due to the potential legal ramifications in the event of any dispute over the ownership of the work and breaches of copyright. On that basis, it is unlikely that the show's creators would feel it prudent to engage in depth with transformative fandom practices, but in "The Monster at the End of This Book" it is clear that The Powers That Be are aware of certain kinds of fan engagement with the show, most specifically the dialogue between fans on the message board Television Without Pity. The first clear example of this is when Dean stumbles upon a website where the fans opine on narrative weaknesses or plot flaws in the "Supernatural" series. He reads a scathing review posted by online user Simpatico out loud, scoffing at their description of the books' recent narrative arc as "craptastic." Simpatico was not a random name, but the real-life avatar of a regular poster on the *Supernatural* Television Without Pity message boards, a message board which receives further attention in "The Real Ghostbusters" (5.09) with the characters Demian and Barnes, both of whom were named after Television Without Pity users. Dean responds "screw you" to the critique leveled at the series by Simpatico, a moment which enables the producers to respond to and dismiss fan criticism on forums which offer scathing reviews. K.T. Torrey observes that "what makes the brothers' discovery of the 'Supernatural' novels and its fan-driven metatext unique is that these works make explicit the Winchesters' lack of authority over their own lives" (166). This is something that Dean in particular appears to struggle with, both in the context of the books themselves and, later, in respect of the transformative works created by the fans of the series.

The first observation made by Dean during his online browsing is a light-hearted example of his competitiveness with Sam, when he discovers the existence of Sam Girls and Dean Girls. For the viewer involved in transformative fandom, it becomes more uncomfortable when Dean discovers the existence of the slash fan. He asks what a slash fan is and, looking distinctly ill at ease, Sam explains, "Sam *slash* Dean. *Together.*" This prompts a horrified reaction from Dean, who quickly shuts the laptop down, saying, "[t]hey do know we're brothers, right?" A robust dismissal of Wincest follows, which Dean describes as "sick." Within the diegesis of the show of course Dean's reaction is not surprising and represents how a real person might be expected to react upon discovering the existence of erotic fan fiction pairing himself and his younger brother. However, it was ultimately the choice of the fictional narrative to so explicitly highlight the existence of Wincest in the first place, and to have Dean, understandable as his reaction may be, soundly condemn it. With a few pithy snippets of dialogue, the practices of Wincest shippers and creators had been exposed to the condemnation of the brothers that were, at the time, the primary objects of

Supernatural fandom's transformative practices, and had exposed the practices of transformative fandom to the scrutiny of the public wider audience.

This "exposure" of a practice which involves posting transformative works online might seem like a contradiction in terms, but although theoretically accessible to everyone, fan fiction has typically been primarily of interest to fans actively seeking it out. Fandoms have fought hard to allow all types of content to exist within fandom spaces and have long resisted attempts to shut down transformative works on grounds of moral censorship. As fan activities become more public and the language of fandom part of mainstream parlance, the conversations within fandom communities have also shifted and a new wave of purity policing and intra-fandom censorship has arisen with the increased popularity of non-journal based online platforms, such as Tumblr, where most of *Supernatural* fandom now operates in conjunction with several large chat-based groups hosted on platforms such as Discord. Due to concerns around legal ramifications, unless they have experience of other transformative fandoms, The Powers That Be are unlikely to have a deep, nuanced understanding of the conversations happening within those fandom spaces, and how participants in largely female dominated spaces, are impacted by vitriolic intra-fandom ship wars, anonymous messaging functions, anti-culture and the desire of a vocal minority to shut down the creation of so-called "problematic" fan fiction and the sites that host those works, such as Archive of Our Own (Minkel 2018). As I will go on to explain, *Supernatural* demonstrates a certain naiveté in its representations of certain modes of fan behavior and incomplete understandings of the demographic that engages with them, seemingly failing to appreciate how certain narrative decisions impact those spaces which are so important to the participants creating within them.

Of course, some fans enjoyed the nod to Wincest shipping. Schmidt suggests that "there is something emotionally alluring for fans about the idea of being known" (2.8). However, as Felschow has observed, not all fans were happy. Whilst some saw the reference to transformational fandom as "playful and inclusive," others responded more negatively, finding the discovery and Dean's reaction to it "harsh and demeaning" (1.2). Tosenberger, too, comments on the mixed reaction to the episode from the fandom, referring to the "shock wave" it sent through the community and critiquing the way the scene appeared to "poke fun at the level of devotion and emotional investment in the series" as it "outed those fans who write Sam/Dean slash" ("Love! Valor! *Supernatural!*" 1.3). This idea of outing the fans might sound like an inconsequential complaint, but for the reasons outlined above, it left some fans exposed to intra-fandom censorship. As K.T. Torrey notes, by explicitly name-checking Sam/Dean slash, the episode "exposed Wincest fans to meta-commentary from the series' producers via the Winchesters [...] and opened fan reading and writing practices that had typically enjoyed a more robust fourth wall between fan activity and canon creator to a wider audience. The practice of writing Wincest attracted criticism from both other *Supernatural* fans and members of the general public who were, like Dean, repelled by Wincest's incestuous content" (168). The mainstream press has typically been quick to offer unsolicited, poorly researched and often negative perspectives on fan fiction. The revelation of the popularity of erotic works of fan fiction focused on an incestuous brotherly relationship attracted a certain amount of media scrutiny. This brought conversations around the ethics of producing fictional works featuring incestuous ships into the broader public domain, at a time when such discussions were already becoming increasingly volatile even within the relative safety of fandom spaces, Perhaps the *Supernatural* creators had anticipated such a controversial topic would generate publicity for the series, but they were unlikely to understand the ramifications and the silencing impact of shame on participants within those communities. As Gray suggests, "the media attention is not surprising, but neither is the discomfort of the fans who feel betrayed" (21).

Season 5's "Sympathy for the Devil" (5.01) introduces Becky Rosen, a "Supernatural" fangirl, with the online username SamLicker81, who is first shown working on a piece of Wincest fan fiction. The idea of a slash writer as a girl who is in love with the male object(s) of her erotica is a tired and reductive depiction of the fangirl and one which is frequently offered by people seeking to understand why female dominated space has a fascination with male/male fiction. It does little to subvert more negative readings of slash as a fetishist practice engaged in by straight women lusting after attractive male bodies. As Felschow observes, *Supernatural*'s engagement with its transformational fandom through Becky is "not an overt invitation to participate, but a demonstration that the producers/writers of the program are aware of exactly what their fandom is doing" (6.6). They serve as a reminder to fandom that The Powers That Be are watching, albeit from a distance. Shortly after the episode aired, a LiveJournal account was created under the SamLicker81 username and the complete copy of Becky's fanfic, "Burning Desires," was uploaded to that account and crossposted to the LiveJournal Wincest community. The person behind that account has, to my knowledge, never been revealed. It is entirely possible the journal was a fan run RPG account, but it could also have been created by people involved with the show, reinforcing that sense that the spaces which are used for transformative modes of fan engagement are on the radar of the creators. Those involved with the show therefore straddle a hybrid space, where they know just enough about transformative fandom to be able to work it into the show, but not enough (due to potential concerns over legal ramifications if they actively engaged with fan fiction) to develop a full understanding of the communities and shippers they name-check.

Becky is clearly played for comedic effect, and the audience is invited to enjoy the joke of her erotic fan fiction and her fascination with Sam. Judith May Fathallah, writing about Becky in "Sympathy for the Devil" (5.01) and later episode "The Real Ghostbusters" (5.09), suggests that fans can laugh along with Becky and her resistance to the conventions of masculine heroism. Drawing on Mikhail Bakhtin's theories of resistant laughter, Fathallah suggests that "Becky can be read as refusing to take seriously the official, dominant story line, inviting those not privileged in mainstream society to appropriate the narrative for their pleasure" ("Becky Is My Hero" 1.2). Although Fathallah makes a convincing point, there is something imbalanced about the laughter Becky generates, as it is always a one-way dialogue in which the fans themselves have no voice. As Felschow notes, although the show might poke as much fun at its own creation as it does the fangirl inspired by it, the self-referential jokes at the expense of the creators do not carry the same implications: "while Kripke and company may be laughing at themselves, they do so from the comfort of the writers' room, a serious position of power" (6.6). Even within her article, which offers an alternative and more positive read of Becky amidst a largely negative response from the fandom, Fathallah adds an important caveat to the idea of laughter as a tool of resistance. She notes that the fangirl who can laugh with Kripke and the creators involved with bringing Becky to the small screen can only do so from a position of relative privilege: "she must be secure in the conviction that hegemonic stories of female passivity and traditional heterosexual unions are not the only legitimate ones, which implies a degree of education in feminist and gender studies" ("Becky Is My Hero" 4.2) otherwise she is particularly vulnerable to feelings of mockery and shame. Within the home, Fathallah offers the fact that some fan fiction writers are intensely private about their endeavors, even with their own families, which could leave those "practically dependent on those hegemonic narratives" nervous about being discovered. If they are open about engaging with fan activity, it is possible that an unsympathetic partner might believe all fangirls find refuge in fandom for the same reasons as Becky ("Becky Is My Hero" 4.2). Those who might find it the hardest to laugh along with the show's depiction of Becky might be precisely those people who get the most from the relatively safe, creative community spaces fandom offers.

It might be easier to enjoy Becky as an exaggerated extreme of fan behavior if the positioning of the fangirl as overly invested in the objects of her fandom—her "affective hysterics and sexual advances" (Busse, "Geek Hierarchies" 82)—weren't so routinely mocked and derided in other forms of discourse. Kristina Busse writes persuasively about the gendering of the good fan and raises the so-called "Twilight Ruined Comic-Con" debacle at the 2009 San Diego Comic-Con, during which the popularity of *Twilight* and the female fanbase it brought with it to the convention circuit was met with significant backlash and outright resistance. Becky's fangirl falls into that mode of "frenzied and hysterical squeeing" ("Geek hierarchies" 74) which was so heavily criticized in that instance. Busse suggests that reactions to a particular kind of female-coded fan behavior is something other fans are quick to dismiss together with "their interests, their spaces, and their primary forms of engagement," a hierarchy of fans determined by their behavior and activities they engage in, which Busse links to "gender discrimination […] on the level of the fan, the fan activity, and the fannish investment" ("Geek Hierarchies" 75). "Season 7, Time for a Wedding!" (7.08) is *Supernatural's* meanest and most uncomfortable depiction of the transformational fangirl. In this episode Becky's hyperbolic fangirling has become a rabid obsession, fuelled by isolation. Becky kidnaps Sam and uses a love potion to make him marry her in Las Vegas, a shotgun wedding which is later annulled when the impact of the potion wears off. Becky tells Sam—whilst he is tied to the bed and gagged—that she only ever felt understood on online message boards. In the same episode she is ridiculed and mocked by a former school classmate, and Crowley passes scathing commentary on her appearance, saying, "I'm sure you have a wonderful personality, dear."

Becky's actions in the episode are driven by her erotic and romantic interest in the male lead of her stories, which has become impossible to contain. Becky's romantic idealization of Sam has very little to do with her shipping interests. This heteronormative sexualization of the practice of slash fiction writing and the misogynistic portrayal of the rabid fangirl is a depressing extension of a deep suspicion of female-driven fan practice that continues to persist in media discourse. Aaron Hicklin's now infamous interview with Benedict Cumberbatch contemptuously passed judgment on Sherlock fandom's "rapacious slash fiction community" turning Cumberbatch's Sherlock into a "lustful cock monster." The slew of opinion pieces following the unprecedented success of fanfic turned pro-fic *Fifty Shades of Grey* were similarly scathing, with a piece for the *Guardian* describing fan fiction as everything from "disturbing" and "postmodern and aesthetically bankrupt" to an "incomprehensible mess" (Morrisson). Although many published authors might meet with similar criticisms, at least they are being paid for the pleasure. It is typically genres associated with women, like fan fiction and the romance genre, which attract such scathing opinion pieces about their literary quality. To canonize the very stereotypes that are so frequently used in a derogatory way to criticize the fangirl and her pursuits was a particularly poor choice which did nothing to serve the broader narrative arc of the season. The episode shifts Becky from a figure of fun to something substantially more depressing. Lisa Macklem observes that "[t]his curiously bitter version of fandom comes at a time when Gamble was under siege from fans who were not happy about the direction she was taking with the show" (42). It is possible that this episode reflects the then showrunner's first-hand experience of fans lobbying those involved with the show, but whatever the drivers, the episode reads like a cautionary tale passing judgment on female desire and transformational fandom. It plays into critiques of female fans as being "too obsessive, too fanatic, and too invested" (Busse, "Geek Hierarchies" 73) and suggests there is a darker side to affect and female sexuality.

As Busse observes, "the fan hero remains relentlessly gendered" ("Geek Hierarchies" 82) in *Supernatural*, and Becky's heroic agency is limited. Tosenberger notes that the show's misogynistic overtones "were especially egregious in 'Ghostbusters'" ("Love! Valor! *Supernatural!*" 1.6). Becky lures Sam and Dean to a "Supernatural" fan convention, which the author, Chuck Shurley, also attends. Several critics have commented on the odd choice to depict the convention audience as predominantly male, given *Supernatural*'s large female fanbase (Tosenberger, "Love! Valor! *Supernatural!*"; Busse, "Fan Labor and Feminism"), another indicator perhaps that the writers and producers might have awareness of fan activity, but don't fully understand it or the demographics of the convention-going *Supernatural* fanbase. This gendering of this form of creator-sanctioned fan engagement might suggest that certain reductive assumptions have been made by the producers about the gendered difference between the preferred modes of activity engaged in by affirmational fandom practice on the one hand, and transformational fandom on the other.

Becky's role is not entirely reduced to comedic relief; as Fathallah points out, "it is her comprehensive fannish knowledge that provides the vital information for the broader myth arc narrative" ("Becky Is My Hero" 3.4) at the end of "The Real Ghostbusters." However, she is not involved in any of the heroics. The affirmational fans who cosplay and live-action role-play might also be mocked by Dean, but unlike Becky, two male live-action role-players, Demian and Barnes, become part of Dean and Sam's heroic quest to defeat the monster of the week. Although space was made for queerness when Demian and Barnes are revealed to be a couple, as is common in *Supernatural*, the reveal is played largely to allow Dean to react with surprise upon being confronted with male queerness. The early seasons in particular are noted for gay jokes, and this reveal is another example of non-heteronormative sexuality being played for laughs. The male cosplayers, however, are sympathetically drawn, as they guide Dean towards a moment of enlightenment, in a way Becky cannot accomplish, so suspicious are the brothers of her modes of fannish engagement and her motivations. Becky ends the episode having got together with Chuck. The established milieu at that point in the series appears to be that men get to be heroes and women get to be wives and girlfriends. Even Chuck, who doesn't fit the mold of an archetypal hero, has his moment towards the end of the episode when he stops one of the ghosts from killing a conference attendee and keeps the rest of those gathered safe in the room, insisting that nobody leaves. It is this moment of heroism that piques Becky's interest, as the shot cuts to her looking flustered after Chuck's uncharacteristic display of chivalry. In this manner, Becky's "access to heroism is confined to sex with a heroic man" (Tosenberger "Love! Valor! *Supernatural!*" 1.6).

Fan Fiction: You Can't Spell Subtext Without S-E-X

The 200th episode of the *Supernatural* series, Season 10's "Fan Fiction" (10.05), has been described as a love letter to the show's fans. Having read about suspicious disappearances, Sam and Dean visit an all-girls school where some students are in the midst of rehearsing a fan-penned musical inspired by the "Supernatural" books. It transpires that Marie, the pivotal fangirl in the story, is the target of Calliope, the Goddess of Epic Poetry and one of the nine Muses, who inspires creators, manifesting into characters from a story to protect the story from those who seek to prevent it from being told. Once the story is complete, Calliope eats its creator. Marie and her friend Maeve are very different from Becky, and the episode generated a much more positive reaction from fans and pro-fandom pop culture writers than other metatextual fangirl focused episodes (e.g., Romano, "*Supernatural*'s 200th Episode Is a Fitting Tribute to Its Fangirls"; Lea, "*Supernatural* Season 10 Episode 5 Review: Fan Fiction"). The episode contains affectionate references to fandom-originated terms such as the Samulet, the name given to the amulet eight-year-old Sam gave to young Dean in "A Very Supernatural Christmas" (3.08) and demonstrates an understanding of the language of fandom and intra-fandom discourse with a reference to "transformative fiction" and an argument between the fans over canon divergence. The episode also features smart, likeable fangirls who have no time for Sam and Dean trying to infiltrate their space, such as when Sam tries to engage Maeve in conversation about his own musical theatre past and, unimpressed, she takes a call on her headset and asks him not to touch anything. The show contains a powerful rendition of *Supernatural*'s unofficial theme tune "Carry on Wayward Son" and humorous, self-referential songs like "A Single Man Tear," referring to Dean's tendency to cry One

Perfect Tear (the term commonly used by fandom). The song "A Single Man Tear" seems designed to capture the original sentiment of the One Perfect Tear, in a nod, perhaps, to where the term originated on the Television Without Pity noticeboard, as the "Single Manly Tear of Emo Angst." The incorporation of the word "Man" into the song title certainly captures the spirit of fandom discussions around the vulnerabilities of Dean's constructed, blue-collar masculinity. Ultimately, for the most part, the episode left fandom feeling warm and positive instead of mocked.

There is something distinctly celebratory about Marie's musical, yet the episode requires further interrogation. Any perceived threat to Dean's masculinity or the possibility of male queerness is quickly quashed when it is introduced into the text. When the brothers arrive and Dean grasps what is happening, he is appalled by the nature of the show, commenting, "if there was singing it would be classic rock not this Andrew Floyd Webber crap" and he continues, "I'm going to need fifty jello shots and a hose to get this stink off me" ("Fan Fiction"). This is in part an in-joke about Dean's love of classic rock and the way his outward portrayal of masculinity has been read by many as a façade (see for instance Bruce, "The Impala as Negotiator of Melodrama and Masculinity in *Supernatural*," or Brennan, "'Jensen Ackles is a [Homophobic] Douchebag': The 'Politics of Slash' in Debates on a TV Star's Homophobia"), but it is also consistent with Dean's long-standing tendency to dismiss pursuits he associates with femininity or campness. Tosenberger explores this in her article on folklore in *Supernatural*, pointing out how Dean responds to fairy tales in "Bedtime Stories" (5.03), in which "Dean's snide, defensive comments spring from the centuries-long linkage of fairy tales with women" ("'Kinda like the folklore of its day'" 5.8) and his belief that "fairy tales are a dodgy, unmanly form of folklore" ("Kinda like the folklore of its day" 5.7). Musical theatre has a long-standing connection with queerness (Dvoskin 19), and with male queerness specifically, considered "a sacred preserve of gay men" (Savran 59). In early seasons Dean made gay jokes which thankfully appear to have been phased out, but he continues to react to anything which calls into question his heterosexuality and, by extension, hypermasculinity, with a degree of aggravation. Various critical angles on Dean's performative masculinity have been offered, with many observing that Dean views homosexuality as a "threat" (Brennan 251). In "Fan Fiction" Dean's reaction suggests that the mode of performance—musical theatre—is not a genre he would choose to capture the story of his life. In the same way he reacted to fan fiction with horror in "The Monster at the End of This Book," he is initially derisive about the association of Dean Winchester with anything as potentially queer coded as musical theatre.

Dean's discomfort is reinforced when he sees the two female characters playing Dean and Sam stand particularly close to one another. In another metatextual moment, Dean comments, "[y]ou know they're brothers, right?" an echo of the same comment in "The Monster at the End of This Book." In welcome contrast, in "Fan Fiction," Marie (the Wincest shipping fangirl) can answer back, rolling her eyes at Dean's comment and explaining that it is all in the subtext. As others have convincingly argued, homoerotic incestuous readings find support in the text (Tosenberger, "'The Epic Love Story'" 0.1). Although Dean's reaction to being confronted with incestuous readings of his relationship with Sam is understandable, the way the show continuously positions those readings as peculiar is frustrating when a subtextual reading of the narrative invites them. When the barrier of incest is removed, Dean's reaction is no better. Two girls playing Dean and Castiel hug and he and reacts with horror, assuaged when he learns the two are a real-life couple. This is an example of Dean's inconsistency when it comes to queerness. Upon being confronted with queer female sexuality he seems at ease, in comparison to his reactions when his own heterosexuality is called into question. His discomfort returns when Marie discloses that Destiel is explored in the second act, with the line, "you can't have subtext without S-E-X." Dean then breaks the fourth wall as he looks at the camera head on and gives the viewer an unimpressed look. Many fans enjoyed this moment, because of its move away from the heteronormative depiction of fangirls, to acknowledge the show's queer female fanbase and in the case of the two girls playing Dean and Castiel, Dean's response is affirmative. However, I am not convinced the episode is so queer-positive. Dean is unable to entertain any discussion about Destiel when he and Sam return to the Impala. The exchange echoes "Playthings" (2.11) when Dean described being read as gay as "troubling." When Dean is confronted with people assuming he and Sam are a couple, "troubling" is perhaps an apt word, given their familial relationship. However, even when the barrier of incest is stripped away, Dean still exhibits a more aggressive response to people speculating about his sexuality than does Sam. In "Fan Fiction," although the suggestion of Dean and Castiel having any romantic inclinations towards one another might be equally surprising for Dean—Castiel is, after all, his best friend—his reaction is still one of bemused discomfort, in contrast to Sam who also shares a close relationship with Castiel and seems far more preoccupied with light-hearted speculation about the pronunciation of ship portmanteaus.

This response is not atypical for Dean. He exhibits significant unease when confronted with people who call into question his heterosexuality that arguably extends beyond the understandable unease in relation to Wincest. When he encounters queer female fans, Dean seems to find that far less problematic. When he reads the girls in the play as "Dean" and

"Castiel," their intimacy is troubling to him, but when their real names are supplied, and he learns they are girlfriends, he refrains from passing further comment. It is male gendered queerness, and more specifically, allusions to his own queerness, that Dean finds unsettling. Despite his change of attitude towards Marie and the other cast members as the episode progresses, he does nothing which explicitly undoes his earlier horror at the suggestion that any homoerotic subtext might be underlying his relationship with Castiel. By the end of the episode Dean might have come to appreciate Marie's fictional production, but he makes it very clear that it has no basis in reality. He encourages the fans to "put as much sub into that text as you possibly can" yet distances himself from the queer reading explicitly on several occasions: "I have my version and you have yours"; "I don't [believe it] […] like, at *all*." The transformational fandom may have felt gratified by an episode which offered much more thoughtfully crafted perspectives on the fangirl than Becky Rosen, and one which celebrated her energy and passions, but Dean's denials remain robust and explicit. Although it is not up to Dean to interpret the text for the audience, the episode appears to suggest that whilst there is room for queerness between fans, and in the transformative works they produce, it has no place in a narrative of masculine heroism.

Fathallah applies Derrida's notion of "hauntology," something which is present but not part of the ontology of being, to make a case for a specter of queerness, a "queer hauntology" which is constantly present in Sherlock, causing narrative disruptions which reveal Sherlock's heterosexuality and masculinity to be performative ("Moriarty's Ghost" 491). Fathallah explains how Sherlock is, on the surface, an "investment in a well-known model of white British neoimperial masculinity" (492) and goes on to explain how Sherlock's nemesis Moriarty comes to manifest as a queer specter offering "persistent challenges that haunt the dominant order" (498), exposing the charade of performative masculinity and what Fathallah refers to as straight-face. Although the British television series is very different from *Supernatural* in genre, form and content, there are some similarities that make this argument worth dwelling on. Dean Winchester, like Sherlock, is an instantly recognizable example of a masculine stereotype, in Dean's case, white, American, working class masculinity. As Julia Wright observes, he is the "the stoic blue-collar hero" who "inhabits stereotypical narratives of lower-class dysfunction" and whose particularly recognizable brand of American underclass masculinity is "repeatedly read as a mask or performance" (15).

The episodes in which Dean is confronted with queer readings of himself can be read as disrupting Dean's narrative of aggressive hetero-masculinity, subverting the surface image he crafts with his porn, skin mags and fleeting encounters with women. When Dean is confronted with something which threatens his hetero-masculinity, he responds badly, albeit his responses are consistent with the world of blue-collar American masculinity Dean, in particular, inhabits. In "Fan Fiction," Dean's response to finding out that he is the lead in a musical is to want to shower, similar to his response to discovering that Jensen Ackles is wearing make-up in "The French Mistake," where he describes himself in a scene clearly played for humor as a "painted whore." Throughout the series, *Supernatural* makes much of the heterotopic space of mirrors, including frequent references to funhouse mirrors which offer a distorted view of reality. It is the way others read Dean, in contradiction to his understanding of himself, or alternatively, in a way that he fears might expose an aspect of himself he has thus far kept closeted or hidden, that become Dean's queer specter. When Dean is at his most comfortable, he engages with pursuits which shift the façade of performative hetero-masculinity, such as one of his funniest fanboy moments, when he meets Dr. Sexy in "Changing Channels" (5.08). Dean not only appears flustered and giggly in the presence of the handsome, television doctor, but he also reveals his interest in watching the kind of daytime television soap opera more commonly associated with a female viewing demographic, in his detailed knowledge of the show: "part of what makes Dr Sexy sexy is that he wears cowboy boots, not tennis shoes" ("Changing Channels"). He appears relatively at ease when he is in control of the situation, and more uncomfortable when third parties read Dean in a way which is contrary to the way he sees himself. In this sense, the fangirl is a critical part of the narrative disruption which reads Dean's hetero-masculinity as performance and explicitly identifies it as such within the narrative. Transformational fandom, is, to an extent, Dean's queer hauntology.

On its surface, "Fan Fiction" appears to empower the fangirls of transformational fandom. When Dean tells Marie the "true" story of what really happened after Carver Edlund's series of novels concluded, he is met with laughter from Marie, who describes the story as like a bad piece of fan fiction, offering to send him links to better alternatives. However, there are subtle moments when the series takes control back over its own narrative. The viewer understands that the first half of the show follows Edlund's stories and the second act is Marie's self-penned ending. The second act is robustly mocked, with even the goddess Calliope saying she can't bear to sit through the second act one more time: "There's robots. And tentacles. In space. I can't even" ("Fan Fiction"). Calliope is clearly not being positioned as a fangirl, but her status as a Muse is important in assessing the interplay between transformative works and the show's narratology. She kidnaps people who want to prevent Marie's story from being told, an echo of

Becky kidnapping Sam to make him part of her imaginary story. Calliope too is obsessed with a story being told and will do anything to make it happen. Calliope is unsuccessful and is destroyed, but if she had been successful she would have eaten the story's creator before the play concluded. This could be a reference to fandom eating itself, a broader commentary on the darker side of a relationship between a writer and a fan that wants to see a story told at all costs, or, given Calliope's status as a Muse, a comment on how creators can be consumed by their creations.

Finally, the appearance of author Chuck Shurley reaffirms the author's place in the narrative. He has viewed Marie's play, and says it is not bad. For some, that is confirmation from God himself that fan fiction and its creators have their place, an affectionate validation of the heart, passion and creative talents of the fangirl. On another read, it is the author reminding the audience of his presence and signaling a return to the creator sanctioned narrative. Just as the creators, writers and producers cannot engage with transformative works for legal reasons, the viewers never get to see Marie's robotic, space inspired, gender-bending second half. With Chuck's appearance, much like Dean's distancing of himself from Marie's interpretation, he gives permission to transformational fandom to create as they wish but serves to remind the viewer the author is very much alive and reasserts his narrative control.

The Girl with the Dungeons and Dragons Tattoo

Through the character of Charlie Bradbury the series engages with a different kind of fangirl. The choice of actress Felicia Day, a geek culture favorite, is an important one for the character. Day created the popular original web series *The Guild* (2007–2013), based on her experiences with gaming. She is a popular fixture on convention circuits and has appeared in several Joss Whedon creations, such as *Buffy the Vampire Slayer* (1997–2003) and *Dr. Horrible's Sing-Along Blog* (2008). On screen, Day's character, Charlie, is a hacker and tech nerd who works for Leviathan Dick Roman but ends up close to Sam and Dean Winchester, making multiple appearances in Season 7 through to Season 11, when her character is killed off. Charlie is first introduced in "The Girl with the Dungeons and Dragons Tattoo" (7.20) and is characterized in a positive way, a welcome queer character (she is a lesbian) in a show with little meaningful LGBT representation. Unlike the fans of the "Supernatural" book series, Charlie is an affirmational fan. Her status as a fangirl is underscored through a multitude of pop culture references, from her description of Leviathan Dick Roman as like the "eye of Sauron" to the Hermione Granger figurine on her desk. She drinks out of a

Wonder Woman mug, has *Star Wars* memorabilia in her home, a reminder on her notice board about San Francisco Comic-Con, and a Princess Leia tattoo she got when she was drunk at Comic-Con. She wears a t-shirt with Carrie Fisher's Princes Leia on the front. Her screen saver is Liv Tyler's Arwen from the *Lord of the Rings* film franchise, and when Sam convinces her to hack Dick Roman's computer, he does so by asking what Hermione Granger would do in her position. Charlie is a fan who goes to conventions, financially invests in the franchise through the purchase of memorabilia and appears to subscribe to, rather than play transformatively with, the vision of the creator. She is, as Busse puts it, "the constructed fan," the good fan who "combines all the positive fan qualities such as sustained viewer interest and commercial viability while engaging fannishly in ways preferred and controlled by the studios" ("Geek hierarchies" 78).

The type of fan practices Charlie engages in are referenced again in the Season 8 episode, "LARP and the Real Girl" (8.11). In this episode, Charlie is LARPing as the Queen of Moondoor, and several LARPers are killed off by supernatural means. As usual, Dean is typically scathing about fan practices, referring to the Shadow Orcs as the "shadow dorks" and playing with the name Albus Dumbledore, the Headmaster in the Harry Potter books, with a reference to "Dumbledork." Unlike his approach to transformational fandom, however, Dean is not threatened by the practices of the LARPers. To the contrary, he gravitates towards the traditionally masculine coded game play strategies, and becomes an active part of the game, leading the other players into battle, with the same enthusiasm he has previously displayed for assuming stereotypically masculine roles in episodes such as his Clint Eastwood-esque turn in "Frontierland" (6.18).

Charlie's modes of fan engagement aren't objectionable to Dean, and they form an immediately close bond. Even though she later confesses to having read the books, she never suggests she engaged with the transformational side of "Supernatural" fandom, although her actions suggest she is certainly familiar with online fandom. She mentions the username Becky-Winchester176 as the online user who uploaded the unpublished "Supernatural" texts, which is met with a shudder from Sam. While Charlie is welcome and accepted into their space, and treated to an extent as an equal, Becky has been cast out. Because Charlie has an early camaraderie with Dean, she seems more easily able to make statements that Dean finds objectionable from fangirls that openly position themselves as fan fiction writers. She comments that "you guys fight like an old married couple" after finishing the "Supernatural" series and describes Castiel as "dreamy" (9.04). In "LARP and the Real Girl," she casts Dean as her handmaiden and puts her queen's crown on Dean's head as she is about to leave. For Dean, Charlie's interest in more masculine coded creator-sanctioned fandom pursuits, technical knowledge, hactivism, gaming prowess and similarly forward and flirty approach with women that Dean favors, enables her to make comments that others can't. Her interest in gaming is also a timely and important recognition and affirmation of female gamers, after the vicious targeting of women within the gaming industry, so-called "Gamergate."

For a show with an awareness of certain elements of its own fandom and a seeming interest in geek culture trivia, the death of Charlie was a disappointing twist. The so-called dead lesbian trope, also known as bury your gays, is a significant issue due to popular media's tendency to kill off gay or bisexual women with bloodthirsty vigor. As Autostraddle observed in 2016, queer women on television—already disproportionately low in number—have tended to meet unhappy ends (Riese). Narratively, one of the deepest frustrations from fans was not only the death of another queer woman on television, but also the fact that Charlie's death seemed so futile and narratively inconsistent. Killing off Charlie is another example of the show engaging with certain aspects of fan discourse, but perhaps being more naïve to other conversations happening within fandom communities, as the death of Charlie was soundly criticized by many popular online publications as well as the fandom itself.

Although Charlie is treated with less suspicion by fan favorites Sam and Dean than Becky and Marie, she ultimately fares little better. Like Becky and Marie, Charlie finds her modes of textual interpretation called into question in "Slumber Party" (9.04). She meets Dorothy from *The Wizard of Oz* (1900), one of her favorite childhood stories, and is told that everything she believed to be true about the story was wrong. Much like the transformational fan, she ends "Slumber Party" entering into the fictional world of Oz, to create her own adventures. She has agency and more of a place within *Supernatural*'s story, but that agency is limited, and her refreshing perspective is silenced by the time the show reaches its 11th season. The outcry over Charlie's death was understandably vocal, and perhaps this influenced the decision to reverse Charlie's death through the medium of an alternate universe. In "Bring 'Em Back Alive" (13.18) Dean enters the Apocalypse and encounters an alternate reality version of Charlie, living in a brutal, dystopian nightmare world, ruled by the Archangel Michael. In the Apocalypse, Charlie leads the resistance and is first shown being captured and taken by Michael's angels for interrogation and public execution. In "Exodus" (13.22), Charlie joins the other resistance fighters in moving from the Apocalypse into the world of Sam and Dean, and by the end of that season we learn that Rowena and Charlie are "road tripping it through the South West" ("Let the Good Times Roll," 13.23), which implies that there may be more of Charlie Bradbury in *Supernatural*'s future. It is not clear what the show has planned for Charlie, but even in her miraculous return from the dead, her "fight" ("Bring 'Em Back Alive") takes place offscreen, much like her battles in Oz. During the season finale she is, once again, offscreen, and the returning Charlie has not yet enjoyed the immersion in the main narrative arc that made her queer, geeky, fangirl counterpart such a fan favorite.

Conclusion

To keep the scope of this analysis relatively contained, my focus has been primarily concerned with meta fictive devices used within the narrative of the fiction of *Supernatural*, as opposed to a paratextual analysis of the interactions between fans and producers, creators and cast in spaces like fan conventions. However, it seems pertinent to note that even within those creator sanctioned spaces, the fangirl who displays an interest in transformative works and slash ships has been routinely policed and shut down by those involved, particularly Jensen Ackles. The topic of whether or not actors and creators on the convention circuit should entertain questions about shipping is a complicated one. On the one hand there is an argument that shows like *Supernatural* profit from having a large slash fandom, and deliberately engage in subtextual strategies to keep those ships alive with an eye on the profits. The argument follows that, where the questions would not muddy the legal copyright waters, those on the convention circuit should be open to addressing questions about queer subtext and same-sex ships. On the other hand, there is the understandable concern that allowing such questions might open the floodgates to intra-fandom ship wars which in some fandoms are loud and vitriolic, or that ship-related questions become the primary focus of the convention appearance at the expense of fans who wish to engage with the show, its creators and actors, without any explicit discussion about shipping practices in transformative fanworks.

There are many fans who engage with transformative fandom that dislike convention questions about slashing and shipping. Just as some fans were uncomfortable with Wincest being outed so publicly in "The Monster at the End of This Book," placing shipping related questions at the forefront of the convention circuit brings something fans prefer to keep within fandom spaces under the scrutiny of a much wider public gaze. Whilst some fans advocate for bringing fan practices out of the closet of secrecy and shame, others feel strongly about protecting the sanctity of an ever-crumbling fourth wall between fan and creator. There is the very real potential for such questions to be handled poorly; indeed, they frequently are, because they are being answered by people with little or no understanding of transformational fandom, either because they can't engage directly with it for legal reasons, or because they simply have no interest in exploring that side of fan activity. The situation is further complicated in the case of *Supernatural* which also has a number of "real person fiction" or "RPF" ships, pairing the various actors in the show together, as opposed to the characters they play. Although there is nothing wrong with RPF, a number of RPF ships have historically attracted extreme "tinhat" or "truther" minority elements, who construct conspiracy theories around the belief that the two actors in question are in a closeted, secret relationship, beliefs which sometimes lead to the harassment of the celebrities in question. It is understandable that actors would prefer not to engage with questions that might fuel those kinds of conspiracies.

Whether or not those working on a television series which demonstrates a peripheral awareness of slashing and shipping practices and works in-jokes into the narrative should be held to account at conventions is a tricky question on multiple levels, not least because of the potential legal ramifications that restrict creators from getting too close to the transformative aspects of their fandom. However, the paratextual perspectives are relevant when seeking to understand how working slash fiction into the narrative informs queerbaiting discussions and to tease out why fans might feel slighted by the speed with which slash shipping questions are shut down, particularly when there is an inconsistent approach between restricting questions related to same sex ships versus discussions of opposite sex ships. There is a power imbalance inherent in the fan/creator relationship. Ackles can give the audience a disapproving look when the matter of Destiel subtext is scripted explicitly into the show, but his fans have no right of reply to that judgment, beyond social media and blog posts, where those involved with the series are able to cherry pick the discussions they wish to engage with and the ones they don't. Even through Marie, the fangirl of "Fan Fiction," her perspective is created and shaped by those in ultimate control of the narrative.

Producer intent is critical to the question of queerbaiting, and this is why *Supernatural*'s metatextual episodes are illuminating. Through these episodes the producers explicitly acknowledge they are aware of the large slash ships, making homoerotic subtext and in-jokes which flirt with the ships in question feel more deliberate. The Powers That Be have demonstrated in the most explicit way that they know what fandom is slashing and shipping, by making it part of the *Supernatural* canon. This makes it easier to gravitate beyond the pleasures of undertaking subjective, subtextual queer readings, to a point where a belief forms that the in-jokes and subtext is there by design, potentially as part of a long-running narrative strategy, something some fans firmly believe with regard to Dean's sexuality.

If it is indeed the case that those involved with the show are intentionally paying fan service to large slash ships in canon subtext, it begs the question as to whether the series plans to continue relying on coded homoeroticism to fuel the practices of transformational fandom, whilst retaining the maximum commercial viability of the franchise. For all fans of the show, including those who enjoy playing with the canon in transformative works, commercial success is preferable to the series ending, so if the status quo is maintained it might be difficult to see the harm. However, in 2018, fans are understandably far less tolerant of franchises which keep the S-E-X in the subtext when it comes to queer relationships, when opposite sex relationships are frequently made explicit. Making being gay or bisexual the punchline for in-jokes directed at observant shippers combing the narrative for moments of queerness starts to leave a bitter taste, particularly for LGBT people within fandom. Having killed off one of its most successful queerly diverse and female characters, it is arguable that *Supernatural* might be wise to consider the way it flirts with homoerotic possibility, and hopefully the resurrection of Charlie Bradbury's character might offer some much-needed queer diversity.

The series might have explicitly celebrated transformative works, but that arguably creates a problem of its own. Free fan fiction and other types of transformational fan labor (such as gif creation and vidding) offer fans the queer content they are seeking and encourage continued investment in a franchise which might never intend to turn subtext into text. As Persephone Garnata commented in an email to popular multi-fandom podcast Fansplaining, "the fans continue to consume problematic franchises and then churn out 'corrective' fics and headcanons" (Klink and Minkel), in a manner which enables a show to continue to profit from harmful queerbaiting tactics. As Kristina Busse has robustly identified, "the danger to fan culture has become the co-optation and colonization of fan creations, interactions, and spaces rather than earlier fan generations' fears of litigation and cease-and-desist orders" ("Fan Labor and Feminism" 111). *Supernatural* takes the fangirl and inserts her into its diegesis, yet frequently reminds the audience that the author is, quite literally, God, and that whilst queer readings of Dean Winchester in particular might be "educational" ("Fan Fiction"), they cannot hope to find canonical purchase.

When *Supernatural* invokes metatextual comments on where the power of authorship is located, fangirls do not triumph. In Becky's case it is the attentions of Chuck that bring her partially inside the circle of trust, and she spends much of her time seeking Sam's approval and romantic interest. In Marie's case, she cares little about Dean's view of her interpretation, but she seeks Chuck's approval, something she is tacitly provided with in a way that encourages her to continue telling stories off screen. Even the fan-positive, queer, unabashedly geeky Charlie is encouraged to create her own, extra-textual adventures in Oz, and her character arc concludes with her death serving only as a catalyst for the later masculine heroism of the Winchesters' narrative arc, the weaknesses of which is exposed through Charlie's death. Becky is ousted from the circle of trust in attempting to make Sam part of her romantic and sexual fantasies, Marie runs the risk of being eaten by her Muse as she tries to tell her own story, or, alternatively, the writers run the risk of being eaten by the fans of the show they have created, and Charlie is killed for a book, the Book of the Damned, she is in the process of translating (and interpreting) at the time of her death. Even Apocalypse Charlie, much like Charlie in Oz, continues to fight the good fight offscreen, in an alternative universe that diverges from the main narrative arc of the show, returning to Sam and Dean's universe only to promptly disappear on a road trip.

Writing about the revival of David Lynch's series *Twin Peaks*, Diane Och notes that there is a "construction of quality TV as specifically masculine and auteurist" (132). She observes the "continuing project to masculinize and thus legitimate television is visible in how the feminine and the popular are positioned outside the quality television genre" (133). With its metatextual incorporation of the practices of its own transformational fandom into the text, *Supernatural* has, so far, given tacit permission for the fandom to continue its activities, but has also suggested those female fandom driven interpretations of homoerotic subtext have no place in the dominant narrative of performative, hetero-masculine heroism, which is consistently valorized. The paratextual dialogue between producers and fans has imbedded power imbalances and legal restrictions around copyright and chain of title, which limits the extent to which the interpretive work of transformational fandom can infiltrate affirmational, creator-sanctioned fan spaces. The dialogue between fan and creator is not an equal one.

If there is to be any representative queerness in the core characters that *Supernatural* takes into the future, where, then, might it be found? The one glimmer of hope is that in a throwaway comment, Chuck Shurley appeared to allude to himself as bisexual ("Don't Call Me Shurley"), and at critical moments within *Supernatural*'s metatextual episodes the audience has been reminded that the narrative power is located with the author-god, because it is he who knows the ending. A popular reading of Dean's panic when he is confronted with male queerness is that he is a closeted bisexual, exhibiting internalized, biphobic tendencies. There are compelling reasons for Dean's sexuality having remained undisclosed for such a long time, which, if such a reveal transpired, would invite questions around the silencing of queerness in hero arcs and the narrative of white, American, blue-collar

Masculinity. These important, topical debates are deeply relevant to contemporary discussions of the construction of American manhood and a subversion of hetero understandings of the "macho man" Dean idolizes, from Hollywood Westerns of Reagan's America, to his fan-boy interest in the areas of geek culture where men are presumed to be dominant.

However, not everybody views Dean through the same lens and not all fans are seeking any canon depictions of queerness through the main characters. My reading of Dean would undoubtedly please many *Supernatural* fans, but it is one which other fans would be opposed to seeing canonized. Although *Supernatural* provided some textual validation for queerness through Castiel's declaration of love for Dean, its extent was limited and occurred in the penultimate episode, which aired after this book was in press so cannot be explored here. Ultimately, in *Supernatural*, the author is, quite literally, God. In transformative fandom, however, the fangirl has ultimate control. The author is dead, and even when canon might disappoint, slashers and shippers are still free to imagine and re-imagine the queer possibilities that the series offers, through transformative works.

Works Cited

Brennan, Joseph. "'Jensen Ackles Is a (homophobic) Douchebag'": The 'politics of slash' in debates on a TV star's homophobia." *Celebrity Studies*, vol. 8, no. 2, 2017, pp. 246–261.

Bruce, Melissa N. "The Impala as Negotiator of Melodrama and Masculinity in *Supernatural*," *Transformative Works and Cultures*, no. 4, 2010, http://dx.doi.org/10.3983/twc.2010.0154. Accessed 13 Nov. 2018.

Busse, Kristina. "Geek Hierarchies, Boundary Policing, and the Gendering of the Good Fan." *Participations: Journal of Audience and Reception Studies*, vol. 10, issue 1, 2013, pp. 73–91.

_____. "Fan Labor and Feminism: Capitalizing on the Fannish Labor of Love." *Cinema Journal*, vol. 54, no. 3, 2015, pp. 110–115.

Campbell, Anna. "Queerbaited: Homoeroticism & Homophobia in *Supernatural* in the Age of the Internet." *Medium*, 2016, https://medium.com/@queensnknaves/queerbaited-homoeroticism-homophobia-in-supernatural-in-the-age-of-the-internet-e8b80ffb0b4b. Accessed 13 Nov. 2018.

Centrumlumina. "AO3 Census: Gender Identity and Categorisation." *Tumblr*, 2014, http://centrumlumina.tumblr.com/post/94545453362/gender-identity-and-categorisation-this-data-is. Accessed 13 Nov. 2018.

_____. "AO3 Census: Sexuality." *Tumblr*, 2014, http://centrumlumina.tumblr.com/post/62840006596/sexuality. Accessed 12 Nov. 2018.

Collier, Cassandra M. "The Love That Refuses to Speak Its Name: Examining Queerbaiting and Fan Producer Interactions in Fan Cultures." Master's thesis, University of Louisville, 2015, Available at: http://ir.library.louisville.edu/etd/2204. Accessed 13 Nov. 2018.

Cruise, Eliel. "Fans Take *Supernatural* to Task for 'Queer Baiting." *Advocate*, 2014, https://www.advocate.com/bisexuality/2014/07/17/fans-take-supernatural-task-queer-baiting. Accessed 13 Nov. 2018.

Dvoskin, Michelle Gail. "'Listen to the Stories, Hear It in the Songs': Musical Theatre as Queer Historiography." PhD thesis, The University of Texas at Austin, 2010, 253; 3417496

Fathallah, Judith May. "Becky Is My Hero: The Power of Laughter and Disruption in *Supernatural*." *Transformative Works and Cultures*, no. 5., 2010, http://dx.doi.org/10.3983/twc.2010.0220. Accessed 13 Nov. 2018.

_____. "Moriarty's Ghost, or the Queer Disruption of the BBC's Sherlock." *Television and New Media*, vol. 16, no. 5, 2015, pp. 490–500.

Felschow, Laura. "'Hey, Check It Out, There's Actually Fans': (Dis)empowerment and (mis) representation of Cult Fandom in *Supernatural*." *Transformative Works and Cultures*, no. 4, 2010, http://dx.doi.org/10.3983/twc.2010.0134. Accessed 13 Nov. 2018.

Gennis, Sadie. "*Supernatural* Has a Queerbaiting Problem That Needs to Stop." *TV Guide*, 2014, http://www.tvguide.com/news/supernatural-queerbaiting-destiel-1089286/. Accessed 13 Nov. 2018.

Gray, Melissa. "From Canon to Fanon and Back Again: The Epic Journey of *Supernatural* and Its Fans." *Transformative Works and Cultures*, no. 4, 2010, http://dx.doi.org/10.3983/twc.2010.0146. Accessed 13 Nov. 2018.

Herzog, Alexandra. "'But This Is My Story and This Is How I Wanted to Write It': Author's Notes as a Fannish Claim to Power in Fan Fiction Writing." *Transformative Works and Cultures*, no. 11, 2012, http://dx.doi.org/10.3983/twc.2012.0406. Accessed 13 Nov. 2018.

Klink, Flourish and Minkel, Elizabeth. "Episode 65: Fandom and Capitalism." *Fansplaining*, 2018, http://fansplaining.com/post/169619454448/transcript-episode-65-fandom-and-capitalism. Accessed 13 Nov. 2018.

Lea, Becky. "*Supernatural* Season 10 Episode 5 Review: Fan Fiction." *Den of Geek*, 2014, http://www.denofgeek.com/tv/supernatural/32923/supernatural-season-10-episode-5-review-fan-fiction. Accessed 13 Nov. 2018.

Macklem, Lisa. "I See What You Did There: SPN and the Fourth Wall." *Fan Phenomena: Supernatural*, ed. Lynn Zubernis and Katherine Larsen, Intellect Books, 2014, pp. 35–44.

Minkel, Elizabeth. "The Online Free Speech Debate Is Raging in Fan Fiction, Too." *The Verge*, 2018, https://www.theverge.com/2018/11/8/18072622/fanfic-ao3-free-speech-censorship-fandom. Accessed 13 Nov. 2018.

Ng, Eve. "Between Text, Paratext, and Context: Queerbaiting and the Contemporary Media Landscape." "Queer Female Fandom," edited by Julie Levin Russo and Eve Ng, special issue, *Transformative Works and Cultures*, no. 24, 2017, http://dx.doi.org/10.3983/twc.2017.917. Accessed 13 Nov. 2018.

Nordin, Emma. "From Queer Reading to Queerbaiting: The Battle Over the Polysemic Text and the Power of Hermeneutics." Master's thesis, Stockholm University, Stockholm, 2015. http://www.diva-portal.org/smash/get/diva2:839802/FULLTEXT01.pdf. Accessed 13 Nov. 2018.

obsession_inc. "Affirmational Fandom Vs. Transformational Fandom." *Dreamwidth.org*, 2009, https://obsession-inc.dreamwidth.org/82589.html. Accessed 13 Nov. 2018.

Och, Dana. "All Laura Palmer's Children: *Twin Peaks* and Gendering the Discourse of Influence." *Cinema Journal*, vol. 55 no. 3, 2016, pp. 131–136.

Polasek, Ashley D. "Traditional Transformations and Transmedial Affirmations: Blurring the Boundaries of Sherlockian Fan Practices." "Sherlock Holmes Fandom, Sherlockiana, and the Great Game," edited by Betsy Rosenblatt and Roberta Pearson, special issue, *Transformative Works and Cultures*, no. 23, 2017, http://dx.doi.org/10.3983/twc.2017.0911. Accessed 13 Nov. 2018.

Riese. "All 198 Dead Lesbian and Bisexual Characters on TV, and How They Died." *Autostraddle*, 2016, https://www.autostraddle.com/all-65-dead-lesbian-and-bisexual-characters-on-tv-and-how-they-died-312315/. Accessed 13 Nov. 2018.

Roach, Emily E. "Cosplay, Drag and the Transformative Nature of Living Out Your Fandom." *The Mary Sue*, 2017, https://www.themarysue.com/dragging-pop-culture-through-cosplay/. Accessed 12 Nov. 2018.

_____. "How Queerbaiting Discussions Show Heteronormativity Is Alive and Well." *The Mary Sue*, 2017, https://www.themarysue.com/queerbaiting-and-heteronormativity-on-tv/. Accessed 13 Nov. 2018.

Romano, Aja. "*Supernatural*'s 200th Episode Is a Fitting Tribute to Its Fangirls." *Daily Dot*,

2014, https://www.dailydot.com/parsec/supernatural-episode-200-fan-fiction-takes-on-fangirls/. Accessed 13 Nov. 2018.

Schmidt, Lisa. "Monstrous Melodrama: Expanding the Scope of Melodramatic Identification to Interpret Negative Fan Responses to *Supernatural.*" *Transformative Works and Cultures*, no. 4, 2010, http://dx.doi.org/10.3983/twc.2010.0152. Accessed 13 Nov. 2018.

Shakeri, Sima. "Television Has a 'Bury Your Gays,' Queerbaiting, and LGBTQ Representation Problem." *Huffpost*, 30 June 2017, www.huffingtonpost.ca/2017/06/30/queerbaiting-bury-your-gays-tv_a_23005000/. Accessed 28 Dec. 2018.

Thomas, Ardel. "Queer Victorian Gothic." *The Victorian Gothic: An Edinburgh Companion*, edited by Andrew Smith and William Hughes, Edinburgh University Press, 2012, pp. 142–155.

Torrey, KT. "Writing with the Winchesters: Metatextual Wincest and the Provisional Practice of Happy Endings." *Journal of Fandom Studies*, vol. 2, no. 2, 2014, pp. 163–180.

Tosenberger, Catherine. "'The Epic Love Story of Sam and Dean': *Supernatural*, Queer Readings, and the Romance of Incestuous Fan Fiction." *Transformative Works and Cultures*, no. 1, 2008, http://dx.doi.org/10.3983/twc.2008.0030. Accessed 13 Nov. 2018.

_____. "'Kinda Like the Folklore of Its Day': *Supernatural*, Fairy Tales, and Ostension." *Transformative Works and Cultures*, no. 4, 2010, http://dx.doi.org/10.3983/twc.2010.0174. Accessed 13 November 2018.

_____. "Love! Valor! *Supernatural!*" *Transformative Works and Cultures*, no. 4, 2010, http://dx.doi.org/10.3983/twc.2010.0212. Accessed 13 Nov. 2018.

Wilkinson, Jules. "A Box of Mirrors, a Unicorn, and a Pony." *Transformative Works and Cultures*, no. 4, 2010, http://dx.doi.org/10.3983/twc.2010.0159. Accessed 13 Nov. 2018.

Wright, Julia. "Latchkey Hero: Masculinity, Class and the Gothic in Eric Kripke's *Supernatural.*" *Genders 1998–2013*, University of Colorado, Boulder, 2008, https://www.colorado.edu/gendersarchive1998-2013/2008/06/15/latchkey-hero-masculinity-class-and-gothic-eric-kripkes-supernatural. Accessed 13 Nov. 2018.

Breaking the Fourth Wall

Fandom Representation in Supernatural Canon

KIMBERLY LYNN WORKMAN

Introduction

> **METATRON:** What makes a story work? Is it the plot, the characters, the text? The subtext? And who gives a story meaning? Is it the writer? Or you? Tonight, I thought I would tell you a little story and let you decide.
> —"Meta Fiction" (9.18)

Perhaps what makes *Supernatural* work is a combination of elements—the writers presenting the story, the actors giving voice to the characters, and the fans interpreting canon to make it their own. The creative forces behind *Supernatural* have been vocally appreciative of the show's fanbase since the show began. "We're making the show for the fans; we're not making the show for the network," series creator and executive consultant Eric Kripke said in 2007 (Ausiello). As the show continued its journey season after season, that sentiment has not changed. Series stars Jensen Ackles and Jared Padalecki have regularly attended fan conventions where they chat with their fans directly, answering questions and learning how the show touches viewers' lives. Through the fandom, *Supernatural* has become more than just a show, but more a family for both the creators and fans that support them.

Fandom has become so integrated into the identity of the show that the writers sought to give a nod to it within its own canon. *Supernatural* is no stranger to breaking the fourth wall and going meta with its episodes, giving shout-outs to the actors' and creative staff's former projects (*Gilmore Girls* [2000–07], *Lois and Clark: The New Adventures of Superman* [1993–97], *Boogeyman* [2005]), as well as name-checking the creative forces

147

involved in making the show (McG, Jensen Ackles, Jared Padalecki, Misha Collins, Genevieve Padalecki, Bob Singer, Serge Ladouceur, Sera Gamble, Eric Kripke, Clif Kosterman, Jim Michaels, Kevin Park) in several episodes—e.g., "Hollywood Babylon" (2.18), "The Monster at the End of This Book" (4.18) and "The French Mistake" (6.15). But it was the thread of episodes that focused attention on exploring fandom and fan identification that took the meta to the next level. Through a novel series based on Sam and Dean Winchester's lives, an author with god-like powers, and a portrayal of fans who devoted their lives to the interpretation and re-purposing of these media texts, the show turned a mirror onto itself. While this exploration has pleased some and angered others, the episodes worked to show the ultimate truth of fandom—*Supernatural* has always been for the fans, and they are what will keep it going.

A Fandom Within a Fandom: Carver Edlund's Novels and the Winchesters as Fictional Heroes

> **CHARLIE:** I also found this series of books by Carver Edlund. Did those books really happen? Wow, that is some meta madness. Thanks for saving the world and stuff. Sorry you had zero luck with the ladies.
>
> —"Pac-Man Fever" (8.20)

Sam and Dean learn in Season 4 that their lives are being presented as fictional stories by an author named Carver Edlund, aka Chuck Shurley ("The Monster at the End of This Book"). Since 2005, the same year the show premiered, Chuck had written approximately 24 novels that directly recounted many of the cases and episodes of *Supernatural* Season 1, as well as some from Seasons 2 and 3, ending with Dean going to Hell in the novel *No Rest for the Wicked* and marking the final novel published in the original series. Though only 24 novels are specifically shown in the episode, Chuck continued writing them on his own and these manuscripts are later made available to the book fandom through professional ("Meta Fiction," 9.18; "Don't Call Me Shurley," 11.20) and personal means ("Slumber Party," 9.04).

The novels were noted as being "pretty obscure" by Sam, with "almost zero circulation" ("The Monster at the End of This Book"). This parallels the show having low ratings in comparison to programs on larger networks, as well as decreasing ratings during its first three seasons, which raised the threat of cancellation (ABC MediaNet, *ABC Television Network Press Release—Season Program Rankings [Part Two of Two]*; ABC MediaNet, *ABC Television Network Press Release—Season Program Rankings from*

09/18/06 Through 05/20/07; ABC MediaNet, *ABC Television Network Press Release—Season Rankings [Through 5/18]*). Additionally, the novels are said to have ceased publication because the publisher went bankrupt, when in fact the third season of the show was truncated due to the writer's strike and could not air a full 22-episode season.

Through interactions with those involved in making and supporting the "Supernatural" books, and commentary from the Winchesters as they discover aspects of the books and the following they have, the brothers serve as outside observers of the fandom phenomenon. Sera Siege, publisher of the book series, expresses her appreciation of the book characters being "open and in touch with their feelings" ("The Monster at the End of This Book"). This is in line with repeated comments from fans, who recognize the series as being very emotional and full of angst (Jenkins). In 2007, aca-fan Henry Jenkins even went so far as to note the parallel between the monsters of the show and the physical manifestation of emotions themselves:

> In *Supernatural*, the monsters are, in effect, emotional scars and psychic wounds. They represent unresolved emotional issues, often within the context of family life, and they are also external correlatives for the emotional drama taking place in the lives of the series' protagonists. Sam and Dean go out there looking for things that are strange and unfamiliar and they end up seeing themselves and their relationship more clearly [Jenkins].

The physical manifestation of how deep those emotional ties may run has been extended within fandom through the exploration of a potential sexual relationship between Sam and Dean. This fan fiction genre is known as slash, and more specifically Wincest within the *Supernatural* fandom—a mashup of Winchester and incest. Slash is present in the book fandom within the series as well, which the brothers discover during their research. Exploration of the slash fandom is later personified in the figure of super-fan Becky Rosen, a slash writer who has multiple interactions with the brothers over the course of two seasons ("Sympathy for the Devil," 5.01; "The Real Ghostbusters," 5.09; "Season 7, Time for a Wedding!" 7.08).

Additionally, Siege demonstrates the protectiveness that many fans and even the production crew themselves have for the characters, referring to Sam and Dean as "her boys" ("The Monster at the End of This Book"). The episode later delves into the connection fans have with certain characters as well, with the identification of "Sam girls and Dean girls" within the book fandom; the same type of alignment exists within the television fandom. This need to protect and connect with the characters in some way is also noted in the permanent, physical markings fans take on to illustrate their love of the Winchesters. Writer and producer Sera Gamble mentioned in 2008 that she believed the show would reach cult status when fans bore the demon-protection tattoo that Sam and Dean had (Cochran). Siege, like many fans, has the tattoo and thus demonstrates the elevation of "Supernatural"/*Supernatural*, both in television and book form, to a cult phenomenon that transcends its fictional beginnings.

The Word of Chuck: Canon Writing as Just the Beginning

> **CHUCK:** How else do you explain it? I write things and then they come to life. Yeah, no, I'm definitely a god. A cruel, cruel, capricious god.
> —"The Monster at the End of This Book"

During the original introduction to Chuck and the "Supernatural" novels, Chuck states that he thought the stories he was creating were fictitious ("The Monster at the End of This Book"). His novels are revealed to actually be a reflection of reality when his characters confront him, breaking down the wall between creator and character. To explain his ability to affect events in the Winchesters' lives, he is revealed by Castiel to be a Prophet of the Lord; the first reference to such a status within the *Supernatural* canon and a role that Chuck had dreamed about, but did not believe in prior to Castiel's confirmation. However, the question of whether Chuck was aware of his power to direct real-life events is complicated when it is implied ("Swan Song," 5.22) and later confirmed ("Don't Call Me Shurley") that he is the literal manifestation of God.

Even with the evolution of Chuck from proposed prophet to actual God, the character is used throughout as an avatar for series creator Eric Kripke. Chuck's placement within the storyline gave the creative forces behind the show a voice and representation inside the narrative. This included the ability to apologize to fans for episodes that were not well-received. When confronted with his characters, and thinking about his writing, Chuck questions whether they should have had "to live through the bugs … the ghost ship," which references the episodes "Bugs" (1.08) and "Red Sky at Morning" (3.06), both of which Chuck deems "bad writing." This is in parallel to Kripke's own dislike of these episodes (Knight, *Supernatural: The Official Companion Season 1* 50–53; Knight, *Supernatural: The Official Companion Season 3* 45), as well as their lower popularity in comparison to other episodes.

Chuck's apology to the Winchesters about putting them through bad writing is also an acknowledgment that fans had the same ability to comment on the canon being presented. During the Winchesters' discovery of the "Supernatural" book fandom and its following, Dean finds that fans are critical of story elements they do not like; as he notes, "for fans, they sure do complain a lot. Listen to this—Simpatico says 'the demon story line is trite, clichéd, and overall craptastic.' Yeah, well, screw you, Simpatico. We lived it" ("The Monster at the End of This Book"). Inhabiting the outsider perspective, fans have the ability to look at the collective work and single out components that excelled or failed: a privilege the Winchesters do not have, which means that they have to live through whatever is written for them.

However, once they become aware of their status as characters within a fictional structure, the Winchesters also become the outsider viewpoint to explore the narrative being created. The book characters take control of the content and re-imagine it, going beyond the source Chuck provided, just as the show's fans have done. Despite the canon being declared the "Winchester gospel" ("The Monster at the End of This Book"), its status as canon does not negate the potential for free will to change the outcome of the story. Chuck is not necessarily deciding the Winchesters' fate, but instead giving voice to what was destined to happen. And that destiny has the potential to change even after it is written. Dean's actions in the episode deviate from what Chuck had written, thus changing the story after the fact, and this parallels the actions of fans. They can rewrite the canon to create new stories or outcomes for the characters and thus effect change over the narrative after it has been declared as canon. Even if the canon was constructed by the show's writers or God himself ("Don't Call Me Shurley"), that does not mean that they hold ultimate control over its interpretation.

Brother Love: Slash Writers in the Supernatural *Fandom*

> **DEAN:** There's Sam Girls and Dean Girls and …What's a slash fan?
> **SAM:** As in Sam slash Dean, together.
> **DEAN:** Like together, together? They do know we are brothers, right?
> **SAM:** Doesn't seem to matter.
> —"The Monster at the End of This Book"

As mentioned above, among the aspects of fan fiction that are acknowledged as part of the "Supernatural" book fandom is the existence of slash fiction being written about the brothers. While the characters seem perplexed that such a thing could exist, it has been a mainstay of the show's fandom since the beginning. In fact, the first Sam/Dean story ("Reunion," by Jane Davitt) was posted online only one day after the pilot aired, and the creative output for this pairing has not stopped since.

This ongoing fictional exploration of a romantic relationship between the Winchesters is rooted in canonical nods to Sam and Dean's codependent relationship, as well as how some outsiders view this level of intimacy. On multiple occasions within the first and second seasons of the show, the brothers are mistaken for a romantic couple ("Bugs"; "Something Wicked," 1.18; "Playthings," 2.11). This suggests that for people not knowing about the familial relationship that exists between Sam and Dean, their body language reads as more intimate than that in a typical sibling relationship. Slash writers use this idea in their works by exploring the ways that male relationships can be read in a different way when released from the patriarchal expectations of how men are supposed to interact with one another (Meyer 478). In *Supernatural*, the patriarchal expectations are already subverted by the fact that the brothers do not have a typical sibling bond, but one that is much deeper and more intertwined than is usual.

As shown in canon, both Sam and Dean have sacrificed their lives on multiple occasions to keep the other safe. The angel Zachariah explains that "Sam and Dean Winchester are psychotically, irrationally, erotically codependent on each other" ("Point of No Return," 5.18), which sums up the often-exclusionary bond that exists between the brothers, and explicitly acknowledges the sexual element to their bond. Friend and foe alike recognize that Sam and Dean are so committed to the continued existence of each other that there is no room for another person, romantic or otherwise, to remain. Canon has shown that the Winchesters' attempts to attain normalcy with a long-term romantic partner are destined for failure, often at the expense of the partner's life ("Pilot," 1.01) or mental health ("Let It Bleed," 6.21). Even those that come into short, intimate contact with the brothers often end up dead ("Heart," 2.17; "Lucifer Rising," 4.22; "The Song Remains the Same," 5.13; "Unforgiven," 6.13; "The Girl Next Door," 7.03; "Of Grave Importance," 7.19; "Goodbye Stranger," 8.17; "Clip Show," 8.22), as do the countless friends the Winchesters lose along the way. This cursed association with the brothers is also made a point within the "Supernatural" novels, as is the fact that the only people the brothers can rely on are each other, and thus the only long-term happiness Sam or Dean will have is to be shared with his brother alongside him.

Both executive producer Sera Gamble and series creator Eric Kripke have noted that the show is essentially about "the epic love story of Sam and Dean" (Borsellino; Boyum), which could be interpreted as authorial confirmation that Sam and Dean have a connection transcending a typical sibling relationship. And the writers have continued to blur the designation of the

Winchesters' relationship between sibling and something deeper by confirming that Sam and Dean are soul-mates and share a Heaven, something that is only reserved for special cases ("Dark Side of the Moon," 5.16). Fan writers are happy to explore and expand upon these canonical hints, creating a reality in which subtext and text are one and the same.

> **DEAN:** Why are they standing so close together?
> **MARIE:** Reasons.
> **DEAN:** You know they're brothers, right.
> **MARIE:** Well, duh. But subtext. ["Fan Fiction" 10.05].

Convention Culture: Canon Representation of Supernatural Conventions

> **CON HOST:** Welcome to the first annual "Supernatural" convention. At 3:45 in the Magnolia room we have the panel, "Frightened Little Boy: The Secret Life of Dean." And at 4:30 there's "The Homoerotic Subtext of 'Supernatural.'"
> —"The Real Ghostbusters" (5.09)

Delving deeper into the community the "Supernatural" books created, the show seeks to explore conventions as part of the fandom experience. Although Dean and Sam were aware there were fans of the book series, and they had a presence online, it is not until they attend a "Supernatural" convention themselves in the episode "The Real Ghostbusters" that they come face-to-face with the social framework that had built up around the books.

The episode includes a number of elements matching real-life conventions: Impalas in the parking lot for attendees to view, fans dressed as their favorite characters (cosplay), and participatory activities creating bonding experiences between fans. Two important elements in the episode are the representation of scheduled panels to discuss the inner workings of the canonical storylines and question-and-answer sessions where attendees can interact with the creative forces behind the content. These elements are perhaps the most important activities at real-life conventions because they allow fans a chance to provide their own viewpoint on canon interpretation. Even if the creators themselves had certain ideas in mind when writing or performing the work, the interpretations fans provide can vary widely from these original intentions. Fans are allowed to be critical of elements that did not work for them, or highlight those ideas that transcended the context in which they were written and had a personal impact.

Two characters that embody the idea of fandom having personal impact are Demian and Barnes. These male fans, an unusual sight at real-life *Supernatural* conventions, dress up as Sam and Dean in order to live-action role-play (LARP) within the episode's convention setting. They are perhaps one of the most positive representations throughout the series of fandom members, celebrating both the friendship and relationship bonds fans have found through the community of the show. When questioned as to how their friendship began, Barnes mentions that they "met online... 'Supernatural' chat room" ("The Real Ghostbusters"). This has a direct correlation to the television fandom structure, as fans are less bound by geographic limitations when finding others that share their common media interest. Super-fan Becky noted the same type of community bonding in her own fandom experience—"Honestly.... The only place people understood me was the message boards. They were grumpy and overly literal, but at least we shared a common passion" ("Season 7, Time for a Wedding!"). And from within these larger communities, fans can also create smaller, more intimate connections with forum members as the exchanges go on. Friendships and communities may start based on the shared media interest and then grow into a deeper relationship over time. This is mirrored in the connection that Demian and Barnes have, as their friendship led to an off-line romantic relationship between the two. A connection established in the virtual space of the internet shifted into the real world.

Demian and Barnes also touch upon the connection fans have with the content itself. When Dean questions their motivations, he seems unable to understand why people would devote their time and energy to a fictional world instead of their real lives. And it's a question that fans of the show may have had to confront as well, having to justify their interest to those outside the fandom. But the writers of *Supernatural*, through the use of Demian and Barnes, show that they understood this fan commitment:

> DEMIAN: You're wrong you know.
> DEAN: Sorry?
> DEMIAN: About "Supernatural." No offense but I'm not sure you get what the story's about.
> DEAN: Is that so?
> DEMIAN: All right. In real life, he sells stereo equipment. I fix copiers. Our lives suck. But to be Sam and Dean, to wake up every morning and save the world. To have a brother who would die for you. Well, who wouldn't want that? ["The Real Ghostbusters"]

Becky Rosen: A Fangirl Who Embraced the Fantasy

> BECKY: Look, Mr. Edlund. Yes, I'm a fan, but I really don't appreciate being mocked. I know that "Supernatural" [is]

just a book, okay? I know the difference between fantasy and reality.
CHUCK: Becky, it's all real.
BECKY: I knew it!!
—"Sympathy for the Devil" (5.01)

While *Supernatural* writers acknowledge the positive connections between the show and its fandom, they also explore the potential for negative ramifications when objects of fantasy are brought into reality. The breaking of the fourth wall erases the safe boundaries that exist between creator, creation, and fan. Without these boundaries in place, the fans can gain access to the creators through multiple interactions, such as written communication, electronic exchanges, or sometimes in person. These interactions can become extreme and unhealthy, allowing the fan to believe that a more intimate connection exists where none does. This type of behavior is illustrated through super-fan Becky Rosen's journey from fan creator to a fan unbalanced.

Our initial introduction to Becky in Season 5 establishes her as the canonical representation of a fan. She is shown to be someone who collects memorabilia associated with the book fandom, having poster prints of the novel covers *Route 666* and *The Benders* hanging on her walls ("Sympathy for the Devil"). This is an accurate reflection of the practice of many fandom members who collect *Supernatural*-branded posters, pictures, clothing, home goods, and more. However, as her introduction continues, the devotion Becky displays for the books and its characters is shown to go much deeper than that of the casual fan.

Becky is writing Wincest during her first scene in the show, and later tells Chuck that she is also the webmistress at MoreThanBrothers.net, which is understood to be a Wincest website. Her representation as being not only a fan, but a slash fan who writes incestuous fiction about the Winchesters, is a reflection of the activities real-world fans take part in. As previously mentioned, slash had been a mainstay of the fandom since the *Supernatural* pilot aired, and the idea of slash fiction being written about the brothers is incorporated into the show when Sam and Dean first learn about the books and their fandom ("The Monster at the End of This Book"). However, giving a nod to the existence of Wincest in text and having the idea become represented through a physical embodiment are two different matters for some fans. Even with the increase and acceptance of slash in fandom discussions over the years, having the show expose these hobbies to those outside fandom created situations where fans might have had to justify why they were interested in reading or writing about an incestuous relationship, and this could lead to negative repercussions in real life (Counteragent).

The other aspect of Becky's character which is emphasized is her lack of social skills, especially in terms of respecting personal space. Upon meeting her favorite character, Sam Winchester, and confirming that he is indeed real, she immediately places her hand on his chest and comments on how firm he is. She again invades Sam's personal space by the end of the scene and even vocally refuses to cease when he requests that she stop touching him. She blurs her perception of Sam Winchester the fictional character, over whom she has some control as a fan creator, and Sam Winchester the person, who is a virtual stranger to her. This is an uncomfortable, yet legitimate representation of the behavior of some fans who meet the actors at conventions. While the majority of attendees respect the actors' personal space and realize they do not have a more intimate relationship than viewer-actor, there are still some fans who may act in a more intimate nature, touching the actors or engaging in conversations that touch upon topics not normally shared with strangers. Becky brings this aspect of fandom to the forefront as something that exists, even if it is not representative of the entire fandom community.

Later in the season, Becky's blurring of fantasy and reality continues as she becomes closer to Chuck. It was originally established that she had pursued Chuck from afar, sending him letters and gifts in support of his work and perhaps crossing the line of accepted societal interactions between a fan and a creator ("Sympathy for the Devil"). These interactions transform into a more intimate relationship over time, as we learn that Chuck and Becky began dating ("The Real Ghostbusters"). This can be viewed as a way for Becky to become closer to the object of her fantasy, gaining privileged information such as early drafts of the books or unwritten knowledge about Sam and Dean through the creator, thereby escalating Becky's importance within fandom. And Becky also maintains her belief that she and Sam share a more intimate relationship than really exists, taking his faltering and eventual recall of her name as evidence that he has thought about her during their separation. This, too, reflects behaviors that occur within a small subset of fandom members. These fans might engage in interactions with the creators or actors online or in person to the point of being recognized, believing that these exchanges provide them with a privileged status that others cannot attain.

Becky's final appearance to date[1] marks her transition from fan to fanatic ("Season 7, Time for a Wedding!"). She and Chuck break up less than a year into their relationship, with Chuck acknowledging he is at fault ("Swan Song"), and Becky does not appear in canon for another two seasons. By this time, however, it is clear she has left behind her attempts to get closer to the object of her fantasy through the creator and has moved on to trying to directly acquire the fantasy for herself. Her motivation seems to be two-fold, both in seeking a more intimate relationship with the real man behind the character and also in seeking to escalate her social status in her non-fandom life. However, her approach to achieving these goals is obsessive and casts her in the light of a fan unbalanced.

Becky manages to achieve total immersion in the Winchester universe by drugging Sam and tricking him into marrying her. In doing so, she achieves the ultimate status of Mrs. Sam Winchester, which would allow for her to provide for him both as a lover and fellow hunter. Her fantasy begins to fall apart, however, when Sam comes out from under the influence of the drug and fights back against his kidnapping. Repeatedly, as Sam begins to gain control, Becky acts under the assumption that Sam loves her, even though this "love" is just another component in the fantasy world she is creating. Eventually, Becky admits that she knew Sam could not share her feelings, acknowledging the one-sided relationship that exists between fan and character, but her overall portrayal shows the ways in which obsession can cross the line from being harmless to being destructive. This is an issue the fandom community must keep in mind as they devote their time and energy to their shared interest.

More positively, Becky also brings to light the reasoning behind why individuals from different backgrounds and geographic locations are drawn together under a common link. Fans may feel like they don't fit in well within real-life social groupings, whether because of their introvert natures or lack of commonality among their peers, but they can find acceptance within the fandom community. That social connection brings fans together, allowing them to be themselves while sharing their love for a common media interest. As long as that devotion does not turn into destructive obsession, it should be celebrated rather than condemned.

Multiple Interpretations: Fan Ownership in the Supernatural Musical Episode

DEAN: Alright, Shakespeare, you know that I can actually tell you what really happened with Sam and Dean. A friend of mine hooked me up with the unpublished books. So Sam came back from Hell, but without his soul, and Cas brought in a bunch of Leviathans from Purgatory. They lost Bobby, and then Cas and Dean got stuck in Purgatory, Sam hit a dog. Uh, they met a prophet named Kevin, they lost him too. Then Sam underwent a series of trials, in an attempt to close the Gates of Hell, which nearly cost him his life. And Dean, he became a demon, a Knight of Hell actually.
MARIE: Wow.

> **DEAN:** Yup.
> **MARIE:** That is some of the worst fan fiction I have ever heard. I mean seriously where did your friend find this garbage? And not saying that ours is a masterpiece or anything, but jeez. I'll have to send you some fic links later.
> —"Fan Fiction"

The ability to take over the narrative and insert the fan's own interpretations can have positive benefits as well. As seen in the "Supernatural" musical in the episode "Fan Fiction," fans can make connections with the canonical text and align it to their own lives in terms of building and expanding relationships. Fans also illustrate the ideal that once the writer has put the canon out into the world, it is no longer necessarily owned by its creator(s); readers or viewers have the ability to adapt it to suit their own interpretations.

The episode's focus on Marie's transformation of the "Supernatural" text into her own interpretation is mirrored by Dean's initial rejection, but eventual acceptance of her right to do so. The episode also suggests why she felt the need to extend the story beyond the canon being presented, in that the books stopped and she needed to tie up what she saw as loose ends. This is reflective of media fandom's common exploration through fan fiction, extending the story beyond what is presented onscreen to fill in the gaps between episodes or sometimes taking the storyline in entirely new directions through the use of alternative universes. The show's writers or actors do not have the ability to control the text once it is presented; they are simply one part of the creative process:

> **DEAN:** You know? This has been educational. Seeing the story from your perspective. You keep writing, Shakespeare.
> **MARIE:** Even if it doesn't match how you see it?
> **DEAN:** I have my version, and you have yours ["Fan Fiction"].

The episode also becomes something akin to a love letter to the fans, providing shout-outs to former canon, affiliations with the show, and notations from fandom itself. Dean's initial comment of "[w]e got work to do" prior to him and Sam embarking on the case is the same comment Sam made in the pilot. And Dean's encouragement for the actors to "kick it in the ass" is a nod to *Supernatural* director and producer Kim Manners's famous catch-phrase; Manners's legacy has remained a central part of the show and fandom since his death in 2009. The line has been used multiple times in canon ("Abandon All Hope…," 5.10; "Swan Song"; "The Girl with the Dungeons and Dragons Tattoo," 7.20; "Clip Show"; "Fan Fiction"; "Inside Man," 10.17; "Who We Are," 12.22) as a continuing memorial to Manners.

Other mentions within the episode reference short-hand descriptions of emotional exchanges between Sam and Dean, which have become frequent touchstones within the fandom. The song "A Single Man Tear" references Dean's ability to cry a single tear when in the midst of emotional outpouring ("Everybody Loves a Clown," 2.02; "Heart"; "All Hell Breaks Loose, Part 2," 2.22; "In the Beginning," 4.03; "Heaven and Hell," 4.10; "On the Head of a Pin," 4.16; "When the Levee Breaks," 4.21; "The End," 5.04; "I Think I'm Gonna Like It Here," 9.01; "Red Meat," 11.17). This phenomenon has been referenced by the writers, actors, and crew in the production of the show (Jenks1983; Jester). In addition, the episode uses the short-hand of BM (boy melodrama) to reference scenes between Sam and Dean, either in the car or leaning against it, when they are more apt to share their feelings. These types of scenes are a mainstay of the series, and the short-hand is actually used by the writers to reference such events (Thompson).

An ongoing thread in the episode is the presence of the amulet that Dean had worn throughout much of his life: a Christmas gift from Sam when they were kids ("A Very Supernatural Christmas," 3.08). Deemed as the "Samulet" by the fandom because of who gifted it, the amulet became a symbol of the bond shared by the brothers and is also referenced within the musical production. The discarding of the Samulet during the latter half of Season 5 ("Dark Side of the Moon") caused a strong emotional reaction from the fans, although its removal created a benefit for the actor, as Ackles mentioned he had periodically injured himself when the amulet hit him in the mouth during stunts (Knight, *Supernatural: The Official Companion Season 5* 23). This, too, was referenced in the musical production as a nod to the behind-the-scenes knowledge fans have about the show's production.

The "Supernatural" musical celebrates the diverse types of fans and fan interpretations in the fandom and provides a way for the show's creators to give thanks to the fans for supporting their efforts over the years. Although the interpretations of what the canon means might differ among the fans, they are all united in their love for *Supernatural*. As Dean asserts,

> I know I have expressed some differences of opinion regarding this particular version of "Supernatural." But tonight is all about Marie's vision, this is Marie's "Supernatural." So I want you to get out there and I want you stand as close as she wants you to, and I want you to put as much sub into text as you possibly can ["Fan Fiction"].

Conclusion

> SAM: So, why this story, huh? Why, uh, "Supernatural?"
> CALLIOPE: "Supernatural" has everything. Life. Death. Resurrection. Redemption. But above all, family. All sorts

of music you can really tap your toe to. It isn't some meandering piece of genre dreck. It's ... epic!

—"Fan Fiction"

Through the use of the "Supernatural" novels within the show's
canon, the creators break down the fourth wall and provide an outlet by
which they can acknowledge and examine the fandom community that
has supported them over the years. As Jensen Ackles said during the Summer Television Critics Association Press Tour in 2014, "[i]f the fans are
latching onto these characters and coming up with their own creativity ...
if this inspires a conversation, fantastic. It's art, we're entertainment, and
people can draw from it what they will" (Panos). That conversation is continuing, and the *Supernatural* creators have inspired an entire community
of fans to explore canon as a jumping off point in order to see where the
road might lead.

NOTES

1. This book was in press before Becky's reappearance in Season 15.

WORKS CITED

ABC MediaNet. *ABC Television Network Press Release—Season Program Rankings from
09/18/06 Through 05/20/07.* 22 May 2007, https://web.archive.org/web/20110825010107/
http://abcmedianet.com/web/dnr/dispDNR.aspx?id=052207_07.
_____. *ABC Television Network Press Release—Season Program Rankings (Part Two of Two).*
9 May 2006, https://web.archive.org/web/20120118224432/http://abcmedianet.com/web/
dnr/dispDNR.aspx?id=050906_04.
_____. *ABC Television Network Press Release—Season Rankings (Through 5/18).* 20 May
2008, https://web.archive.org/web/20081206014833/http://abcmedianet.com/web/dnr/
dispDNR.aspx?id=052008_06.
Ausiello, Michael. "*Supernatural* Exec: 'We Won't Be *One Tree Hill* with Monsters!'" *TV
Guide,* July 2007, http://www.tvguide.com/news/supernatural-exec-we-8522/.
Borsellino, Mary. "Super Women: *Supernatural*'s Executive Story Editor Sera Gamble."
Sequential Tart, 1 Dec. 2006, http://www.sequentialtart.com/article.php?id=345.
Boyum, Steve. *Supernatural: Season 5 DVD Commentary: The End (5.04).*
Cochran, CP. "Interview: Sera Gamble, Producer and Writer for 'Supernatural.'" *Firefox
News,* 1 Mar. 2008, https://web.archive.org/web/20090409002420/http://firefox.org/news/
articles/1254/1/Interview-Sera-Gamble-Producer-and-Writer-for-quotSupernaturalquot/
Page1.html.
Counteragent. *Good Fourth Walls Make Good Neighbors.* 9 Jan. 2010, https://supernaturalart.
livejournal.com/1796967.html.
Jenkins, Henry. "*Supernatural:* First Impressions." *Confessions of an Aca-Fan,* 14 Jan. 2007,
http://henryjenkins.org/2007/01/supernatural.html.
Jenks1983. *Jensen Ackles Panel @ Jibcon 2 Pt.3.* YouTube, https://www.youtube.com/watch?v=
GA3womJlzKA. Accessed 27 Jan. 2018.
Jester, Alice. "The Winchester Family Business—Interview with *Supernatural* Executive Pro-
ducer Sera Gamble." *Winchester Family Business,* 30 Nov. 2009, http://thewinchesterfamily

business.com/articles/article-archives/interviews/4062-interview-with-supernatural-executive-producer-sera-gamble.

Knight, Nicholas. *Supernatural: The Official Companion Season 1.* Titan Books, 2007.

_____. *Supernatural: The Official Companion Season 3.* Titan Books, 2009.

_____. *Supernatural: The Official Companion Season 5.* Titan Books, 2010.

Meyer, Michaela D. E. "Slashing *Smallville*: The Interplay of Text, Audience and Production on Viewer Interpretations of Homoeroticism." *Sexuality & Culture*, vol. 17, no. 3, Sept. 2013, pp. 476–93. *CrossRef*, doi:10.1007/s12119-013-9190-5.

Panos, Maggie. "Jensen Ackles and Jared Padalecki Open Up About *Supernatural*'s 'Remarkable' Fans." *Pop Sugar*, July 2014, https://www.popsugar.com/entertainment/Jensen-Ackles-Jared-Padalecki-Talk-About-Fans-35278284.

Thompson, Robbie. "Fun Fact, My 1st Day on #Supernatural Writers Kept Referring to 'The B.M.' Scene… I Was SO Confused." *@rthompson1138*, 12 Nov. 2014, https://twitter.com/rthompson1138/status/532399969312206848.

Monsters Make Gender Trouble

Megan Genovese

In the pilot episode of *Supernatural* (1.01), Dean introduces the core concept and narrative structure of the show: "saving people, hunting things; the family business." The Winchester brothers save people by hunting things, most of which turn out to be inhuman. But as becomes clear over the course of the show, the division between human and inhuman is not the same as the division between people and monsters. Many creatures are dangerous and destructive, but monsters threaten much more than life and limb; they transgress the most fundamental truths of human existence. So what makes a monster? As a comprehensive analysis of gender politics in Seasons 1 through 9 shows, *Supernatural* marks the difference between people and monsters with gender trouble. This essay examines this discourse of monstrosity in recurring angel, demon, and fan characters.

This analysis uses the poststructuralist definition of gender as performance. This understanding is informed by the writings of Judith Butler, especially *Gender Trouble*, "Imitation and Gender Insubordination," and *Bodies That Matter*. Butler defines gender as something under perpetual creation, preservation, and modification, both in the sense of the communally created ideal form of gender (i.e., concepts of maleness, femaleness) and in an individual's realization or lack of realization of that gender ideal (i.e., their masculinity or femininity). Most contemporaneous scholars distinguished between gender and the biological status of sex, but Butler contends that this is logically untenable when sex is a linguistically and culturally gendered concept. From this, Butler concludes that there is no blank canvas entity of "the body" on which gender is written, but that the construction of sex/gender "create" the body as something others can perceive. As Susan Hekman briefly summarizes Butler's argument,

> [T]he materiality of sex is constructed through a ritualized repetition of norms; performativity is not an act of "choice," but a reiteration of norms, in this case the "law

162

of sex." What this comes to is that, for Butler, there is no "choice" of gender, because even, or especially, "deviant" gender roles are discursively constructed by the symbolic [68].

In contrast to Butler's theory of gender as performance, *Supernatural*'s creators represent gender as an expression of intrinsic biological sex as it is understood to manifest in genital configuration. Like many cultural texts originating in patriarchal cultures, *Supernatural* adheres to an anachronistic, Freudian dictum that "anatomy is destiny" (qtd. in Diamond 1123). In this biological determinism, one's gender identity is preordained by physical sex, which is considered a neutral, ontological fact of the body. Sex and gender in *Supernatural* are construed as oppositional binaries of strictly segregated physical, psychological, and behavioral traits. Yet Butler's theory of performativity is evidenced in this system, as it requires that characters constantly prove their gender identity by acting correctly masculine or feminine. In addition to positive identification with the appropriate gender model, characters evidence their gender through the rejection of the other. This is particularly true for male characters, for whom "masculinity is defined by its *not* being feminine" because "the most significant thing about being a man is *not being a woman*" (Diamond 1100). That is, gender in *Supernatural* is normative: proved by characters' adherence to norms correlated with their biological sex, troubled by non-normative behaviors, and enforced by a narrative paradigm that rewards normative behavior and punishes non-normative behavior.

The ideological assumptions that define *Supernatural*'s narrative paradigm hinge on this binary, pseudo-biological understanding of gender as a strict dichotomy between male and female characteristics and roles deriving from dimorphic physiology. Social and narrative enforcement of heterosexuality is an inextricable part of binary sex-gender. The Winchesters embody a heroic masculine ideal against whom other male characters are found too antisocially masculine or too effeminate (e.g., the Ghostfacers' failure in their attempts to imitate the Winchesters' heroism). The feminine ideal is a woman the Winchesters can save and desire sexually, but tragic lost loves and mothers who die for their children are also acceptably feminine; women who transgress into masculine roles or are sexually unavailable or aggressive are antagonists or must be written off the show as a narrative consequence for the threat they pose to the integrity of binary sex-gender (e.g., Jo Harvelle repeatedly fails to inhabit the masculine role of hunter, ending in her death).

Supernatural has roots in the horror genre, characterized by dramatized repression of the monstrous that threatens paradigms of normality. In this case, the normative paradigm is binary sex-gender, encompassing all aspects of identity and performance. Its most basic plot structure is the damsel in distress trope, in which the Winchesters save helpless, sexually desirable women from monstrous entities. Monsters in horror demonstrate the theory of the abject, a conceptual framework that divides self from other through symbolic assignment of oppositional category pairs like living/dead, clean/unclean, and healthy/diseased:

> The place of the abject is "the place where meaning collapses," the place where "I" am not. The abject threatens life; it must be "radically excluded" from the place of the living subject, propelled away from the body and deposited on the other side of an imaginary border which separates the self from that which threatens the self. [...] The concept of a border is central to the construction of the monstrous in the horror film; that which crosses or threatens to cross the 'border' is abject. Although the specific nature of the border changes from film to film, the function of the monstrous remains the same—to bring about an encounter between the symbolic order and that which threatens its stability [Creed 9–11].

Because *Supernatural*'s ideology and narrative depend on binary sex-gender and its correlates, human/monster is assigned through categories of gendered/ungendered, straight/queer, and assimilable/unassimilable into this symbolic order. Monsters are those beings that fall into abject categories of identity and behavior, or those who, in their existential rejection of the sex-gender binary, threaten the structural logic of *Supernatural*.

The core symbolic paradigm of *Supernatural* is "a discourse of the monstrous" around gender trouble, and its narrative constitutes an iterative "ritual of boundary guarding through which the civic monster is named, repudiated, and, finally, staked" (Ingebretsen 91). The naming of the abject as monsters is crucial to the construction of a positive identity in horror, and it is in interactions the Winchesters have with beings they designate as monsters that *Supernatural* fulfills its central concept and narrative goal. The Winchesters become heroes by defining and defending the limits of the social order inscribed in binary sex-gender ("saving people"), and successfully destroying the entities that represent the threat of transgressive ideologies of gender and sexuality ("hunting things").

Inhuman characters who may not have human bodies present an inherent challenge to the binary sex-gender paradigm, but inhuman does not automatically equate with monster. Though fantastical texts offer opportunities to go beyond the limits of reality, traditional sexual and social roles tend to remain in place. Dimorphically sexed bodies and gender expectations do not exist in the natural forms of either angels or demons; an angel exists as a "multidimensional wavelength of celestial intent" ("The Third Man," 6.03), and a demon is naturally a billow of black smoke that represents a fundamentally corrupted human soul. Nevertheless, *Supernatural* personifies angels and demons with human gender, both in the bodies they occupy onscreen and the rhetorical constructions around them. Because they all "look like people, not otherworldly monsters" (Fife Donaldson 26), the rhetorical construction of monsters reflects back on humanity its deepest fears about the inadequacy and artificiality of binary sex-gender. Looking at the arcs of recurring angel, demon, and fan characters makes clear that *Supernatural*'s monsters are readily identified and identifiable in gender trouble.

Angels: Monstrous Un-Gendering

When first introduced in Season 4, angels are assumed from their reputation in the Judeo-Christian tradition to be the Winchesters' allies. Individual angels' characterizations develop from that point depending on their relationships with the Winchesters and their goals, and symbolized in gender constructions and connotations. Angels like Raphael become monsters because their antagonism is accompanied by gender trouble, whereas Castiel is never named a monster even when he is temporarily antagonistic to the Winchesters because he remains respectful of binary sex-gender.

Raphael leads the faction of angels trying to bring on the Apocalypse that the Winchesters are attempting to stop throughout Seasons 4 and 5. Raphael and his lieutenants all initially manifest in male bodies and use masculine pronouns, but as they become more aggressive and sinister toward the Winchesters' heroic goals, these gender identities are narratively and rhetorically destabilized, un-gendering them and contextualizing their antagonism as monstrous in *Supernatural*'s symbolic order. For example, in a confrontation with Uriel, one of Raphael's lieutenants in "Heaven and Hell" (4.10), Dean reacts to opposition by calling Uriel's masculinity into question. When Uriel expresses disgust that Dean had sex with a fallen angel, Dean retorts, "What do you care? You're junkless down there, right? Like a Ken doll?" This is an escalation of their previous encounter, when Dean accused Uriel of wanting to destroy a town because he was "compensating for something," implying that Uriel is less than a real man in phallic terms ("It's the Great Pumpkin, Sam Winchester," 4.07). Since genitals define sex that dictates gender, and maleness is defined in large part by heterosexual desire and accomplishment in *Supernatural*'s ideological paradigm, Dean's accusation points out a perceived disconnect between Uriel's claim to a masculine identity and his identity performance that indicates an underlying, monstrous identity that is neither male nor female.

The accusation is meaningless from Uriel's perspective; *Supernatural* implies that angels do not have sexed dimorphic physiologies like humans ostensibly do, and either lack or are strongly discouraged from expressing sexual desire. Uriel's vocal disgust with humanity would suggest he would be proud of his exclusion from the Winchesters' conception of normality. But *Supernatural* draws from the horror genre conventions that give heroes the authority to define human and monster, so it is the Winchesters' perspective and their normative paradigm that audiences are forced to adopt to make sense of the narrative. Uriel is an antagonist, and that gives the Winchesters license to draw the border between human and monster between themselves and him.

Although every angel is biologically sexless according to *Supernatural*'s assumptions, that trait is discursively elevated only in those angels denoted as monstrous. Indeed, it is contradicted when the show means to indicate an angel is on the Winchesters' side and subscribes to the logics of binary sex-gender: developing in parallel with the Winchesters' attempts to circumvent the Apocalypse, Cas's relationship with Meg has sexual overtones, and the fallen angel Anna Milton, who explicitly turned her back on Heaven and adopted a fully mortal physical incarnation, is attracted to and has sex with Dean in "Heaven and Hell." When Anna later decides to reclaim her angelic powers and attempt to forestall the Apocalypse by eliminating Sam, her antagonism and overall rejection of the Winchesters' role as the protagonists of the narrative by circumventing them entirely makes her so monstrous that she is reduced to a completely ungendered "it" and swiftly destroyed ("The Song Remains the Same," 5.13).

This correlation between un-gendering and antagonistic angels made into monsters is most obvious in Raphael. He transitions from a male vessel to a female vessel after the first is destroyed. When the Winchesters first meet Raphael in his new vessel in "The French Mistake" (6.15), their contemptuous response—"Nice meat suit. Dude looks like a lady"—underscores the consistent implication that antagonists' monstrosity is either symbolized by or situated in a lack of a fixed sex-gender identity. Since not all vessels are equally compatible and durable to a given angel, there is also a post-hoc implication that the original male vessel that was partially destroyed by Raphael's usage, despite correlating with Raphael's masculine pronouns, did not reflect Raphael's true, monstrously non-binary self. Additionally, the term "meat suit" is more associated with demons' nonconsensual possession of human hosts than with angels' possession of vessels, which requires genetic compatibility and consent. This terminological distinction implies the monstrous nature of demons by evoking the "transvestite killer" in horror films such as *Silence of the Lambs* (1991) and *Psycho* (1960), men whose monstrosity is symbolized in the literal or figurative putting on of a woman's stolen skin (Tharp 107). Dean's use of the demonic turn of phrase when referring to Raphael's female vessel emphasizes the monstrous implications of Raphael's gender trouble.

The monstrosity of Raphael's lack of a fixed sex-gender presentation is reiterated and emphasized in "The Man Who Knew Too Much" (6.22). Because Raphael has escalated his antagonism to the Winchesters by joining forces with the demon Crowley, the discourse of Raphael's gender trouble escalates as well. With a feminine face and voice, he refers to himself as Castiel's brother, a deliberate dissonance further emphasized when Crowley pointedly vacillates over pronouns, saying things like, "She—*he* has offered me protection against all comers." That even Crowley, a monster himself, can mock Raphael for claiming a male identity while having a female vessel indicates that this particular kind of gender trouble is part of a discourse of monstrosity that is universal within the narrative reality, not merely human. In Raphael's concurrent descent into villainy and identity destabilization, *Supernatural* suggests that trans and non-binary identities are inherently monstrous and insufferable even for other monsters.

Angels' biological lack of sex-gender was made the crux of the Apocalyptic angels' monstrosity. As other angels' character arcs show, though, inhuman sexlessness and flexibility of gender presentation can be minimized when the angel is not antagonistic to the Winchesters and human norms. Castiel, the most commonly recurring angel character, consistently avoids being subjected to a discourse of monstrosity by attempting to abide by the dictates of binary sex-gender and human masculinity as part of his defection from Heaven. His inhumanity is self-evident and often highlighted whenever he temporarily sides against the Winchesters in his inability to understand pop culture references and non-literal speech, references to his inhuman natural form, and misunderstanding of norms of gendered social interaction, but this never becomes the basis of an accusation of monstrosity. Though Castiel takes on female vessels on brief occasions throughout his tenure on the show, including beyond Season 9, these are treated as exceptional interruptions to his normative state as male rather than an expression of angels' normative state that is not tied to specifically sexed or gendered bodies. He even briefly inhabits his vessel's adolescent daughter in "The Rapture" (4.20), but this transition does not become an indication of monstrosity as it did for Raphael because it was in service to the Winchesters.

Constructing monstrosity through the discourse of gender trouble allows ambiguity in inhumanity, "licensing otherwise transgressive energies in limited" instances (Ingebretsen 97). Castiel's most persistent failure of masculinity is the implication in the narrative and in characters' observations that he is romantically or sexually interested in Dean, but this never becomes a discourse of monstrosity. Whereas the implication of queerness articulates much of Crowley's monstrosity, as I will show in the next section, Castiel's implied queerness is allowable because it is not associated with antagonism. In fact, it forms the basis of his willingness to side with the Winchesters. Though Castiel credits both Sam and Dean with teaching him how to fit into the binary sex-gender paradigm, he credits Dean alone with inspiring him to doubt and defect from Heaven, even describing it as something he did out of his personal feelings for Dean. In one of many such instances in "Good God, Y'all" (5.02), Castiel tells Dean, "I killed two angels this week. My brothers. I'm hunted. I rebelled. And I did it, all of it, for you." Perhaps because Castiel does not understand attraction, he never names his feelings for Dean as romantic or sexual, nor does he try to redefine their relationship beyond friendship, leaving his queerness in subtext alone. Instead of initiating a discourse of monstrosity, implied queerness thus only problematizes Castiel's ability to embody human masculinity, putting him on a level with human counterparts like the Ghostfacers whose masculinity similarly falls short of the Winchesters' heroic ideal. Whereas the Apocalyptic angels' gender trouble links with their antagonism to become a discourse of monstrosity, Castiel's "transgressive energies" of inhumanity and possible queerness are mitigated by his deference to the Winchesters' perspective and aspiration to assimilate into the binary sex-gender paradigm.

Demons: Monstrous Sexualities

Like angels, demons on *Supernatural* also become monsters through gender trouble. Their ontological difference from angels is that demons are not a uniquely created species but the "twisted, perverted, [and] evil" result of centuries of torture administered to human souls in Hell ("Weekend at Bobby's" 6.04). This means that when demons are made discursively into monsters, the ways in which they deviate from normative paradigms are marked as doubly distant from humanity: not only the result of inhumanity but also, by definition of what a demon is in *Supernatural*, the total corruption of humanity. Unsurprisingly, then, the discourses of demon monstrosity are different from those applied to angels. Neither Meg nor Crowley ever experiences the kind of discursive un-gendering that marks antagonistic angels as monsters. Instead, demon monstrosity is articulated in their deliberate defiance of binary sex-gender identities and roles through performative excess, especially in their sexuality.

Female characters in *Supernatural* are both inherently distinct from men and dependent on their relationships with male characters for their narrative existence, usually as sexual objects that invite and passively accept male attention. Assertiveness and aggression are exclusive to masculine sexuality and diametrically opposed to feminine sexuality; to summarize these gendered sexual roles, "Masculinity enacts dominance as a means of erotic arousal, and femininity is defined by the erotic nature of its submission" (Krelko 29). The only other valid way to be a woman is to be a symbolically de-sexualized mother, whose existence revolves entirely around her children.[1] A woman who is not a mother and yet refuses to be a sexual object in the heterosexual script, who instead misappropriates the active, aggressive masculine role in sexual situations, is unfeminine. Meg has a reliable female identity based on implications about her centuries-past former life as a human and especially on her penchant for young and attractive female host bodies. She can possess male bodies, as she does Sam in "Born Under a Bad Sign" (2.14), but Meg's monstrosity is not in un-gendering her female identity, but in her performance of masculine sexuality in spite of it.

She reacts to insults, threats of violence, and actual violence with innuendo that exposes the sexual subtext of violence in the horror genre. If Meg is thrust into situations where a human woman would suffer symbolically sexual violence and await the male hero, she instead becomes sexually aggressive as a defense mechanism. When the Winchesters capture Meg in "Devil's Trap" (1.22), she deliberately sexualizes the situation, teasing, "You know, if you wanted to tie me up, all you had to do was ask," adding that the Winchesters "hitting a girl" is "kind of a turn on." Meg's aggressive strategy of turning her victimization back onto her male attackers is similar to the way that the Winchesters downplay and deny their physical and emotional vulnerability when captured or injured. This shows her incompatibility with the fundamental correlation between femininity and victimization in *Supernatural*, marking her as unassimilable into the show's symbolic order.

Going a step beyond resistance to the damsel in distress trope, Meg deliberately inverts its normative structure to victimize and humiliate the Winchesters. By usurping a masculine role and making the Winchesters objects of sexualized violence, Meg defamiliarizes the most basic plot device facilitating the horror genre discourse of monstrosity: the male heroes saving the damsel in distress from the sexually predatory monster. In an example of this inverted trope in "Caged Heat" (6.10), Meg ties Dean to a chair, straddles his lap, and asks him to explain the Winchesters' recent activities. When Dean remains silent, she declares herself "officially over the foreplay," menaces him with a knife, and demands, "Satisfy me, or I please myself!" Forcing a reversal of gender roles makes the Winchesters sexualized victims with no recourse for salvation, since relying on a rescuer would also undermine their dominant masculinity. In doing so, Meg corrupts the prescriptive roles of binary sex-gender that underpin *Supernatural*, exposing their artificiality and unnatural imposition on even the narrative reality built around them.

The critical point about female demons' monstrosity is that it is tied to non-normative sexuality. Meg's discourse of monstrosity starts with her adoption of stereotypically masculine sexual aggression, denial of passive feminine sexuality, and concerted efforts to feminize the Winchesters, but the way the Winchesters name Meg as a monster truly excludes the abject from the normative. Though she never actually has sex in these situations, her monstrosity is named in the Winchesters reviling her with "derogatory epithets that are qualitatively inapplicable" to anyone but "women who embody sexual deviance" (Nurka 316; 315). Labeling Meg as a slut ("Are You There God? It's Me, Dean Winchester," 4.02), whore ("Caged Heat"; "Reading Is Fundamental," 7.21; and "Goodbye Stranger," 8.17), and skank ("Reading Is Fundamental") does not indicate the quality of her individual monstrous acts; it symbolizes the nature of feminine monstrosity generally in *Supernatural*, namely that it manifests from a failure to comply with a normative passive role in sexual and narrative scenarios. Notably, these derogatory epithets are closely correlated with female demons rather than with human women who also defy *Supernatural*'s narrow parameters of femininity, albeit in lesser magnitude. This suggests that, while certain crimes against norms of femininity are punishable only by death (e.g., Jo Harvelle's failed claim to a masculine hero identity as a hunter), crimes like Meg's are so egregious that they can only be found in demons: monsters that are both narratively and symbolically irredeemable (for more on evil or dangerous femininities in *Supernatural*, see Beliveau & Bolf-Beliveau).

Crowley's discourse of monstrosity is also rooted in non-normative gender performance, especially of his sexuality. A crossroads demon who usurps the throne in Hell after the Winchesters stop the Apocalypse, Crowley is an opportunist who either works with or against the Winchesters as suits his current interests. Crowley has a stable male identity, firmly rooted in his human past as a Scottish tailor who sold his soul to enlarge his penis. While this detail pokes fun at male anxieties, it does not disrupt the assumptions and symbolic order around binary sex-gender rooted in physical endowments. He has one instance of gender trouble when he temporarily possesses Linda Tran in "What's Up, Tiger Mommy?" (8.02) that does instigate the discourse of monstrosity, but not through un-gendering. In response to the Winchesters' demands that he "[g]et out of her," Crowley invokes a metaphor for possession that implies an extensive sexual history with female partners. Dean's reframing suggestion that Crowley is "getting in touch with [his] feminine side" does not deny his masculinity, but implies its deficiency according to *Supernatural*'s binary understanding of sex-gender, that "to be a man, above all else, is to be the opposite of a woman" (Krelko 54). Crowley's monstrosity is rooted in his easy acceptance of this accusation as compatible with his original assertion of heterosexual experiences, tacitly claiming that he can be feminine without disrupting his male identity.

Indeed, Crowley's performance of his gender identity as equally compatible with stereotypically feminine and stereotypically masculine traits is antithetical to *Supernatural*'s representation of ideal masculinity embodied in the Winchesters as competitive, anti-feminine, and exclusively heterosexual. The Winchesters enact their masculinity according to a model of hegemonic dominance that demands a constant struggle to prove one's own masculinity and strip other men of theirs, a competition in which subordination is a feminizing symbolic rape. The problem that Crowley poses to *Supernatural*'s normative paradigm is that he undermines the assumption that femininity precludes a masculine affinity for power and dominance. Crowley shows equal comfort in positions of masculine dominance and feminine subordination. While they are still in an uneasy alliance in their search for Purgatory in "The Man Who Knew Too Much," for instance, Crowley reminds Castiel he is "the bottom in this relationship," using the normative model of male dominance over another man as feminizing sexual penetration. But when their power dynamic abruptly flips in "Meet the New Boss" (7.01), Crowley accepts his subordination with good humor, joking that Castiel "like[s] to bend them right over" and inviting, "Let's go." By showing no fear at the prospect of being seen as feminine and symbolically raped, Crowley transgressively implies that the Winchesters' competitive performance is the product of insecurity contingent on a normative ideology of masculinity rather than a fact of maleness.

Going beyond simply allowing himself to be feminized in power relationships, Crowley actively associates himself with femininity and particularly with queer sexuality. Queerness is a failure of masculinity in *Supernatural*'s ideological paradigm because "homosexual men deviate from the hegemonic male standard" of voracious heterosexual viability and appetites and are "generally assumed to be effeminate" (Krelko 20; 34). *Supernatural* introduces Crowley in "Abandon All Hope…" (5.10) as he closes a crossroads deal with a banking executive who is selling his soul for solvency. Crossroads deals are sealed with a kiss, and when the bank executive balks at closing with Crowley rather than the "very young, attractive lady" demon who had first worked with him, Crowley offers him the choice of "cling[ing] to six decades of deep-seated homophobia, or giv[ing] it up and get[ting] a complete bailout." This is the first same-sex kiss on *Supernatural*, and this initial, overt link between Crowley and queerness is consistently reiterated across Crowley's appearances over the next four seasons.

Association with homosexuality in and of itself is not enough to make Crowley a monster, but it becomes the discourse of his monstrosity in juxtaposition with his antagonism. The monster "registers the moment where human integrity is threatened" (Ingebretsen 2); when Crowley poses a threat to the Winchesters' integrity, physical and otherwise, this threat is always associated with his queerness. For example, in his most direct assault on the Winchesters' heroic identities in "Clip Show" (8.22), Crowley successfully cows them into submission by threatening to kill "everyone [they have] ever saved," though the two examples seen on screen are pretty young women whose relationships with the Winchesters had romantic overtones. He expressly articulates the relationship between the Winchesters' rescue of these "damsels in distress" and their identities both as heterosexual men and as heroes is his motivation in doing so. "What's the line?" he asks mockingly,

> Saving people, hunting things: the family business. Well, I think the people you save, they're how you justify your pathetic little lives. The alcoholism, the collateral damage, the pain you've caused—the one thing that allows you to sleep at night, the one thing, is knowing that these folks are out there, still out there happy and healthy because of you, you great big bloody heroes! They're your life's work, and I'm going to rip it apart[.]

This is monstrous in itself because Crowley is threatening the foundations of *Supernatural's* narrative integrity in undermining the damsel in distress trope. However, this declaration, which appears in a conversation that takes place over the phone, is bookended by overt performances of queerness. Though Crowley's purpose in contacting the Winchesters is to issue the threat quoted above, he takes the time for "first things first" and flirtatiously asks, "What are you wearing?" Then, with his purpose accomplished and the Winchesters reeling from watching one previously saved damsel die in front of them, Crowley finishes with a flourish of calling the Winchesters "my darlings." By framing Crowley's intensive attack on the Winchesters' heroism with his non-normative gender performance and sexuality, *Supernatural* contextualizes Crowley's performances of femininity and queerness in spite of his male identity as signifiers of monstrosity.

Fans: Metatextual Monsters

Supernatural is unique in its inclusion of its fandom within the textual body of the show through a series of pulpy novels written, published, and popularized within the narrative universe that detail the Winchesters' heroic journey. Given the nearly one to one parallel between episodes and books, the fans depicted in *Supernatural* reflect the show's perceptions of the fans of *Supernatural*. Most of these fans are human, but Metatron, one of only two recurring fan characters, is an angel. Metatron is grouped with the fans rather than with the angels because his monstrosity does not originate in his inhumanity but in his fannish activities.

Angels and demons are close to the border between humanity and the abject by dint of their inhuman lack of normatively sexed bodies, readily facilitating discursive construction as monsters. Most of *Supernatural*'s textual representations of its fans are human, yet where non-fan characters like Jo Harvelle and the Ghostfacers are framed in terms of the gender roles they fail to adhere to, fans are subject to a complex construction that frames them instead in terms of monstrosity. Instead of individual punishment for not living up to the demands of binary sex-gender, *Supernatural* collectively excommunicates fans from humanity. This section will examine *Supernatural*'s representations of its own fandom generally through the end of Season 9 and then closely examine the two recurring fan characters, Becky Rosen and Metatron.

Supernatural's representation of its fans as monstrous is not an isolated incident of hostility. Historically, fans have been defined by inappropriate modes of consumption that are excessive and proprietary relative to broader cultural valuation of rationality and legal ownership of media properties. Though scholarly understanding and public perceptions of many fannish behaviors have largely shifted in favor of fans, industry studios and creators still often resent fans' interventions in and reactions to media productions as much as they rely on fan enthusiasm for publicity and profits. This leads to an often implicit, sometimes contradictory distinction between good fans and bad fans. The source of fan monstrosity in *Supernatural* is not in the fan identity *per se*, or necessarily in being a fan of the "Supernatural" books, but in a specific viewing attitude that subordinates the male hero to women's gaze (see also Coker & Benefiel) and/or is interested in queer subtext and the activity of writing fan fiction. *Supernatural* consistently represents the participants in these kinds of transformative fannish activities as monstrously disruptive to the core ideology and generic structures of the show.

The perceived disproportion of fans' attachment and dedication to their favorite texts is evident in the evocative designation of such fans as "cult fans." *Supernatural* represents "the cult fan [as] both a boon and a burden," avidly consuming the show but proving difficult to please (Felschow 5.8). In "The Monster at the End of This Book" (4.18), the Winchesters stumble upon the existence of the "Supernatural" book series while on a case that takes them into a used bookshop. The first representation of fans is the shopkeeper's casual mention that the books "[d]idn't sell a lot of copies" but instead "had more of an underground cult following," suggesting a small but intensely invested readership. Upon investigating further, Dean marvels first that "[t]here's actually fans" of the Winchesters' fictionalized exploits, and then remarks, "For fans, they sure do complain a lot." This starts to draw the line between good and bad fans. The antagonistic view *Supernatural* has of some of the show's fans can be understood as the manifestation of frustration that these fans often do not fit the model of an audience that only consumes, but rather talk back to the show and repurpose it in different ways for antithetical purposes.

In addition to being overcritical, the fans are "outlaws in the sense that they do not use the programming offered to them as intended" (Costello & Moore 14). The intended purpose of *Supernatural* is stated in the "saving people, hunting things" shorthand and consistently articulated in its use of horror genre tropes, including the discourse of monstrosity: it is about the difference between people and monsters in terms of a binary sex-gender paradigm as shown through the perspective of humanity's heroes, the Winchesters. Instead of simply receiving this meaning, though, fans use their own lenses to critique and repurpose the show. Though different fans have different interpretations, *Supernatural* singles out and names as monsters those fans with interpretations that contradict the central symbolic order of binary sex-gender by focusing on the Winchesters' moments of femininity and homoeroticism rather than their masculine dominance; in other words, these fans celebrate the moments in which they are closest to crossing the border with monstrosity rather than farthest away from it. For example, when the Winchesters visit a fan convention in "The Real Ghostbusters" (5.09), the fans are excited for panels entitled "Frightened Little Boy: The Secret Life of Dean" and "The Homoerotic Subtext of 'Supernatural.'" *Supernatural* shows that these interpretations of the text are fundamentally wrong through Sam and Dean, who were already taken aback by the excess of fans' enthusiasm and react to the announcement of the panels with disbelief and anger, miming violence at the books' author for participating in and thus endorsing the viewing attitude evidenced in the panel topics.

Through this kind of narrative discourse, *Supernatural* portrays this particular subsection of its fans as a group that has "failed in their humanity" through a specific misinterpretation of the text they persist in holding despite textual resistance to it, and enacts "a ritual of civic repudiation" against them (Ingebretsen 96). The Winchesters respond with revulsion to this specific fan culture as emblematic of an ontological monstrosity within that fan identity. For example, Sam discovers that, in addition to "Sam girls and Dean girls" who express sexual or romantic preference for one of the brothers, there exists in the "Supernatural" fandom something called a "slash fan." An obviously disgusted Sam explains that "slash" refers to "Sam-slash-Dean, together," and that it "[d]oesn't seem to matter" to fans that the Winchesters are brothers. Recoiling, Dean protests, "Oh, come on. That—that's just sick" ("The Monster at the End of This Book"). In this reference to the popular incest slash pairing commonly referred to as Wincest, *Supernatural* allows no ambiguity in its condemnation of both the pairing and its perpetrators as that which "is (or at least ought to be) personally unthinkable" (Ingebretsen 97). The source of monstrosity is the taboo of incest, but the incarnation of incest as an interest emblematic of the specific kind of *Supernatural* fan the show singles out confers that monstrosity on the fans themselves.

The two recurring fan characters, Becky and Metatron, are the best examples of the creators naming, repudiating, and symbolically staking these fans as monsters. Unsurprisingly, the harshest treatment is a reaction to the most dangerous of fan activities: writing fan fiction, better known as fanfic. Many fan activities are dangerous in that they impose fans' own interpretations on the narrative of *Supernatural*, fundamentally challenging "discursive and productive monopolies" held by the show's institutionally sanctioned creators (Johnson 291). Fanfic is especially dangerous, though, because it constitutes "a rebellion against the system" of hegemonic social norms that underpin the narrative and the production and regulation of those norms through institutional channels (Costello & Moore 136). Fanfic is the pinnacle of fans failing to be content in their prescribed role as audiences that only consume.

Where other fan activities dispute the creative intent of *Supernatural*, writing fanfic commands control over the narrative itself and potentially overturns the text's normative paradigm of binary sex-gender and the symbolic order of monstrosity in gender trouble. Just as writing fanfic poses a more direct threat to the integrity of the narrative than other fan activities, characters who write fanfic pose a more direct threat to the Winchesters than other fans, as is made evident in the Winchesters' interactions with Becky and Metatron. Becky writes fanfic that shifts the Wincest slash pairing from an interpretation of homoerotic subtext to an unambiguous, fully realized text that other fans can consume alongside and in the same way they do the "Supernatural" books ("Sympathy for the Devil," 5.01). Her domain of influence may be limited to her website, MoreThanBrothers.net, but fans like Becky, who are able and willing to create fanfic that directly contradicts the official text of "Supernatural" and *Supernatural*, undercut their singular authority over narrative reality. In doing so, these fans also reject *Supernatural*'s ideological basis in binary sex-gender that precludes homosexuality in any form, but especially in incest.

Even while giving them minor roles that acknowledge their value to the franchise, *Supernatural* represents these fans as delusional and incompatible with the narrative reality to remind the rebellious fandom "of who exactly is in charge" (Felschow 6.6). Becky Rosen is an exceedingly unflattering portrait of a fangirl. She is described by a friend as "so pathetic, it actually loops back around again to cute." As an avatar of fans, Becky just accepts this cruel description: "I know what I am, okay? I'm a loser, in high school, in life," who feels a sense of belonging only on online fan message boards ("Season 7, Time for a Wedding!" 7.08). Though she protests, "I know the difference between fantasy and reality," Becky immerses herself so deeply in what is ostensibly fiction that, even in the absence of any evidence, she believes the books are real before she meets the Winchesters. She is obsessed with Sam and, after meeting him, makes a fool of herself by fawning over him and refusing to acknowledge his discomfort when she caresses his chest ("Sympathy for the Devil"). Convinced that Sam returns her interest, Becky embarrasses herself further by trying to let him down gently when she begins dating someone else. "I'm not going to lie," she tells Sam seriously. "We had undeniable chemistry. But like a monkey on the sun, it was too hot to live. It can't go on." Sardonically, Sam assures her he will "find a way to keep living" after the disappointment ("The Monster at the End of This Book").

The relationship does not last, so Becky's third and final appearance on *Supernatural* as of this writing, in "Season 7, Time for a Wedding!" brings her obsession with Sam back in full force. Becky decides that having Sam accompany her to her high school reunion will prove her worth to her former bullies. She is still portrayed as delusional to the point of idiocy, again convincing herself that Sam "already love[s her] deep down" to justify her methods of coercing him to be her date. In a turn for the sinister, Becky forces Sam into abandoning Dean and marrying her by drugging him with a magical roofie, and when the spell fails, she ties him to a bed. Whereas other female characters have come between the Winchesters through their genuine relationships with one of the brothers, Becky is unable to generate the kind of heterosexual desire in the heroes that female characters are supposed to be able to do. Sam tries to convince her to release him with the promise that she could find love without the need for coercion, and Becky sadly says, "That's sweet, but I'm not so sure." She ends her three-episode recurring arc in complete humiliation, the Winchesters' warning to stay away from them ushering her out.

Supernatural also uses the character Metatron to portray fanfic writers as monsters. Though he is an angel and shares many of the attitudes characteristic of the Apocalyptic faction described earlier in this essay, Metatron is symbolically aligned with fans like Becky. They both have multiple identities, one name corresponding to their "real" lives and one to their fannish lives. Also like Becky, Metatron is willfully deluded about the shape of reality and his place in it. He is portrayed as a "petty, unliked, unloved angel" who has an overinflated opinion of his natural charisma, abilities as a writer, and his own importance in the world ("Do You Believe in Miracles?" 9.23). He tries literally to rewrite *Supernatural*'s reality from within to make himself the hero and the Winchesters the monsters according to his own symbolic order. Just as Becky is introduced writing fanfic at her computer and speaking of the Winchesters as if they were characters she has control over, the episode that features Metatron most prominently, "Meta Fiction" (9.18), situates him at a typewriter, writing what he calls the "script" for his preferred narrative. A megalomaniac who understands that "[w]hen you create stories, you become gods of tiny, intricate dimensions unto themselves" ("The Great Escapist," 8.21), Metatron poses a threat to the Winchesters and the narrative integrity of *Supernatural* that is exponentially larger than Becky manages through incest erotica. Enabled by inhuman power as an angel that increases his threat, Metatron's temporary imposition of his monstrous interpretation of the show is accompanied by a "Metatron" title sequence to replace the usual one. The representation of fanfic texts through Metatron's failed attempt to usurp the protagonist role portrays them as a blighted version of the proper narrative of *Supernatural*.

If Becky's arc had not been sufficiently explicit, Metatron's narrative in Season 9 is filled with moments designed to directly condemn fans as monsters. Anomalously breaking the fourth wall to speak directly to the audience in the pointedly titled "Meta Fiction," Metatron looks up from his typewriter to muse, "What makes a story work? Is it the plot, the characters, the text? The subtext? And what gives a story meaning? Is it the writer? Or you? Tonight, I thought I would tell you a little story and let you decide." As is revealed later in the episode, this speech takes place as he is gloating to Castiel that he and the Winchesters are at Metatron's mercy and will be forced to play the doomed villains in Metatron's twisted narrative. In usurping the identity of creator while overturning the essential symbolic order of the show, Metatron engages in an antagonism that is symbolically aligned with his fannish author identity and transmuted by the threat to binary sex-gender into monstrosity. As Metatron is an avatar of the fan author, his ultimate disarmament and defeat serves as a reminder to the fan authors in the audience that the canon text will always trump fans' interpretations and alternate narratives. Less subtly, the angels who side with Metatron are referred to as his fans. While Dean is speaking to one such "fan" in "King of the Damned" (9.21), he breaks the fourth wall to say to the audience, "Just because you're hot for [a character], just because you know everything about them, doesn't mean that you actually know them." Sam chimes in to add that the objects of fans' adoration do not "even know [they] exist," let alone care.

Supernatural never has the Winchesters literally kill their fans, but the symbolic destruction of a particular fannish identity through their disdain for and ridicule of the avatars of fans accomplishes the same goal. Becky exits the show in complete disgrace, a symbolic staking as effective in destroying her as an onscreen death; Metatron turns out to be too little of a threat to bother killing and ends up in prison to serve later plot functions, his role as fan avatar concluded. His monstrosity is discursively ended not by his redemption or death, but by the narrative conclusion that the antagonism of bad fans is simply not worth worrying over. This revision of the position articulated against Becky, perhaps because of the backlash against the conclusion of her arc, suggests the show has come to accept and ignore the existence of such fans. Metatron's end puts such fans beyond the border between humanity and monstrosity, but also discursively denies any danger of such fans successfully upending the symbolic order that defines the narrative reality of *Supernatural* itself. Thus, *Supernatural* symbolically stakes its metatextual monsters.

Coda

Supernatural is, as of this writing (2018), in its 15th season. Angels and demons are still prominent species on the show, still subject to the same discourses of monstrosity, though changing societal norms around trans identities have precluded the kind of overt transphobia seen in Raphael's arc. Fans made a significant appearance onscreen in the 200th episode, "Fan Fiction" (10.05), in which, perhaps after negative feedback about previous fan representations, the show struck a more conciliatory tone. As with the end of Metatron's arc, "Fan Fiction" portrays alternate fan interpretations, including the celebration of the Winchesters' femininity and queer subtext, as an acceptable but contained alternate narrative. The fans putting on an original "Supernatural" musical can have their version of the story, and Sam and Dean will even find some enjoyment in watching it, but *Supernatural* does not incorporate or adopt any of their attitudes or interpretations. When the episode ends, the fans' version of the story is over and the "real" narrative goes on, with the Winchesters still embodying a narrow, heteropatriarchal heroic masculinity; the queer subtext between Dean and Castiel remains unacknowledged and unconsummated. Monsters still make gender trouble.

Notes

1. Linda Tran exits because her son would no longer be part of the narrative, literally announcing that she will wait for Kevin to become a vengeful ghost and then let him kill her. Though Jody Mills's femininity is not problematized by her (ultimately fruitless) romantic pursuit of Bobby, that is because her femininity is anchored in her de-sexualized role as a mother, first to her dead child, then to the Winchesters, and then to Alex and the other "wayward sisters."

Works Cited

Beliveau, Rolf, and Laura Bolf-Beliveau. "'A Shot on the Devil': Female Hunters and the Identification of Evil in *Supernatural*." *Supernatural, Humanity, and the Soul: On the Highway to Hell and Back*, edited by Susan A. George and Regina M. Hansen, Palgrave Macmillan, 2014, pp. 111–123.

Butler, Judith. *Gender Trouble: Feminism and the Subversion of Identity*. Routledge, 1990.

_____. "Imitation and Gender Insubordination." *The Lesbian and Gay Studies Reader*, edited by Henry Abelove, Michèle Aina Barale, and David M. Halperin, Routledge, 1991, pp. 307–320.

_____. "Bodies That Matter." *Feminist Theory and the Body: A Reader*, edited by Janet Price and Margrit Shildrick, Routledge, 1993, pp. 234–245.

Coker, Cait, and Candace Benefiel. "The Hunter Hunted: The Portrayal of the Fan as Predator in *Supernatural*." *Supernatural, Humanity, and the Soul: On the Highway to Hell and Back*, edited by Susan A. George and Regina M. Hansen, Palgrave Macmillan, 2014, pp. 97–110.

Costello, Victor, and Barbara Moore. "Cultural Outlaws: An Examination of Audience Activity and Online Television Fandom." *Television & New Media*, vol. 8, no. 2, 2007, pp. 124–143.

Creed, Barbara. *The Monstrous Feminine: Film, Feminism, Psychoanalysis*. Routledge, 1993.

Diamond, Michael Jay. "Masculinity Unraveled: The Roots of Male Gender Identity and the Shifting of Male Ego Ideals Throughout Life." *Journal of the American Psychoanalytic Association*, vol. 54, no. 4, 2006, pp. 1099–1130.

Felschow, Laura E. "'Hey, Check It Out, There's Actually Fans'": (Dis)empowerment and (Mis)representation of Cult Fandom in *Supernatural*." *Transformative Works and Cultures*, no. 4, 2010, http://dx.doi.org/10.3983/twc.2010.0134. Accessed 8 March 2015.

Fife Donaldson, Lucy. "Normality Is Threatened by the Monster: Robin Wood, Romero and Zombies." *CineAction*, no. 84, 2011, pp. 24–31.

Hekman, Susan. "Material Bodies." *Body and Flesh: A Philosophical Reader*, edited by D. Welton, Blackwell Publishers Inc., 1998, pp. 61–70.

Ingebretsen, Edward J. "Staking the Monster: A Politics of Remonstrance." *Religion and American Culture*, vol. 8, no. 1, 1998, pp. 91–116.

Johnson, Derek. "Fan-tagonism: Factions, Insinuations and Constitutive Hegemonies of Fandom." *Fandom: Identities and Communities in a Mediated World*, edited by Jonathan Gray, Cornel Sandvoss, and C. Lee Harrington, New York UP, 2007, pp. 285–300.

Krelko, Rebecca Elizabeth. "Homophobia, Humor and Male Rape: *Family Guy*'s Role in the Modern Construction of Hegemonic Masculinity." Honors thesis, Ohio University, 2013.

Nurka, Camille. "Feminine Shame/Masculine Disgrace: A Literary Excursion Through Gender and Embodied Emotion." *Cultural Studies Review*, vol. 18, no. 3, 2012, pp. 310–333.

Tharp, Julie. "The Transvestite as Monster: Gender Horror in *The Silence of the Lambs* and *Psycho*." *Journal of Film and Popular Television*, vol. 19, no. 3, 1991, pp. 106–114.

"Driver picks the music"

Tracing Supernatural's Long Road Trip to Discovering Fan Identity

Laurena Aker

Navigating the relationship between fans and creators of a popular television show is one of the most mystifying yet critical aspects of modern media production. Fans' loyalty and fervent involvement can make the difference between a show's long-term success and short run cancellation. The paradox faced by showrunners is how to encourage fans' engagement, and assimilate their input, without compromising the show's artistic integrity. Fans' opinions are as varied as the people who comprise the fandom, often advocating diametrically opposite creative directions with equal zeal.

As American television's longest consecutively running science fiction series (Ollis), *Supernatural* has had time to explore the dynamics of the fan/producer relationship. The SPNFamily (*Supernatural's* fandom identity) kept the show on the air for 15 years through fragile start-up uncertainties, a tumultuous writers' strike, a network buyout and several executive team turnovers. Whereas shorter-term shows dare not risk alienating their audiences by questioning fan behavior through meta commentary (or can't spare the screen time to even address the topic), *Supernatural's* intrepid spirit and loyal fanbase have emboldened its writers to courageously examine the nature of participatory fandoms. Tracing *Supernatural's* portrayal of popular culture fans, their behaviors and their role in the creative process reveals distinct strategies and evolving stages in the show's view of itself, its relationship with its fans and the creative tension they exert on the show. Adapting the lessons *Supernatural* has learned in its journey may help lead the entertainment industry to a truer understanding and partnership with loyal fans.

"I'm a big fan": Fan Depictions in Supernatural's *Recurring Characters*

Exploring fans' attachment to their passions was perhaps written into *Supernatural*'s genetic signature. Only 18 minutes into the first episode, Dean, the elder of the monster hunting duo of Sam and Dean Winchester, defends his right to be an avid rock and roll fan with an emphatic declaration to his brother, "Driver picks the music, shotgun shuts his cakehole!" ("Pilot," 1.01), Since that initial introduction to Dean's priorities, fandoms were injected into most lead characters' profiles. As the story's most developed personalities, fandom passions are typically only one facet of their multi-dimensional lives; thus, their fan portrayals are genuinely relatable.

Dean most often embodies the fan experience. Besides his dedication to classic rock, Dean's mastery of pop culture movies enriches the series with a wealth of fan references and creative scenarios. For example, his love of Westerns establishes the comical context of "Frontierland" (6.18) and "Tombstone" (13.06). In both instances, Dean dons the period costumes of his heroes (stopping short of calling it cosplay) and enthusiastically recites an encyclopedic knowledge of their lives. His fanboy dedication elicits some pushback from his brother, in "Frontierland":

SAM: You're obsessed with all that Wild West stuff.
DEAN: No, I'm not.
SAM: You have a fetish!
DEAN: Shut up. I like old movies.
SAM: You can recite every Clint Eastwood movie ever made, line for line!

Sam finally acquiesces and, acknowledging the stress-reducing attributes of costumed pretense, joins his brother in a simulated medieval battle while Dean reenacts memorized excerpts from *Braveheart* (1995) ("LARP and the Real Girl," 8.11).

As much as Dean endorses and enjoys the light-hearted side of fandoms, he also suffers from one of its afflictions: star-struck anxiety. Dean's usual glib eloquence repeatedly devolves into stuttering awkwardness when he recognizes his celebrity idols ("Hollywood Babylon," 2.18; "Changing Channels," 5.08; "Rock and a Hard Place," 9.08; and "Beyond the Mat," 11.15). Of course, Sam teases his brother about it:

DEAN: Dude. Dude! Gunnar freakin' Lawless!
SAM: Groupie much?
DEAN: Shut up. Should I go say hi? I should go say hi. I'm gonna go say hi. Hi, s-sir. I, uh, saw you ... saw you standing over here and told my brother that I ... I should come over and say hi ... so I came over and, uh.... Hi. ... I...I got to tell you. I ... worshipped you, growing up ["Beyond the Mat"].

Dean inherited many of his fan passions from his father ("Dream a Little Dream of Me," 3.10), authentically illustrating the origin of many fan interests, and affirming fandom activities as quality family time. Dean fondly remembers "Dad's favorite" wrestler, wrestling matches as "one of the few times I ever saw him actually happy," and their wrestling outings as "one of the nicest things dad ever did for us." Similarly, Sam associates the family's wrestling diversions with his "first crush." His unconvincing denial that he was not "one of those guys that had [his idol's] poster above his bed" betrays his flustered embarrassment over the common fan practice of plastering bedrooms with celebrities' pictures ("Beyond the Mat").

Sam and Dean share other childhood fandoms as well. When the brothers are transported into a cartoon world in "Scoobynatural" (13.16), they both admit to watching *Scooby Doo, Where Are You!* (1969–70) as children. Dean then exemplifies fans' impulse to defend a pop culture icon's legacy:

SAM: We're in *Scooby-Doo!*
DEAN: […] This is like a dream come true.
SAM: Your dream is to hang out with the Scooby Gang?
DEAN: These guys, they're our friggin' role models! […] It doesn't matter if we die. Scooby-Doo could die! And that's not happening, not on my watch. I'd take a bullet for that dog!

Reluctantly, Sam also confesses a childhood interest in magic ("Criss Angel is a Douchebag," 4.12), a life-long fascination with serial killers (a "freaky fetish" according to Dean in "Thin Lizzie," 11.05), and an admiration of Mahatma Gandhi ("Fallen Idols," 5.05). Although none of these are technically fandoms for Sam, they give Dean ammunition with which he can tease his brother: "You couldn't have been a fan of someone cool? Really? Gandhi? … Let me get this straight. Your ultimate hero was not only a short man in diapers but he was also a fruitarian? That is good. Even for you, that is good" ("Fallen Idols").

Teasing, or fan shaming, accompanies virtually every lead character's exhibition of fan behavior in *Supernatural*. Even the brothers' surrogate father, Bobby Singer, isn't spared when he admits to being a Tori Spelling fan ("You Can't Handle the Truth," 6.06). Quick retorts between the brothers are common, but ironically Dean is the most vocal critic of all. During the case that introduces Dean to live action role playing (LARPing), an investigator mocks a LARPer, saying, "He lived alone, which was a real shocker, considering his place is full of toys" (i.e., collectibles). Dean later adds "And I thought *we* needed to get out more" ("LARP and the Real Girl"). Although it may seem hypocritical that a fan would espouse such harsh criticism of other fans, Lynn Zubernis and Kathy Larsen observe that "fandom has internalized a significant degree of shame about being a fan" (*Fandom at the Crossroads* 57). This partially explains why Dean epitomizes "a man who has fannish tendencies but denies them" (Coker and Benefiel, "The Hunter Hunted" 97). Proud of his virile image, Dean struggles to reconcile his "no chick-flick" ("Pilot") masculinity with his deeply rooted fanboy distractions. Insecure in his fan identity, he delivers the expected derision of fandom practices even as he himself participates in them. Dean's admission to one of his movie star idols summarizes his, and often fans', conflicted feelings about fan identity: "I know it's … really uncool to say this, but I—I'm a big fan" ("Hollywood Babylon"). Having lead characters alternate between subversion and support of fandom behavior is an effective, multilayered strategy that enables *Supernatural* to simultaneously explore both sides of the fandom debate and for its producers to empathetically acknowledge the shame fans often feel and the cynicism they face, while slyly repeating that criticism themselves.

Even though Sam never wins the argument that his fan interests are "cool" and fan shaming persists in the show, *Supernatural's* duality convincingly presents pop culture knowledge as a social advantage. As the James Dean persona of the duo, Dean legitimizes fandom's allure, while the brothers' best friend, the angel Castiel, is routinely chastised for not understanding pop culture references. Even when Castiel participates in the common fan custom of "knee deep binge watching" marathons ("Thin Lizzie"), he reinforces his unworldly awkwardness by confessing to not understanding the practice. The angel Metatron personifies the other extreme, having read a "metric ton of books" ("Don't Call Me Shurley," 11.20). Finally reaching his limit of frustration with Castiel's pop culture ignorance, Metatron uses the fandom lexicon to reverse Castiel's naiveté: "Would it have killed you to pick up a book, watch a movie? Here. I know it's a bit of a retcon, but it's gonna make this whole conversation a lot easier." Then, mind-melding with Castiel, he concludes, "I just gave you every book, movie, and TV show I have consumed in the last couple of millennia" ("Meta Fiction," 9.18).

Supernatural's most obvious proponent of the fan experience is Charlie Bradbury. Introduced in Season 7 ("The Girl with the Dungeons and Dragons Tattoo," 7.20), Charlie differs from lead characters in that being a fantasy and science fiction fan is a primary component of her identity. She is an expert gamer and accomplished information technology professional, but instead of being a lonely, awkward nerd who lives in her parents' basement, Charlie is a spunky, smart, queer hero. In a perfect match-up of character and actress, *Supernatural* writer Robbie Thompson specifically envisioned internet maven Felicia Day for the role (Aker). The strategy of featuring a female fandom icon was a huge success. Charlie became one of the series' most beloved characters, affectionately showcasing fans' attributes. Like Dean, Charlie's parent sparked her fan passions (her mother's bedside reading of *The Hobbit* [1937]). Charlie's workspace flaunts her love of *Star Wars* and *Harry Potter*, she unapologetically explains fan convention attendance with "Girl's gotta get her collectibles," she unabashedly immerses herself in her interests, and she uses fandom terminology to connect fantasy and reality: "I'm a wee bit obsessive. If 'wee bit' means completely. I also found this series of books, by a Carver Edlund? Did those books really happen? Wow. That is some meta madness" ("Pac Man Fever," 8.20).With her binge into the Edlund book series (discussed later), Charlie transitions from being the perfect genre fan to *Supernatural* fans' de facto representative within the show—she and fans share the same knowledge of the brothers' lives, and she is living every fan's dream of interacting with Sam and Dean. Charlie makes everyone comfortable with their fan identity, even Dean, because, according to Thompson, Charlie is "able to access the secret geeky part of Dean" (Richards). Charlie is integral to seven episodes until her brutal murder in Season 10 ("Dark Dynasty," 10.21), a decision that was universally unpopular with fans and a contributing factor to the episode registering the lowest ratings the series had experienced to that date (Baron; "*Supernatural* Ratings, All Seasons by Episode"). Producers noted fans' outcry, and Charlie's alternate universe counterpart (also played by Felicia Day) returned in Season 13.

Throughout the series, *Supernatural*'s lead and recurring characters provide a steadfast framework within which fan identity is explored. While these characters aren't always supportive of fan culture, they successfully supplant both stereotypical caricatures and denial of fans' existence with informed, reasonably accurate fan portraits. *Supernatural*'s short term and non-recurring characters further explore the fan/producer relationship. Their depictions of fan passions start out humorously but become increasingly negative over time.

"Guilty pleasure": The Daring Curiosity of the Early Years

As early as Season 2, *Supernatural* supplements its lead characters' casual inclusion of fan behaviors with characters and plots that are entirely defined by fandom concepts. In the initial stage of this focus on producers' and consumers' roles, commentary is carefully balanced, remarking as much about the entertainment industry, specifically the horror genre, as about the fans who support it. Criticisms are softened within a context of humor, parody or fantasy.

"Hollywood Babylon" is *Supernatural*'s first foray into studying film and television production for fans' consumption. In this early episode,

Dean becomes predictably (and humorously) engrossed in his cover as a studio production assistant for a horror movie. The movie's stereotypical horror scenarios, poor quality production, overly dramatic cast and trite executive production squabbles parody the horror genre, with which *Supernatural* identifies. The episode ends with Dean having a satisfying tryst with the star actress before the brothers walk "into the sunset," a painted backdrop that is rolled away as the camera pans out. The entire storyline spoofs the entertainment industry but rewards Dean's fannishness by giving him ultimate access to his idol. Dean's detailed genre knowledge is critical to solving the case, additionally affirming the value of fans' passions. Overall, fans come out looking better than moviemakers.

The first time a fan is at the center of a *Supernatural* plot is in the episode "Monster Movie" (4.05), which features a shapeshifter who transforms into classic horror films' powerful monsters. Realizing that movies have taken over the delusional fan's life, the story's characters repeatedly remind each other (and fans) of the difference between fantasy and reality, saying "*X-Files* is a TV show. This is real," "Life ain't a movie!" and "You can't make [movies] real!" The shifter's reply offers one theoretical explanation of fans' motives: "Life is small, meager, messy. The movies are grand, simple, elegant. I have chosen elegance." Ultimately, the dissociative monster drops all pretense. Offering the show's first profile of an extreme fan's psyche, the fan relates that his childhood was brutally abusive, and that he felt powerless and alienated from society. In movies, he saw characters that were "strong," "feared" and "beautiful" so he assumed their identities to become "Commanding. Terrifying."

In contrast to "Hollywood Babylon," "Monster Movie" honors old horror movies but paints a disturbing portrait of a fan as an ostracized individual who is "lonely," feels "different," and blurs the boundaries between reality and fantasy. The affront is softened by making the fan a supernatural creature, and fandom into a desperately needed tool to cope with childhood trauma (a strategy that equally applies to Dean's retreat into pop culture, "Mint Condition," 14.04). Further, although the fan is a "monster," viewers are distracted from the insulting undertones by the episode's light-hearted motif of black and white filming, plus title card, credits, music and even an "intermission" placard that are reminiscent of classic movies. Thus, while the story depicts an unflattering fan stereotype, every attempt is made to place the message in the context of fiction versus reality.

"Changing Channels" (5.08) is another courageous departure from the show's normal format. In a daring extrapolation of the entertainment industry, the brothers are transported to "TV-land" and forced to play roles in enormously exaggerated television shows. Recognizing their surroundings, Dean confesses his "guilty pleasure" of being "a fan" of the inane soap opera in which they are trapped. Like "Hollywood Babylon," "Changing Channels" parodies studios' nonsensical programming, but it also mildly and humorously parodies the fans who loyally watch manufactured dramas, striking the perfect balance of criticizing the entertainment industry's absurdity without over-playing vapid fan stereotypes.

Eric Kripke, the show's creator and showrunner at the time, fondly recalled intentionally targeting "other TV genres we [wanted to] have fun with. We knew we wanted to parody *CSI* and *Grey's Anatomy*, because they were our timeslot competition" (Knight, *Season 5* 49). The *Grey's Anatomy* parody section has special resonance for *Supernatural* fans. While Dean's favorite character, "Dr. Sexy MD," clearly invokes Patrick Dempsey's character, nicknamed "McDreamy," fans of both shows will recognize the more significant Easter egg: when Sam is puzzled as to why a medical show has a ghost on it, the viewers in on the joke recall that Denny Duquette appeared in several *Grey's Anatomy* episodes as a ghostly presence. Duquette was played by Jeffrey Dean Morgan, who also plays the Winchester patriarch on *Supernatural*. This intertextual moment functions complexly, not merely to allow fans to delight in their inside knowledge but also to provide subtle metatextual implications as to why Dean is so fond of this show. The extra-diegetic echoes comment on how one's emotional engagement with a particular show can be deepened and complicated by echoes of other shows. *Supernatural*'s gamble paid off, and the episode remains a fan favorite.

Season 6 contains *Supernatural*'s boldest, funniest meta exploration of shows and their fans. In "The French Mistake" (6.15), Sam and Dean are again transported to a parallel universe, arriving on the set of a TV show named *Supernatural*. Making itself the object of the parody, the alternate reality show shares the same storyline, cast and production teams as the real show; while relationships, personal lives and interactions with "*Supernatural* fans" are all greatly exaggerated. Symbolically and ironically, the creative team is eventually killed by their own mythology. Confirming that the episode was specifically intended to comment on dynamics within the entertainment industry, Jared Padalecki ("Sam") told *Variety*, it was a "really cool way to make fun of ourselves [...] and the industry." He went on to say, "So many people take themselves too seriously in this business, and that was a nice way to bring ourselves back down to earth" (Prudom).

Three of the four episodes in this first stage of conspicuously experimenting with fan identities and the boundaries and legitimacy of the entertainment industry were written by Ben Edlund, a brilliant humorist. Edlund's finesse helped *Supernatural* deftly satirize both producers and consumers. Even though Edlund remained with *Supernatural* through

Season 8, the next phase of the series' exploration of fans and their passions is much more bluntly critical.

"You're the crazy ones": Pushing Back on Superfans

Season 5's "Fallen Idols" is *Supernatural's* first uncompromising, harsh commentary on fans' devotion. The story features a demigod who transforms into popular or historical idols, and then consumes the idols' most devout fans. Read through a meta lens, a creator (the god) takes pleasure in killing superfans (the most devout fans), who are consumed by their obsessions:

> SAM: Professor Hill was a Civil War nut. He dug Lincoln.
> DEAN: Cal must've been a James Dean freak. He spent 17 years of his life tracking down the guy's car. So you're saying that we've got two super-famous, super-pissed-off ghosts killing their super-fans?

In this conversation, the brothers (who have mistaken the god for ghosts) refer to the deceased superfans as a "nut" and a "freak." When Sam, who plays the fan in this episode, finds an obscure clue that helps them solve the case, Dean calls him a "geek." While this is no worse than the brothers' razzing in other episodes, all of the fans depicted in this episode are scorned. The fan who spent years of his adult life looking for James Dean's car is duped by a fake. Even fans who turned their passions into professions are mocked, such as the professor who taught history, and the curator who preserved public figures in a wax museum. Valuing authenticity, he adorned his collection with genuine memorabilia, boasting, "there isn't another place like us, not anywhere." He personally was a fan of "The Fonz" (*Happy Days*, 1974–84), and proudly wore Fonzie's leather jacket, "seasons two through four." Rather than being impressed, the brothers are condescending, with Sam commenting, "W–wow. Yeah, that's—that's really cool-ish." The god's final form is Paris Hilton, who plays herself. Her fans are two stereotypical, mindless teen girls. Paris finally voices criticism of people who idolize celebrities: "You people. You're the crazy ones. You used to worship gods. But this? This is what passes for idolatry? Celebrities? What have they got besides small dogs and spray tans? You people used to have old-time religion. Now you have *Us Weekly*."

Paris Hilton's self-deprecating speech indicts herself and other celebrities as shallow and unworthy of fans' devotion. This continues *Supernatural's* tradition of criticizing the entertainment industry's producers as well as its consumers. Further, her role as the carnivorous god could be interpreted as an implicit criticism of Hollywood's insatiable appetite for consuming the money, time and attention of consumers without respecting them in return. If this is indeed the moral of the story, its punch line delivery isn't as effective as some of *Supernatural*'s other parodies in mitigating criticisms of fans (both inside and outside the entertainment context). "Fallen Idols" deserves credit as having a preponderance of pop culture references, but in sharp contrast to "Hollywood Babylon," fans (especially superfans) are served up as the main course.

Supernatural's ridicule of teenage girls continues in "Live Free or Twihard" (6.05), a crossover commentary about vampire lore. Aired in 2010, the episode reiterated *Supernatural*'s pop culture awareness by mocking the global craze of *Twilight,* an apropos vogue that tempted *Supernatural*'s showrunner Sera Gamble: "we poked good-natured fun at the [vampire] genre as a whole but *Twilight* was definitely a larger target because it's wildly popular and ripe for parody" (Knight, *Season 6* 34). Unfortunately, the parody includes a disparaging depiction of *Twilight*'s "Twihards" (young *Twilight* fans, Kubiesa 117) by the episode's men. Kristen's (the missing girl, whose name clearly echoes that of *Twilight* star Kristen Stewart) dad laments, "girls are hard," Dean calls the girls "emo chicks," and the episode's vampire, Boris, refers to his naïve victims as "horny" and "stupid little brats."

Supernatural's embittered depiction of fans largely subsides until "Thin Lizzie." This episode has Dean theorize that an assailant is "some psycho fan who's seen too many slasher flicks" and "some crazed fan." When Sam objects to the plausibility of Dean's rationale, Dean delivers a backhanded insult to fans, saying the murderer must have been "actually competent." As in "Fallen Idols," superfans are specifically targeted. When Dean notes a Lizzie Borden collection in the home of a fan who is "obsessed but harmless," superfans and collectors are portrayed as law breakers and stalkers:

> DEAN: Heh. Boy, you are a Lizzie Borden.... I don't think fan covers it.
> LEN FLETCHER [the fan]: That's superfan. And curator. [...] I'm not exactly allowed at the inn anymore. There's a minor restraining order. And there's a gag order not to talk about the restraining order.

This "superfan curator" goes to conventions, leads live chats, hosts a blog and sells his collection on eBay, all common fan activities. He additionally has a phobia of being touched, a stereotypical fan characteristic. While he is derided the entire episode, he ends up being a hero in the story, a tactic *Supernatural* occasionally uses to soften the blow, as an "all in good fun" wink to its fans.

Is his redemption enough to assuage the slander that he and by representation, superfans, endure throughout the episode? There are certainly very real examples of psychotic superfans stalking and harming celebrities, so his depiction is not an entirely fictitious exaggeration. *Supernatural's* lead actors have themselves admitted to troubling encounters with fans ("Jensen Ackles," @Tonniann_Rose), a reality that would likely be known to the show's writers. Still, rather than respect and impartially investigate his activities, the stalker/hero is the object of stereotypical superfan ridicule. Whether the writers' parting words on the topic reflect their real view of superfans or are a diplomatic capitulation is debatable, but this isn't the only time this conflicted presentation of superfans appears in the series (see the discussion of "The Monster at the End of This Book," 4.18, later in this essay).

Supernatural's most negative depiction of fandom thus far is in "Rock Never Dies" (12.07). If Season 2's "Hollywood Babylon" is a humorous, tactful parody of the entertainment industry and its fans, "Rock Never Dies" is an explicit, cynical redux (Dean even references "Hollywood Babylon" by mentioning his and Sam's prior trip to Los Angeles). Reimagining Dean's intimate access to his idol ten years earlier, a superfan is granted wild sexual encounters with a disillusioned, aging rock star, Vince Vincente, who has been possessed by Lucifer. The fan, Roseleen Greenfield, recounts how she has loved the rock star since she was "a normal kid" at 16, enduring "younger girls'" mockery for her fandom tattoos (echoing teen girls' defamation). Avowing "I never stopped loving you. And I never will," she pulls out her tooth to prove her devotion, then, akin to a real Slayer fan's actions ("Slayer"), she carves Vince's name into her chest until "there'll be no fixing those scars." Roseleen defends the star's self-mutilation requests, saying she was trying to make him "happy," then demands to be allowed to attend his show.

Obviously, this is an extreme case, yet the senseless devotion of the band's entire fandom is repeatedly referenced. Escalating fan criticisms in prior episodes, Lucifer (in the form of the rock idol) narrates his version of the "Fallen Idols" goddess Leshii's condemnation of pop culture infatuation: "the music [...] was just an excuse to worship, to adore. See, humans have always been desperate to put someone or something above them [...] It takes a Kim Kardashian, a whatever Justin Bieber is. A me. They're enjoying the ride."

He also specifically spurns superfans:

> VINCE: I've had my fill of the diehards. They already love me. Religion, celebrity, Twitter—it's all the same rules. If you're not gaining followers, you're losing followers. I want a different crowd tonight. New fans.
> MANAGER: Look, getting a new audience is great for social media visibility, which is great for overall buzz, but they're fickle. They don't spend any money on music. They have no loyalty [...]
> VINCE: I don't care. I want fresh blood.

Repeating the paradigm of concurrently satirizing consumer and producer, the "star-making" industry is equally ridiculed. The rock star's manager is a judgmental caricature obsessed with social media who brags, "I'm in P.R. I've worked for sexists, racists, even politicians. My job is making saints out of devils." The star's music producer, Russell Lemons, "started daily meditation, yoga, green juice. Helps to keep the ego and the anger in check." Dean also repeatedly besmirches Los Angeles, saying it is inhabited by "image-obsessed narcissists." *Supernatural*'s producers then have the superstar express a poignant meta-criticism of the show and its supporters:

> This is all meaningless. Heaven, Hell, this world. If it ever meant anything, that moment is past. Nothing down here but a bunch of hopeless distraction addicts, so filled with emptiness, so desperate to fill up the void, they don't mind being served another stale rerun of a rerun of a rerun. You know what my plan is? I don't have one. I'm just gonna keep on smashing Daddy's already broken toys and make you watch.

Within the episode's story, this is Lucifer spewing his perverted manifesto of wanton destruction and the uselessness of God's, i.e., "Daddy's," creations. Taken as such, his view isn't shocking. The tirade's meta-references to *Supernatural*, however, open up far more troubling interpretations. The phrases "Heaven, Hell, this world" and especially "rerun of a rerun of a rerun" refer to the context of *Supernatural*'s universe, so while the comment doesn't literally mention *Supernatural* fans, it is hard not to hear that implied meaning. The closing phrase, "I'm just gonna keep on smashing Daddy's already broken toys and make you *watch*" (emphasis added), has more relevance to the television show than to Lucifer's mindset. "Daddy" in the show's context is Eric Kripke, and his "toys" are the characters of the show or the show itself. So the sub-text reading is that the show's stories are all meaningless now, if they ever meant anything at all; *Supernatural* fans are a "bunch of hopeless distraction addicts" who never tire of the show's reruns (which is fairly close to the truth); and its writers don't have a plan for the show but are just going to "break" the show while fans mindlessly watch.

The slam is delivered by guest star Rick Springfield, who portrays Lucifer in three episodes of *Supernatural*'s twelfth season. As with Felicia Day, Springfield's casting was as much about the actor as the role. Did *Supernatural*'s writers use a musician and actor whose career spans 45 years to voice their own concerns about *Supernatural*'s multi-decade relevance? Are they saying they believe the show has already continued well past its prime?

Perhaps the point is that only Lucifer, and the "Idols'" goddess Leshii and "Twihards'" vampire Boris, could have such bleak opinions, thus identifying negative views as "monstrous." That interpretation doesn't mitigate Dean and Sam's belittlement of fans in these unsettling episodes, though. Those prior episodes' plots are also more fantastical and don't specifically impugn the *Supernatural* family, so they could be defended as cautionary tales, or views over the fence at other fandoms. "Rock Never Dies" innuendoes go one step further to be specific to *Supernatural* itself and its fandom. They aren't masked by humor or set in an alternate reality, nor are there redeeming counterpoints that walk them back from the brink. It is puzzling to see a show that has been so successful and owes so much to its fandom become so cynical, accentuating extremes and including derogatory messages that devalue itself and fans'—any fans'—intelligence and worth. The optimistic view would be that the translation from fantasy to reality was not intended. After all, if the writers wanted to overtly comment on *Supernatural* or its fans, their messages could have been more openly delivered within their previously established *Supernatural*-meta myth arc.

"The 'Supernatural' books are all I got": Meta Commentary on Supernatural and Its Fans

By Season 4, *Supernatural*'s plotline dared to place Sam and Dean in a biblical Apocalyptic battle between Heaven and Hell, with God himself as a spectator. Kripke recalled his mindset about introducing God to the plotline: "Let's go for it." He liked "the recklessness of it," daring the writers to "be as bold and risky as we can, and if we fall flat on our face, then so be it [...] no one can accuse us of playing it safe" (Knight, *Season 5* 10).

With these stakes, the show's "go for broke" attitude launched a run of meta-episodes that explore the show's relationship with its fans within the context of its own story. This meta trajectory begins with "The Monster at the End of This Book" when the brothers discover a series of books that document every detail of their lives. The books were written by Chuck Shurley, a prophet who is canonically confirmed in Season 11 to be God (the ultimate universe creator), under the penname Carver Edlund, a splice of two *Supernatural* producers' surnames. The book series has the meta title of "Supernatural," content that exactly parallels the television series, and a loyal fanbase that imitates the TV show's real fans. The books are referenced in at least 11 episodes in seasons 4 through 11, and then are introduced as the entire premise of Season 15.

In a 2014 *Variety* interview, Eric Kripke admitted introducing books that mirrored the show "would give us an opportunity to really poke fun at what we're doing in *Supernatural*, and that was really fun for me [...] it was our first serious meta episode" (Prudom). It was a bold experiment that allowed the writers to express opinions about themselves and the show's fandom simply by writing their editorials within the context of the books.

The high-risk venture yielded some of the best, and the worst, episodes of the series.

Consistent with the show's early fandom representations, initially both writers and fans are satirized, with exaggerations used to shroud critique. Chuck (the writers' avatar) is a paranoid, alcoholic recluse. The books' publisher (identified in an interview by series writer Sera Gamble as "Sera Siege," itself a name combining Gamble's with that of another *Supernatural* writer, Julie Siege) is the quintessential obsessed fan, who proudly reveals the show's iconic tattoo on her backside as evidence of her dedication, and refuses to cooperate until the brothers convince her (by exposing their own tattoos and demonstrating equal mastery of "their" lives' details) that they are also superfans. Further testing fans' sense of humor, the brothers lambaste a Wincest (romantic coupling of the brothers) fan fiction archive.

The exposé episode shocked many fans, who realized that not only were their activities known to the show's producers, but they were fair game for being broadcast and judged. Fans no longer had an amorphous secret society, invisible in their consumption and interpretation of the show. Laura Felschow observed of the writers pulling back the curtain on themselves and fans, "while Kripke and company may be laughing at themselves, they do so from the comfort of the writers' room, a serious position of power." She went on to observe that the writers' criticisms of themselves did not completely ameliorate slights to fans because, "jokes made at the writers' and fans' expense have unequal costs." Felschow concluded, "'The Monster at the End of This Book' can be seen as a reminder to *Supernatural* fandom, delivered with a smile, of who exactly is in charge."

The meta-parallel between the show and its fandom is taken further when "Supernatural" superfan Becky Rosen is introduced in "Sympathy for the Devil" (5.01). As a Wincest writer and Carver Edlund's "number one fan," Becky resumes the "Monster Movie" fantasy versus reality debate:

> **BECKY:** Look, Mr. Edlund. Yes, I'm a fan, but I really don't appreciate being mocked. I know that "Supernatural"'s just a book, okay? I know the difference between fantasy and reality.
> **CHUCK:** Becky, it's all real.
> **BECKY:** I knew it!!

Despite professing to have a firm grasp on reality, Becky becomes the archetype of a stalker fan. In her second appearance ("The Real Ghostbusters," 5.09), Becky tricks the brothers into attending her "Supernatural" fan convention by faking an emergency. Becky's actions spark embarrassed apologies from Chuck and frustrated ridicule from the brothers. Two other convention attendees, Demian and Barnes, are initially portrayed as equally eccentric as Becky. Like the fan at the center of "Monster Movie," Demian testifies that fandoms attract people who lead uninteresting lives:

DEMIAN: In real life, he sells stereo equipment. I fix copiers. Our lives suck. But
to be Sam and Dean; to wake up every morning and save the world; to have a
brother who would die for you—well, who wouldn't want that?
DEAN: Maybe you got a point. You two don't make a bad team yourselves. How do
you know each other anyway?
DEMIAN: Oh, well, we met online. "Supernatural" chat room.
DEAN: Oh. It must be nice to get out of your parents' basement, make some friends.

This short exchange encapsulates the producers' conflicted portrayal
of fans. Demian's penetrating insights about the "Supernatural" story provide Dean with desperately needed perspective and motivation to continue
his journey, much the same way that real fans' appreciation of the actors
reenergizes them to keep telling their story. Melissa Gray observes of the
conflicted fan depictions in the "Supernatural" meta episodes: "As a nod
to the importance of fandom to *Supernatural*, [producers] have not been
committing gratuitous fan portrayal. In every episode in which they've
appeared, not only have fans played a role vital to the plot, but their fannishness is also vital to their role. [...] This usefulness ameliorates some
of the antipathy displayed toward the portrayal of the fans." Dean and the
writers' closing words, though, reiterate insulting fan stereotypes.

Kripke admitted that the writers' experiences with fans crept into their
convention concept, saying, "Chuck's question and answer panel was a little
exaggerated because we were going for comedy, but the way certain people
really try to punish you with their questions, how they're really aggressive in
terms of pointing out the flaws of the show, that part can sometimes be pain-
fully accurate" (Knight, *Season 5* 53). Kripke occasionally interacted with
fans online, so many of the convention's activities, including the writers'
fears of being attacked with literally aggressive questioning, might have been
grounded in a kernel of truth and be generously judged as accurate extrap-
olations. The writers' portrayal of the composition of the convention's audience is closer to parody than reality, however. Whether this was for dramatic
effect, reflected casting choices or betrayed a disconnect between writers'
perceptions and the reality of the fandom's demographics is unknown.

Attempting to balance the meta-critique, "The Real Ghostbusters"
repeats the tactic of "Hollywood Babylon" for producers including themselves in the parody. The convention is ineptly hosted by Chuck Shurley,
who is both the books' creator and the avatar for the show's creator (and, to
add another layer of parallel, is portrayed by the actor Rob Benedict, who
co-hosts *Supernatural*'s real fan conventions). *Supernatural*'s writers used
Chuck to specifically spoof themselves, reflecting Season 5's bold (but still
humorous) nature: "You guys know what I do for a living? Could you tell
me? 'cause I don't. I'm not a good writer. I've got no marketable skills. [...] I
gotta live, all right? The 'Supernatural' books are all I've got."

In recalling the introduction of the "Supernatural" meta concept into the plot, Kripke told *Variety* that he couldn't get enough of the "insanity" of writing Chuck Shurley and the books into the plotline: "Every single time Bob [Singer, co-showrunner] would say to me, 'this is the one where we've gone too far.' [...] I responded, 'Don't you see? We can *never* go too far, there is no too far'" (Prudom).

Unfortunately, Becky's next portrayal may have indeed "gone too far." In "Season 7, Time for a Wedding!" (7.08), fans are presented as irrational criminals when Becky bewitches Sam with a love spell, marries him, ties him to a bed, gags him, and holds him captive. Unlike "Hollywood Babylon," where the fan and celebrity have a consensual, comical romp, this "marriage" implies date rape by a fan. This is the most direct affront to female *Supernatural* fans written thus far into its storyline. If Becky's actions weren't damning enough, the writers went further to have Becky vilify herself and other fans:

I know what I am, okay? I'm a loser. In school, in life. Guess that's why I like *you* so much. [...] you had that whole character arc about being a freak, and ... I can relate. Honestly, the only place people understood me was the message boards. They were grumpy and overly literal, but at least we shared a common passion.

As so many times before, Becky helps the brothers in the end, but this "redemption" is inconsequential as Sam (rather justifiably) remains mockingly skeptical of Becky, and Dean refers to fans as "crazy groupies." In a 2016 interview, Emily Perkins, the actress who portrayed Becky Rosen, offered: "Becky was meant to be a loving poke, not a literal representation of fans as deviants" (Booth and Bennett). Unfortunately, the humor fell flat for a fandom that was insulted by the episode's hugely unflattering fan depiction.

In a massive course correction, the next time *Supernatural* used the books to comment on the show's fans was its 200th episode, "Fan Fiction" (10.05). Written by Robbie Thompson (Charlie Bradbury's creator), the episode is regarded by many fans as one of the best of the series. Symbolically relinquishing control of the story to the fans, the episode features a girls' high school musical, written and produced by a student who envisioned her own ending to the "Supernatural" saga. Coming full circle, Chuck Shurley (i.e., Kripke), with a broad smile and the words "Not Bad," endorses fans' right to interpret his story, and Dean admits that fans' interpretations of the text are no less valid than the creators' interpretation:

DEAN: You know? This has been educational. Seeing the story from your perspective. You keep writing, Shakespeare.
MARIE: Even if it doesn't match how you see it?
DEAN: I have my version, and you have yours.

Supernatural Fan/Producer Centric Episodes

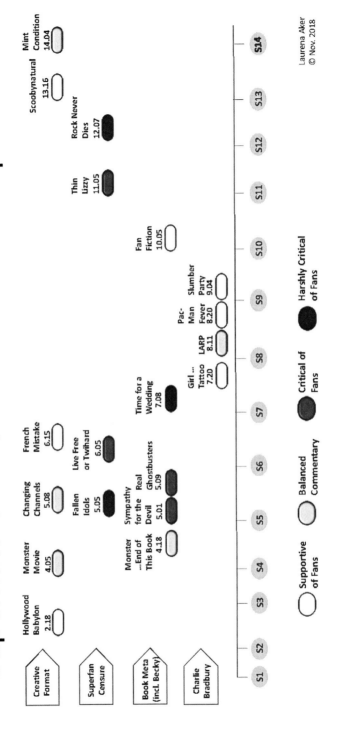

Laurena Aker
© Nov. 2018

Supernatural's executive team promoted the episode as their "love letter" to fans. Thompson confirmed, "our intention was to try to do something that really honored the history of the show and the symbiotic relationship with the audience" (Paulina). Executive Producer Robert Singer confirmed that "what we wanted to do in this love letter to the fans is to say to the fans, 'we realize how much of your love has made us what we are'" (Byrne). The sentiment was echoed by *Supernatural*'s then showrunner Jeremy Carver: "It's our love letter to the fans. Many aspects of the fandom are going to see themselves represented in many different ways and in the most loving way possible." His next statement reflects the show's long-standing practice of pairing fan commentary with self-criticism, and the producers' view of the complexity of the fan/producer relationship: "It's an episode that takes a long, loving look at the show, warts and all. And we're the first to admit our mistakes or our inconsistencies, and I think long-time fans will have a lot of fun seeing where we acknowledge this one big, happy, messy family that we're all part of" (Prudom).

After the series' "love letter" to fans, the "Supernatural" meta concept reappears in Season 14, launching the basis of Season 15. In the boldest move yet, Chuck's relationships with Becky, Sam, Dean and Castiel are all transformed by revealing that their reality had always been defined by fiction, further blurring any sane boundary between the two concepts. Until that story's ending is known, the final verdict on whether the fans or producers come out ahead in *Supernatural*'s massive meta experiment is yet to be determined.

Conclusion

In his discussion of fan depictions in primetime television, Lincoln Geraghty concluded, "Despite the assertion that fans are part of mainstream media, recent work still highlights the fact that extreme stereotypes serve to counter any steps made toward a sympathetic and informed representation of fandom and fan-related practices." *Supernatural*'s producers have thus far been on both sides of the aisle in their portrayals of fans within the show. Lead characters routinely mock fan practices, even though they themselves realistically and positively exhibit those same passions. Short term characters fall back on stereotypical depictions—excessive, pathological, frightening loners. Even when specifically referring to itself and its own fans, *Supernatural*'s representations vacillate between scathing satire and gushing admiration. Cait Coker and Candace Benefiel humorously concur, stating, "*Supernatural* is particularly aware of the thin line between acknowledging fans and mocking them, often not so much straddling the fence as awkwardly falling first on one side and then another, to the dismay of all parties" ("It's a Guilty Pleasure"). This indecision is counter intuitive, as one might expect to see a direct correlation between fans' steadfast loyalty and the show's endorsement or positive portrayal of fandom behavior. In reality, the irony is that SPNFamily's long term support has given *Supernatural*'s producers near limitless latitude to experiment with fandom tropes in ways that few shows can (summarized in Figure 1). Variations in fan depictions can be partially explained by the biases and talents of individual writers, from Eric Kripke's mischievousness and Ben Edlund's humor to Robbie Thompson's supportive fandom insights. Much has also been written substantiating that *Supernatural*'s resistance is steeped in the producers' desire to establish dominion over *Supernatural*'s text against the ever-increasing creative pressures exerted by its fandom. Through Becky, producers went so far as to portray their work being kidnapped and violated by fans, but three years later in a milestone that wouldn't have been achieved without fans' unfailing support, *Supernatural* acknowledged fans' right to the text and sincerely thanked them. Showrunner Sera Gamble perfectly summed up producers' conflicted reality: "we keep pulling the wacky trick of getting renewed […] because you showed up and watched. And told your friends. And jumped on the internet. And praised us and bitched us out and generally became one of the strongest and most passionate fandoms ever" (Knight, *Season 5* 7).

In retrospect, the discord in Dean's fandom identity is a window to the soul of the show, perfectly reflecting the ambivalence in *Supernatural*'s portrayal of fandom. Maybe Sam's more recent advice to Dean, "Be proud of your hobbies. It makes you who you are" ("Celebrating the Life of Asa Fox" 12.06), reflects the producers' evolving understanding of fan identity. "Mint Condition" (14.04), *Supernatural*'s 14th season Halloween episode, is another step in the right direction. A major entry in *Supernatural*'s fan identity journey, this ghost story is again based on Dean's penchant for horror films. The episode's three main characters, all passionate fans who have turned their interests into a profession, present a broad range of fan profiles. A comic book shop worker is the stereotypical lonely "piece of work" with poor "impulse control" who lives in his mother's basement, but he is a "good friend" who is spoken of lovingly by his coworkers. The shop is co-owned by a man who is a courageous, slightly less eccentric collector and Dean's counterpart; and a smart, mature young businesswoman who is also a comic book aficionado and Sam's "twin." The multiplicity of these fan portrayals is encouraging, recognizing that there are as many different fan profiles as there are people within fandoms.

This episode, plus Sam's recognition of Dean's "hobbies" and

Supernatural's "love letter to fans," are all hopeful harbingers that *Supernatural*'s long road trip to discovering fans' identity has led it to leaving behind stereotypes and insecurities, arriving at a destination that exemplifies an insightful understanding of fans and a trusting, mature fan/producer partnership. Despite a few negative detours along the way, hopefully *Supernatural*'s strong bond with its undeniably close fandom leaves a lasting impression that picks us where Charlie Bradbury left off and honestly, accurately honors most fans' true nature and contribution to television and society. This should be another milestone *Supernatural* adds to its long list of accomplishments. The entertainment industry and fandoms everywhere would benefit from the breakthrough.

WORKS CITED

Aker, Laurena. "Robbie Thompson!—C2E2 Panel with Supernatural Writer Extraordinaire Part 2." *The Winchester Family Business*, 28 June 2016, www.thewinchesterfamilybusiness.com/articles/article-archives/con-reports/20000-robbie-thompson-c2e2-panel-with-supernatural-writer-extraordinaire-part-2. 23 May 2018.

Baron, Steve. "Wednesday Final Ratings: 'Arrow,' 'Nashville,' & 'The Goldbergs' Adjusted Up; 'American Idol,' 'Criminal Minds' 'Supernatural' & 'Blacki-ish' Adjusted Down." *TV by the Numbers*, 7 May 2015, tvbythenumbers.zap2it.com/sdsdskdh279882992z1/wednesday-final-ratings-arrow-nashville-american-idol-criminal-minds-supernatural-blacki-ish-adjusted-down/400544/. 23 May 2018.

Booth, Paul and Lucy Bennett. "Interview with Emily Perkins, Actor in 'Supernatural.'" *Seeing Fans: Representations of Fandom in Media and Popular Culture*, edited by Lucy Bennett and Paul Booth, Bloomsbury Academic, 2016, pp. 153–156.

Braveheart. Dir. Mel Gibson. 1995. Film.

Byrne, Craig. "Supernatural #200: Robbie Thompson & Robert Singer Talk 'Fan Fiction.'" *KSiteTV*, 11 November 2014, www.ksitetv.com/interviews-2/supernatural-200-robbie-thompson-robert-singer-talk-fan-fiction/46519/. Video. 15 June 2018.

Coker, Cait and Candace Benefiel. "'It's a Guilty Pleasure': Gendering Cultural Consumption, Masculine Anxiety, and the Problem of Dean Winchester." *Metafiction, Intertextuality, and Authorship in* Supernatural, edited by Anastasia Klimchynskaya, McFarland, 2019. Forthcoming.

_____. "The Hunter Hunted: The Portrayal of the Fan as Predator in Supernatural." Supernatural, *Humanity and the Soul: On the Highway to Hell and Back*, edited by Susan A. George and Regina M. Hansen, Macmillan, 2014. pp. 97–110.

Felschow, Laura E. "'Hey, Check It Out, There's Actually Fans': (Dis)empowerment and (mis)representation of cult fandom in *Supernatural.*" *Transformative Works and Cultures 4.*"Saving People, Hunting Things" (2010), pp. 134–142. 25 June 2018, journal.transformativeworks.org/index.php/twc/article/view/134/142.

Geraghty, Lincoln. "Fans on Primetime: Representations of Fandom in Mainstream American Network Television, 1986–2014." *Seeing Fans: Representations of Fandom in Media and Popular Culture*, edited by Lucy Bennett and Paul Booth, Bloomsbury Academic, 2016 pp. 95–106.

Gray, Melissa. "From Canon to Fanon and Back Again: The Epic Journey of 'Supernatural' and Its Fans." *Transformative Works and Cultures* 4. "Saving People, Hunting Things" (2010), pp. 146–149. 25 June 2018, journal.transformativeworks.org/index.php/twc/article/view/146/149.

IMDb. www.imdb.com/.

"Jensen Ackles and Jared Padalecki at Q&A for Season 14 EW Preview." *YouTube*, uploaded by Supernatural Conventions, 2 October, 2018, www.youtube.com/watch?v=e2QGBdpo118. 29 October 2018.

Knight, Nicholas. *Supernatural: The Official Companion Season 6.* Titan Books, 2011.

_____. *Supernatural: The Official Companion, Season 5.* Titan Books, 2010.

Kubiesa, Jane M. "'Breaking All the Rules': Team Twilights and Cross-Generational Fan Appeal." *Fan Phenomena: The Twilight Saga,* edited by Laurena Aker, Intellect Books, 2016. pp. 116–24.

Ollis, Holly. "Re: Fact Confirmation Request." Received by Laurena Aker, 24 October 2018.

Paulina. "Exclusive Interview with Robbie Thompson: Nerding Out & Discussing Every *Supernatural* Episode He Wrote." *Nerds and Beyond,* 19 March 2018, www.nerdsandbeyond. com/2018/03/19/exclusive-interview-with-robbie-thompson-nerding-out-discussing-every-supernatural-episode-he-wrote/. 15 June 2018.

Prudom, Laura. "'Supernatural' at 200: The Road So Far, An Oral History." *Variety,* 11 November 2014, variety.com/2014/tv/spotlight/supernatural-oral-history-200-episodes-ackles-padalecki-kripke-1201352537/. 12 January 2018.

Richards, Dave. "'Supernatural's' Robbie Thompson on Felicia Day and the Return of Charlie." *CBR.com,* 28 October 2014, www.cbr.com/supernaturals-robbie-thompson-on-felicia-day-and-the-return-of-charlie/. 15 June 2018.

"Slayer—Crazy Fan." *YouTube*, uploaded by AzurePhase, 6 November 2009, www.youtube. com/watch?v=4L8sBoXi_jQ. 29 October 2018.

"*Supernatural* Ratings, All Seasons by Episode." *The Winchester Family Business,* n.d., www. thewinchesterfamilybusiness.com/articles/ratings-all-spn-seasons. 10 January 2018.

Supernatural Wiki: A Supernatural Canon and Fandom Resource. www.supernaturalwiki. com/Supernatural_Wiki. 23 May 2018.

Tolkien, J. R. R. *The Hobbit.* George Allen & Unwin, Ltd., 1937.

Ulaby, Neda. "The Few, the Fervent: Fans of 'Supernatural' Redefine TV Success." *NPR,* 15 January 2014, www.npr.org/2014/01/15/262092791/the-few-the-fervent-fans-of-supernatural-redefine-tv-success. 25 June 2014.

The Winchester Family Business. thewinchesterfamilybusiness.com/.

Zubernis, Lynn and Katherine Larsen. *Fandom at the Crossroads: Celebration, Shame and Fan/Producer Relationships.* Cambridge Scholars Publishing, 2012.

_____. "We See You (Sort Of): Representations of Fans on *Supernatural*." *Seeing Fans: Representations of Fandom in Media and Popular Culture,* edited by Paul Booth and Lucy Bennett, Bloomsbury Academic, 2016. pp. 139–152.

@Toniann_Rose. "OMG." *Twitter,* 1 October 2018, 3:31 p.m., twitter.com/it/status/10468600 56048951296. 29 October 2018.

Coda

Engaging with Engagement:
Following a Creator/Creating Followers

LISA MACKLEM *and* DOMINICK GRACE

While *Supernatural* is known for its very meta-treatment of its own fans, the show also examines fans from other perspectives. Though figures such as Chuck Shurley/God and Metatron most explicitly represent the trope of the writer as godlike creator on the show—with Chuck/God literally the author of the universe, as well as a series of pulp horror novels about Sam and Dean Winchester, and Metatron, in his own attempt to become God, both explicitly a would-be author himself and critic of the work of his predecessor—the show invokes multiple iterations of creators producing works over which they have difficulty maintaining control, a situation analogous to that between any creator and the fan base that may follow his or her work. As Metatron asks, "who gives a story meaning? Is it the writer? Or you?" ("Meta Fiction," 9.18). The "you" conflates character and audience, suggesting both fans and characters have agency; fans, like characters, can try to seize control of the narrative. The first reference to fans in the show occurs in Season 1 in "Hell House" (1.17) when Harry Spengler and Ed Zeddmore unknowingly create a Tulpa through the engagement of the fans of their online site. Reality television is the bane of television writers, and Ed and Harry represent both reality television and the very worst of YouTube creators like PewDiePie or Logan Paul. Ed and Harry have little knowledge of their fans past ensuring that they have a following to advance their own careers. Harry and Ed are seen from the beginning as the complete opposite of Dean and Sam, who are selflessly trying to save people. Ed and Harry's interactions with their fans and with Dean and Sam make an interesting contrast to *Supernatural*'s treatment of its own fanbase and the fan/creator relationship. Ed and Harry are far from godlike, but Metatron fails just as spectacularly at securing a devoted fanbase.

200

In the first season, Ed and Harry's first appearance in "Hell House" sets them up as comic relief and foils to Dean and Sam Winchester. In fact, the episode is meant to be light as it also features a prank war between the two brothers. Ed and Harry are scared, inept amateurs, though they claim to be professional paranormal investigators in "Hell House" and supernaturalists in "#thinman" (9.15). Their entire motivation is becoming famous and having sex by preying on fans of the supernatural. Dean and Sam, by contrast, are selfless, brave professionals, and their motivation, as always, is hunting things, saving people. They do their best to remain unnoticed and to keep most of the world's population in the dark about the supernatural. In "Hell House," both teams are set up as fanboys in their own rights. Dean as a music fan recognizes one of the symbols on the wall of the Murdoch house as the logo for the band the Blue Öyster Cult, whose music is also featured in the episode as Dean is singing along to it while driving. Ed and Harry are Tolkien fans as Ed blurts out "Sweet Lord" and Harry finishes "of the Rings" when they are frightened by the appearance of Mordecai. When things start to get out of hand, Harry wants to quit, but Ed insists that they keep going, asking WWBD—what would Buffy do? The reference is to *Buffy the Vampire Slayer*, the show on the WB that really paved the way for other genre shows and *Supernatural* in particular. Dean later mocks Ed and Harry for their action figures that are still in the packaging. It's clear that Ed and Harry are representative of the stereotypical geek fan, who is male, not well-socialized, and still lives with his parents.

The emphasis on Ed and Harry, however, isn't as fans but as the unwitting conduit for the creation of the Tulpa through the harnessing of fan engagement. Craig Thurston and his cousin Dana decide to amuse themselves by starting the urban legend of Mordecai Murdoch as a prank, in keeping with the theme of the episode. Dana happens to use a Tibetan symbol that harnesses the thoughts of those following the legend, resulting in the Tulpa. The fans of the site who embellish the legend change how the Tulpa looks, acts, and can be killed; the fans are the creators. Sam and Dean try to get them to take the site down, but Ed insists that they have an obligation to their fans and the truth. Of course, they don't actually know what the truth is. In exchange for taking down the site, Dean and Sam tell Ed and Harry another version of Mordecai which will allow them to kill Mordecai. They know that Ed and Harry are lying about taking the down the site and are counting on them not taking it down, but they don't count on the fans crashing the site when the information is posted. The change doesn't take because the fans can't empower it, so Dean burns the house down while Ed and Harry get some great new footage. Later, Ed and Harry get what they think is a call from a Hollywood producer who wants to put their show on the air, but it is actually Sam pranking them. Despite Sam and Dean's key role in what happens being on their videos, Ed and Harry are happy to take all the credit for the creation and leave to sell the rights to their video. It's clear from this episode that the writers/producers of *Supernatural* knew the power of an audience to get a show made and on the air in Hollywood and that their perspective was from the industry standpoint and reflects the politics of the industry. Fans themselves can be seen as a type of monster that writers lose control of. It's also clear that Ed and Harry are foils to the writers themselves as writers/producers who are willing to exploit the creation of others for their own gain, something legitimate writers abhor and copyright laws prohibit.

In "Ghostfacers" (3.13), which was the first *Supernatural* episode back after the writers' strike in 2009, Ed and Harry's reality ghost hunting show represents an issue from that writers' strike: television writers were worried that they would lose their jobs to reality shows, which are cheaper to produce because they don't officially employ writers and nonetheless garner huge audiences. Metatron's speech in "Meta Fiction" actually begins with several questions about authorship: "What makes a story work? Is it the plot, the characters, the text? The subtext?" Even reality television makes use of these elements. Of course, reality shows are as much "written" as any television show, it's just that the scripting takes place during the editing process. Ed and Harry essentially highjack the entire episode, which features special credits and an introduction by Ed and Harry in smoking jackets and lounge chairs, doing their best imitation of Masterpiece theatre—the farthest thing from Ghostfacers as possible. The tape is destined for "bigwig network executives" and they directly reference the writers' strike and the "lazy fatcat writers!" As the team sets up their base camp in the haunted Morton House, Ed tells them that he "can smell syndication," and that is every creator's hope—to produce enough episodes for the series to be syndicated and thus garner royalties. One of the things that they encounter in the house is death echoes—a dead person stuck in a loop experiencing their death over and over—rather like syndication.

When Dean and Sam also show up at the Morton House, they remember the duo as Hell Hounds, but Ed tells them that that name didn't test well—they've done some consumer research. Unlike how they behave in a "real" episode, Dean and Sam swear, and their mouths are covered by skulls to bleep them. The episode is largely shot by the actors using hand held cameras and body cameras. This parallels other uses of the style, such as *The Blair Witch Project* (1999), the popular horror movie filmed in documentary/witness style and that popularized this approach to horror. This gritty style was used in a similar *X-Files* episode, "X-Cops" (7.12, February 20, 2000), that was filmed on video in real time like an episode of the reality series *Cops*. Lorna Jowett points out that "[v]ideo footage on television news maintains its credibility as the 'real' because of the context in which it is presented. Yet even the news evokes emotional and psychological responses via its use of 'raw' filmed action" (26). "Ghostfacers" also features "confessional moments" which Dean refuses to engage in but which are generally used to help the audience identify more with the characters. Of course, ironically *Supernatural* also features such confessional moments, most often with the brothers either in the Impala or leaning up against it. The end of the "Ghostfacers" episode features one such confession from a starry-eyed Corbett, who is the intern killed during the course of the hunt. By the end of the episode, the action pulls back to reveal that Dean and Sam have been watching the footage that Ed and Harry have put together. Sam remarks that they have both honored Corbett's memory while exploiting his death, which is a good description of what sensationalized reality television does.

The spinoff of Ghostfacers to a web series also reflects the transmedia impulse of fans as well as their continued desire for more *Supernatural*. Hollywood studios and producers recognized the growing presence of fans online and especially on YouTube, engaging in fan produced works, but also engaging with content. Derek Johnson recognizes "the logics of media franchising [...] [that manages] fan texts as multiplicative industrial product ranges in which a number of different spin-offs and parallel market appeals can be made simultaneously to reach different kinds of consumers" (396). *Supernatural* has struggled to find other opportunities, and the web series lasted for only 11 episodes and is featured as an extra on the Season 5 blu-ray/DVD. It is still probably the most successful attempt of the producers to expand the series, which has had two failed embedded pilots for spinoffs as well as an anime series originally geared to the Japanese market. Rather than competing with Dean and Sam, Ed and Harry are less threatening as foils to the brothers and their less successful doppelgängers.

Much as producers/writers recognize the power of online fandom, Ed and Harry also help the Winchester brothers through their online presence—at least in one episode. Self-help videos from Ed and Harry that exploit what they've learned from the Winchesters appear in "It's a Terrible Life" (4.17) to help Dean and Sam, who have been given alternative identities, in which they have no knowledge of the supernatural, by the angel Zachariah. Once again, Ed and Harry aren't truly creators but more exploiters of content. Their YouTube videos never fail to take cheap shots at the Winchesters while they are protected by physical distance. Their videos pop up to help fans of the supernatural in "Thin Lizzie" (11.05) and as recently as Season 14's "Don't Go Into the Woods" (14.16). "Thin Lizzie" centers on a case at Lizzie Borden's house. The house is set up to fake the presence of ghosts, and attracts superfans of the notorious killer. It also highlights

Sam's own fannish passion for serial killers. In the end, however, it isn't a ghost committing the murders but Amara trying to re-write the wrongs of reality; we will return to Amara shortly.

In the last full episode with Ed and Harry, instead of using the Internet to inform the public about the supernatural, they once again turn to exploiting fans. In "#thinman," the darker side of the Internet is showcased. Ed creates the Thinman legend in order to prevent Harry from leaving their partnership to pursue a "normal" life with his girlfriend. Once again, the American Dream is thwarted. The legend is based on a real Internet phenomenon, the created urban legend of the Slenderman, which resulted in several real-life violent incidents and at least one murder. The episode also showcases the obsession people have with the Internet. Harry spends much of the episode Facebook-stalking his ex-girlfriend, and the initial murder happens after a girl takes selfies of herself. The destructive force of the Internet is also showcased in the episode "Halt & Catch Fire" (10.13), when a group of teenagers cause an accident by texting and driving and the ghost subsequently manifests in the Internet. This is also a nice twist on people's use of the Internet to insulate themselves from day to day reality by creating their own narrative. In "Ghostfacers," for instance, Dean asks Maggie if looking through the camera makes her feel better and she answers with an emphatic yes.

Ed manipulates reality by seeding the Thinman legend with photoshopped images to convince Harry. The selfie taken by the first victim, however, is not photoshopped and results in both Dean and Sam and Ed and Harry arriving to pursue the "monster." Once again, Ed and Harry's presence makes things more difficult for the Winchesters. Ed obsesses over the number of their twitter followers—something producers/writers/showrunners have also become obsessed with as easily quantifiable evidence of fan/audience numbers. Dean identifies the two as "fame whores." When Dean and Sam question their authority on the subject, Harry tells them "Amazon me, bitches!" It turns out that Ed and Harry have authored a book: *The Skinny on Thinman*.

Because Harry is more invested in the legend, he presses to continue hunting even after Ed is willing to let Dean and Sam take over. Harry remarks that Sam and Dean don't even have Twitter! This moment is a knowing shout-out to the fact that at the time (March 2014), Jensen Ackles was still resisting joining Twitter—he finally gave in in August of 2014. In fact, most celebrities are contracted to have a presence on social media today. This in-show reference to social media offers another example of the politics of the entertainment industry itself finding its way into the storyline. Unlike many fans, however, celebrities often treat social media merely as an employment obligation rather than a social space, once again engaging in a different way than fans. Fans use social media to engage with each other and to feel a greater sense of engagement to the media properties they love; media producers recognize the economic value of such engagement, so encourage it. The possible rewards of media exposure underlie Harry's appeals to his partner: Harry tries to reinvest Ed by reminding him that they are going to be on Dr. Phil when they solve the case, not Dean and Sam.

Dean and Sam continue to investigate the legend, finding both the photoshopped and non-photoshopped photos, leading Dean to question how something can be both real and fake at the same time. Dean is also shocked to learn that the Thinman has fans. While fictional horrors may attract fans relatively unproblematically, real horrors having fans raises uncomfortable questions about the blurred line between fact and fiction. This knowledge makes Dean change his theory that the first murder was a ghost to speculating about whether this is another Tulpa—as with "Hell House," another instance of avid fan engagement converting the fictional into the real. Ed, however, tells them that no one agrees on the lore, it changes from blog to blog, so the sort of focused fandom that created the Tulpa does not apply here. Instead, we see a version of sectarian fandom, each subgroup pursuing its own preferred version of the object of their desire. Such factions also existed in 2014 within *Supernatural* fandom. In fact, deangirl and samgirl fans existed from the very beginning, to be joined later by Destiel fans and others with particular and differing objects of interest. When Dean presses Ed, Ed responds, "No. We just play supernaturalists on tv," but he's being sarcastic even as he says the highly ironic line.

When the second murder is caught on security tape and then goes up on the Internet, Sam and Dean speculate that the killer might be a demon, one who likes to stab and to watch YouTube. Dean remarks that people will watch the video because people are sick. Sam wonders when viral videos went from cute chimpanzees falling out of trees to killers. Ed finally confesses to Sam and Dean that he made the whole thing up to keep Harry with him, but when they became a crowdsourcing legend, it was awesome to have a following.

Reality and fiction are further confused in this episode when the monster turns out to be two humans. Deputy Norwood considers himself to be the visionary—the one creating the story—while Roger is simply the psycho committing the murders. They had both felt invisible in their own town until they found the Thinman online. They take Dean and Sam prisoner and plan to kill both of them on film, creating their best video yet. Dean points out that they are just copycat killers—they aren't original. The nested commentaries here on how consumers engage with media are complex.

We have here a TV show within which a manufactured online narrative masquerading as real has inspired fans who in turn attempt to create their own "Artistic" narrative, documenting their own killing spree. One could easily here see a critique of fannish over-investment leading to disastrous real-world consequences, if not for the fact that Norwood in the pairing with Roger stands in for the producer of the art. Who is responsible: the fan who appropriates art and repurposes it to horrific ends, or the producer who encourages the sort of fan engagement that can lead to such results?

Ownership of media property is further problematized as the narrative reaches its conclusion. In another twist, Ed and Harry come to the Winchesters' rescue. In yet another online reference, Ed struggles with the pronunciation of meme, calling it "me-me" (his mispronunciation is an amusing commentary on his narcissism). Deputy Norwood is eager to kill Ed and Harry because once they're dead there's no proof that Thinman was their brainchild, and then he and Roger can take possession of the story. Ed and Harry's story seems to come to an end as Harry tells Ed that their relationship is now "complicated," again using Internet speak. Harry then gets a ride from Sam and Dean. It's unclear whether the YouTube videos produced by Ed and Harry that appear in the subsequent episodes are new or predate their apparent retirement in "#thinman." In Season 14's "Don't Go Into the Woods," the clip that Eliot watches is the same as the one from "It's a Terrible Life." As Dean learns to his horror in "Halt & Catch Fire," nothing on the Internet is truly gone.

Ed and Harry represent both Dean and Sam and writers and producers of "reality television" that blurs the lines between fact and fiction. Their storyline examines the interplay between story and fan and the politics of ownership as well. In May 2017, confidential storyboards for the anime series *Voltron: Legendary Defender* were leaked online. As copyrighted material, the images, which had been copied by a fan on a tour of Studio Mir and then posted without Mir's permission, placed Mir in legal jeopardy from Dreamworks, for whom they were producing the animation. While many fans complied with requests to remove the materials and took down the images, one fan attempted to use them to blackmail the studio, demanding that a particular ship, Klance, a ship between the characters Keith and Lance, be made canon, or the images would not be taken down. While extreme and exceptional, this incident nevertheless speaks to the increasing demands from fans to have control over canon. More typical attempts to influence content depend on individual or organized campaigns to get a show modified—such as, for instance, the change.org petition to have Ernie and Bert get married on *Sesame Street* (which garnered over 10,000 signatures), or, to bring it closer to our focus, the various petitions to influence content on *Supernatural*, such as the multiple petitions to make Destiel canon, or at least to provide more fodder for Destiel shippers in the show. (Of the ones of these we have seen, one explicitly not asking for Destiel to be made canon but requesting simply that the petitioners "would like to see more interaction on screen" ["I Support Destiel"] had the most signatures, at 2,428 of a goal of 3,000.)

Audiences have long chosen to use and interpret their entertainment according to their own needs and preferences; Stuart Hall noted practices such as negotiated readings and oppositional readings almost 40 years ago. Now, we see fans setting out to challenge the quasi-godlike authority creators have over their creations, and *Supernatural*, especially, has internalized and explored that dynamic of the tension between the creator and the audience by setting up literal challengers to God for supremacy in the diegetic world. The two with the most fruitful links to fan practice are, perhaps, Metatron and Amara, or The Darkness.

Metatron is a "real" angel, referenced in several Kabbalistic texts, but given that he first appeared in Season 8 of *Supernatural*, well after the show had invested heavily in violations of the fourth wall, the "meta" component of his name clearly resonates with how self-reflexive the show had become and with its concomitant interest in the dynamics of creating (for more on *Supernatural* and the fourth wall, see Macklem). In contrast to characters explicitly coded as fans, such as Becky Rosen, or to ones whose status and behavior can be seen to model fan behavior, such as Ed and Harry, Metatron might not on the face of it seem like another iteration of fandom in the show. However, even from the first time he is referenced in the show ("Reading Is Fundamental," 7.21), his angel status and pop culture status are conflated. When Cas refers to Metatron as the scribe in whose handwriting "The Word" has been inscribed on the stone, Sam responds, "Metatron? You saying a Transformer wrote that?" and remains baffled as Dean corrects him that the transformer was MEGAtron, not METAtron.

In the moment, this is simply a joke, but it has resonances. There's much in a name. Jamil Mustafa has pointed out that the name Metatron is itself a sort of oxymoron, its component parts "meta" meaning above or beyond, and "tron" referring to the subatomic, which he associates with Metatron's remit as a writer: "Metatron writes at every level" (53). The closeness between Meta- and Megatron speaks to the profound difference even a single letter, or phoneme, can make: one gives us an unimaginably powerful angel; the other a tiny plastic toy—or, rather what began as a tiny plastic toy that grew into a massive multi-media franchise, arguably a triumph primarily of marketing rather than of, say, narrative depth or complexity. Transformers themselves transformed quickly from toys to comic books and an animated TV series, aggressively cross-marketed and designed to develop a fanbase of kids who would eagerly consume all the available products. But Metatron is himself something of a transformer, as well; as he emerges as the big bad of Season 9, and his clear agenda is to transform the narrative God has written to fit his own specific desires. His engagement with God, in effect, can be read as a metaphor for an aspect of what Derek Johnson calls "fantagonism," specifically these components: "fantagonism explicitly evokes an *activist* struggle to intervene in industry worlds"; and it also includes "the power of television producers to deploy the text itself as a means of disciplining engagement" (397).

When we first meet him, Metatron can easily be likened to the collector fan. He is an omnivorous reader, having consumed all earthly narratives, and is eager for more. His earliest Earthly function, indeed, is as a sort of reverse mythmaker; rather than providing humans with their defining narratives, he grants them longevity in exchange for new stories—much as fans of serial narrative can grant that serial continued life as long as it continues to satisfy their hunger for narrative. His encyclopedic knowledge is in fact useful as a plot device to provide Cas with the knowledge of culture (especially pop culture) that he has hitherto lacked when in "Meta Fiction" he downloads into Cas's brain all the cultural content Metatron himself has consumed—in a sort of angelic version of peer-to-peer sharing (and perhaps an amusing hearkening back to the initial reference to Metatron himself, confused with a cultural product by Sam). Metatron is, in effect, the deeply invested fan, who knows canon better than the producers of canon do themselves, a notion with which the show has already played in the figure of Becky Rosen, who in the episode "The Real Ghostbusters" (5.09) (itself set at a fan convention replete not only with lovers of "Supernatural" but also with fans who gripe about things they don't like) provides Sam and Dean with crucial information she has derived from Carver Edlund's novels—which Chuck/God himself seems to have forgotten about, or to have neglected himself to share with Sam and Dean.

This leads Metatron into the fantagonistic territory of desiring an active role in the "industry world." When he sets out to set himself up as God he explicitly does so by trying to usurp God's authorial function and to reshape the narrative into what he wants it to be. Metatron explores such questions of authorship in "Meta Fiction," in which the question of who controls a story—author or audience—blurs into the question of whether characters *within* the story also have control. The lines between active agent and passive consumer blur, as Metatron's very meta question, mentioned above, "who gives a story meaning? Is it the writer? Or you?" is not in fact the simple binary it appears to be. The "you" might seem to be the viewer, since Metatron breaks the fourth wall by looking directly into the camera when he asks the question, but diegetically, he is in fact talking to Cas, a person within his reality, *and* someone Metatron also wants to cast in his own story, wherein Cas will assume the villain role to Metatron's hero. Metatron as fan attempting to seize control of the narrative explicitly sets up an adversarial relationship between himself and characters within that story, in which he reverses the roles that fans in the extra-diegetic world—watchers of the show—apply to the same narrative. Metatron is the fan who sees himself as the hero saving his narrative by reforming it; characters within the show, and arguably at least some fans of the show, will impose an opposite construction, reading Metatron as the Big Bad of the season rather than as its hero. Nevertheless, in a way, Metatron is also allying himself with segments of the fanbase that have come to question, challenge and even resist the dominant narrative of the show; this character within the show reflects the feelings of many watchers of the show, and his engagement with the reality he inhabits reflects their desire to see *Supernatural* reshaped to make it into what they want it to be.

Metatron eventually gets the opportunity to confront the author directly, in "Don't Call Me Shurley" (11.20), a complex episode in which Metatron's fantagonistic relationship with God is redefined; he goes from being (as he himself acknowledges) a terrible replacement God and writer to a good editor, helping God edit his autobiography, while also trying to persuade God to reconsider his view of humanity. In effect, fantagonism shifts to a sort of negotiation, in which revising and editing replace wholesale rewriting, and by the end of the episode, Metatron's interventions have persuaded God to do his own revisions, enacted diegetically as, for instance, Sam is suddenly healed, but reflected metaphorically in Metatron's awe and delight as he sits reading God's latest draft. Though this is not the end of Metatron's story, it marks a significant turn in his narrative, both diegetically, as he now realigns himself with God (and the Winchesters) and ends up dying on the side of the heroes, in conflict with Amara—herself another manifestation of an aspect of fandom—and arguably as an allegorical comment on what the show hopes for from its own fans.

If Metatron is the fantagonist eventually reclaimed as ally, Amara can be read in light of Paul Booth's concept of fan euthanasia—the desire some fans eventually develop to see a once-beloved property come to an end after losing what was, to them, its core elements: in effect, the segment of fandom that views itself as jilted lover and becomes desirous of the death of the once-loved artifact; as Booth's subtitle for his essay acknowledges, there's a thin line between love and hate. As Booth notes, "Fan euthanasia reveals moments when fans' desire for an ending overrides the media creator's authority over meaning" (82), and arguably Amara can be read as an allegory of the disaffected fan who desires the destruction of that created by the one she once loved. Though we subsequently learn her backstory, Amara is introduced literally as an infant who must be cared for and nurtured—as a nascent fandom grows early in its relationship with a cultural product. Like fandoms, though, Amara grows quickly and unpredictably, soon being beyond the control not only of the characters but of their diegetic creator—as fandoms can quickly grow and morph, even turning, when they feel rejected, on the initial object of their passion. Amara's narrative invokes the image of the entitled fan, demanding attention from the creator, or she will tear it down. In "O Brother, Where Art Thou" (11.09), for instance, she annihilates a church full of worshippers and when Dean questions why, she says she did so because she "had to get [God's] attention"; "He ignored me. He forced my hand. I had no other reason to harm his chosen. My issue is with my brother, not his creation."

The sister, ignored, tries to destroy the brother's creation to draw his attention; the fan, ignored, attacks the creation to draw the creator's attention. Amara's pattern is to ramp up her attacks in the hope that God will eventually acknowledge her, until ultimately the existence of the entire universe is threatened: if she can't have what she wants, she wants everything dead. However, the genesis of the conflict complicates this simple binary. While God claims she was "Always telling me what to do, making me do what she wanted" ("All in the Family," 11.21), her claim is that her desires conflicted with God's, so he imprisoned her: "I needed solitude and he needed a fan club, so he made all that. Then when I complained, he stuffed me in a hole for eons." Amara blames the creator's design for fans, which creates an interesting (if unintentional) parallel to the destructive results of the attempts Ed and Harry make to garner their own fans for their dubious creations. While from both perspectives, Amara objects to not getting what she wants, God defines her as the active antagonist, while she defines *him* as the oppressor. In effect, both sides of the fan/producer argument are given voice. When Amara continues her destructive path and God argues, "She's baiting me. I can't respond every time. I won't be manipulated," the question of who is responsible, as in "#thinman," becomes complicated. The fan accusation of being baited by subtext (accusations of queerbaiting, for instance, being common among some segments of *Supernatural* fandom—see, for instance, Cruise) is flipped on its head here, as God accuses Amara of using provocative action to bait him. As fans can complain about being manipulated, here God complains that Amara's action is designed to manipulate him. Rather than presenting a disciplining of fan action, or merely depicting Amara as the unruly fan who must be brought to heel, the conflict here distributes responsibility and shows that the strategies of one side are comparable to those of the other.

Once again, as with Metatron, the only possible resolution is through accommodation. Rather than a climactic (or perhaps in addition to a climactic) battle in which one side destroys the other, instead we get a case for compromise and mutual respect. While the creator remains paramount—"When God's gone, the universe—everything will cease to exist," Amara acknowledges in "Alpha and Omega" (11.23)—the ultimate paradigm that resolves the crisis is familial: Dean convinces Amara that because she and God are family, she can set aside the hate. Amara sounds very much like the hurt fan when she tells God, "you went and you made all these other things. I hated them. I hated you for needing something else, something that wasn't me," but she sounds very much like the *Supernatural* fan when she says, "I know that we can't go back to the way things were. I don't want to, but I wish … I wish that we could just be family again." *Supernatural* fandom defines itself as the family, adopting from the show a key paradigm—the family business, placing family above all other considerations—to define itself, and that paradigm is readopted back into the show, reaffirming the centrality of the relationship between fans and producers as familial, and not (or not just) hierarchical or economic. Amara may in some ways acknowledge her fannish failures here, but equally true is that God—and the show—literally would not survive without her—or the fans.

Season 15, the show's final, further complicates such questions by making God himself the Big Bad. If earlier seasons can be (and have been) read as problematically critical of fandom, this final season turns the lens fully inward, questioning whether the producer of media can be as dangerous and destructive as fans have earlier been depicted as being. What we are to make of the implied connection between a deranged god setting out to upend and destroy his creation with the producers of *Supernatural*, who are of course quite literally doing to the show exactly what God is doing to the diegetic world, remains open to interpretation, especially as Season 15 is ongoing as of the time of this writing. However it ends, though, *Supernatural* throughout its run, and to the bitter end, has raised complex and fascinating terms of engagement.

Works Cited

"The Blair Witch Project." Lionsgate, 2010.

Booth, Paul. "Fan Euthanasia: A Thin Line Between Love and Hate." In *Everybody Hurts: Transitions, Endings, and Resurrection in Fan Cultures*, edited by Rebecca Williams, pp. 75–86. University of Iowa Press, 2018.

Buffy the Vampire Slayer. Created by Joss Whedon, WB, 1997–2003.

Caron, Nathalie. "Voltron: Legendary Defender 'Fan' Blackmails Studio to Make a Gay Ship Canon on the Show." *SYFYWire*. 29 May 2017. https://www.syfy.com/syfywire/voltron-legendary-defender-fan-blackmails-studio. Accessed 1 June 2019.

Cruise, Eliel. "Fans Take *Supernatural* to Task for 'Queer Baiting.'" *Advocate*, 2014, https://www.advocate.com/bisexuality/2014/07/17/fans-take-supernatural-task-queer-baiting. Accessed 13 Nov. 2018.

Ghostfacers. Created by Eric Kripke, Space Zombie Films and Wonderland Sound and Vision, 15 Apr. 2010.

Gilligan, Vince. "X-Cops." *The X-Files*, Season 7, episode 12, Fox, 20 Feb. 2000.

"I Support Destiel." *Care2Petitions.* https://www.thepetitionsite.com/702/464/185/i-support-destiel/ Accessed 14 April 2019.

Johnson, Derek. "Fantagonism, Franchising, and Industry Management of Fan Privilege." *The Routledge Companion to Media Fandom*, edited by Melissa A. Click and Susan Scott, Routledge, 2018, pp. 395–405.

Jowett, Lorna. "'Mulder, have you noticed that we're on television?'": X-Cops' style and innovation." *Science Fiction Film and Television.* 6.1 (Spring 2013), pp. 23–28.

Macklem, Lisa. "I Saw What You Did There: SPN and the Fourth Wall." In *Fan Phenomena: Supernatural*, edited by Lynn Zubernis and Katherine Larsen, Intellect, 2014, pp. 34–45.

Mustafa, Jamil. "'You Can't Spell Subtext Without S-E-X': Gothic Intertextuality and the (Queer) Uncanny." In *The Gothic Tradition in* Supernatural: *Essays on the Television Series*, edited by Melissa Edmundson, McFarland, 2016, pp. 51–62.

Appendix One

Episodes Cited

Episodes are cited throughout the volume by episode name and year/season number only, to avoid unnecessary repetition. Full bibliographical information, season by season, is provided below. To find details about an episode, check by the year/season number cited in the essay. All seasons are available on Warner home video, in both DVD and Blu-Ray formats.

Season 1

1.01, "Pilot" (Sept. 13, 2005). Written by Eric Kripke, directed by David Nutter.

1.02, "Wendigo" (Sept. 20, 2005). Written by Eric Kripke, Ron Milbauer, and Terri Hughes Barton, directed by David Nutter.

1.03, "Dead in the Water" (Sept. 27, 2005). Written by Sera Gamble and Raelle Tucker, directed by Kim Manners.

1.04, "Phantom Traveler" (Oct. 4, 2005). Written by Richard Hatem, directed by Robert Singer.

1.05, "Bloody Mary" (October 11, 2005). Written by Ron Milbauer and Terri Hughes Burton, story by Eric Kripke, directed by Peter Ellis.

1.06, "Skin" (Oct. 18, 2005). Written by John Shiban, directed by Robert Duncan McNeill.

1.07, "Hook Man" (Oct. 25, 2005). Written by John Shiban, directed by David Jackson.

1.08, "Bugs" (Nov. 8, 2005). Written by Rachel Nave and Bill Coakley, directed by Kim Manners.

1.09, "Home" (Nov. 15, 2005). Written by Erik Kripke, directed by Ken Girotti.

1.10, "Asylum" (Nov. 22, 2005). Written by Richard Hatem, directed by Guy Norman Bee.

1.11, "Scarecrow" (Jan. 10, 2006). Written by John Shiban and Patrick Sean Smith, directed by Kim Manners.

1.13, "Route 666" (Jan. 31, 2006). Written by Eugenie Ross-Leming and Brad Buchner, directed by Paul Shapiro.

1.14 "Nightmare" (Feb. 7, 2006). Written by Sera Gamble and Raelle Tucker, directed by Phil Sgriccia.

1.16, "Shadow" (Feb. 28, 2006). Written by Erik Kripke, directed by Kim Manners.

1.17, "Hell House" (March 30, 2006). Written by Trey Callaway, directed by Chris Long.

1.18, "Something Wicked" (April 6, 2006). Written by Daniel Knauf, directed by Whitney Ransick.

1.19, "Provenance" (April 13, 2006). Written by David Ehrman, directed by Phil Sgriccia.

1.22, "Devil's Trap" (May 4, 2006). Written by Erik Kripke, directed by Kim Manners.

Season 2

2.01, "In My Time of Dying" (Sept. 28, 2006). Written by Eric Kripke, directed by Kim Manners.

2.02, "Everybody Loves a Clown" (Oct. 5, 2006). Written by John Shiban, directed by Phil Sgriccia.

2.03, "Bloodlust" (Oct. 12, 2006). Written by Sera Gamble, Directed by Robert Singer.

2.06, "No Exit" (Nov. 2, 2006). Written by Matt Witten, directed by Kim Manners.

2.07, "The Usual Suspects" (November 9, 2006). Written by Catherine Humphris, directed by Mike Rohl.

2.08, "Crossroad Blues" (Nov. 16, 2006). Written by Sera Gamble, directed by Steve Boyum.

2.09, "Croatoan" (Dec. 7, 2006). Written by John Shiban, directed by Robert Singer.

2.11, "Playthings" (Jan. 18, 2007). Written by Matt Witten, directed by Charles Beeson.

2.12, "Nightshifter" (Jan. 25, 2007). Written by Ben Edlund, directed by Phil Sgriccia.

2.13, "Houses of the Holy" (Feb. 1, 2007). Written by Sera Gamble, directed by Kim Manners.

2.14, "Born Under a Bad Sign" (Feb. 8, 2007). Written by Cathryn Humphris, directed by J. Miller Tobin.

2.15, "Tall Tales" (February 15, 2007). Written by John Shiban, directed by Bradford May.

2.16, "Roadkill" (March 15, 2007). Written by Raelle Tucker, directed by Charles Beeson.

2.17, "Heart" (March 22, 2007). Written by Sera Gamble, directed by Kim Manners.

2.18, "Hollywood Babylon" (April 19, 2007). Written by Ben Edlund, directed by Phil Sgriccia.

2.20, "What Is and What Should Never Be" (May 3, 2007). Written by Raelle Tucker, directed by Eric Kripke.

2.22, "All Hell Breaks Loose, Part 2" (May 17, 2005). Written by Sera Gamble, directed by Robert Singer.

Season 3

3.02, "The Kids Are Alright" (Oct. 11, 2007). Written by Sera Gamble, directed by Phil Sgriccia.

3.04, "Sin City" (Oct. 25, 2007). Written by Robert Singer and Jeremy Carver, directed by Charles Beeson.

3.05, "Bedtime Stories" (Nov. 1, 2007). Written by Cathryn Humphris, directed by Mike Rohl.

3.06, "Red Sky at Morning" (Nov. 8, 2007).

Written by Laurence Andries, directed by Cliff Bole.

3.08, "A Very Supernatural Christmas" (Dec. 13, 2007). Written by Jeremy Carver, directed by J. Miller Tobin.

3.09, "Malleus Maleficarum" (Jan. 31, 2008). Written by Ben Edlund, directed by Robert Singer.

3.10, "Dream a Little Dream of Me" (Feb. 7, 2008). Written by Sera Gamble and Cathryn Humphris, directed by Steve Boyum.

3.11, "Mystery Spot" (Feb. 14, 2008). Written by Eric Kripke, directed by Kim Manners.

3.12, "Jus in Bello" (Feb. 21, 2008). Written by Sera Gamble, directed by Phil Sgriccia.

3.13, "Ghostfacers" (April 24, 2008). Written by Ben Edlund, directed by Phil Sgriccia.

3.14, "Long-Distance Call" (May 1, 2008). Written by Jeremy Carver, directed by Robert Singer.

3.15, "Time Is on My Side" (May 8, 2008). Written by Sera Gamble, directed by Charles Beeson.

3.16, "No Rest for the Wicked" (May 15, 2008). Written by Eric Kripke, directed by Kim Manners.

Season 4

4.01, "Lazarus Rising" (Sept. 18, 2008). Written by Eric Kripke, directed by Kim Manners.

4.02, "Are You There, God? It's Me, Dean Winchester" (Sept. 25, 2008). Written by Sera Gamble, story by Sera Gamble and Lou Bollo, directed by Phil Sgriccia.

4.03, "In the Beginning" (Oct. 2, 2008). Written by Jeremy Carver, directed by Steve Boyum.

4.04, "Metamorphosis" (Oct. 9, 2008). Written by Cathryn Humphris, directed by Kim Manners.

4.05, "Monster Movie" (Oct. 16, 2008). Written by Ben Edlund, directed by Robert Singer.

4.06, "Yellow Fever" (Oct. 23, 2008). Written by Andrew Dabb and Daniel Loflin, directed by Phil Sgriccia.

4.07, "It's the Great Pumpkin, Sam Winchester" (Oct. 30, 2008). Written by Julie Siege, directed by Charles Beeson.

4.09, "I Know What You Did Last Summer"

(Nov. 13, 2008). Written by Sera Gamble, directed by Charles Beeson.

4.10, "Heaven and Hell" (Nov. 20, 2008). Written by Eric Kripke and Trevor Sands, directed by J. Miller Tobin.

4.12, "Criss Angel Is a Douchebag"(Jan. 22, 2009). Written by Julie Siege, directed by Robert Singer.

4.13, "After School Special" (Jan. 29, 2009). Written by Daniel Loflin and Andrew Dabb, directed by Adam Kane.

4.14, "Sex and Violence" (Feb. 5, 2009). Written by Cathryn Humphris, directed by Charles Beeson.

4.15, "Death Takes a Holiday" (March 12, 2009). Written by Jeremy Carver, directed by Steve Boyum.

4.16, "On the Head of a Pin" (March 19, 2009). Written by Ben Edlund, directed by Mike Rohl.

4.17, "It's a Terrible Life" (March 26, 2009). Written by Sera Gamble, directed by James L. Conway.

4.18, "The Monster at the End of This Book" (April 2, 2009). Written by Julie Siege, directed by Mike Rohl.

4.19, "Jump the Shark" (April 23, 2009). Written by Andrew Dabb and Daniel Loflin, directed by Phil Sgriccia.

4.20, "The Rapture" (April 30, 2009). Written by Jeremy Carver, directed by Charles Beeson.

4.21, "When the Levee Breaks" (May 7, 2009). Written by Sera Gamble, directed by Robert Singer.

4.22, "Lucifer Rising" (May 14, 2009). Written by Erik Kripke, directed by Erik Kripke.

Season 5

5.01, "Sympathy for the Devil" (Sept 10, 2009). Written by Eric Kripke, directed by Robert Singer.

5.02, "Good God, Y'all" (Sept. 17, 2009). Written by Sera Gamble, directed by Phil Sgriccia.

5.03, "Free to Be You and Me" (Sept. 24, 2009). Written by Jeremy Carver, directed by J. Miller Tobin.

5.04, "The End" (Oct. 1, 2009). Written by Ben Edlund, directed by Steve Boyum.

5.05, "Fallen Idols" (Oct. 8, 2009). Written by Julie Siege, directed by James L. Conway.

5.06, "I Believe the Children Are Our Future" (Oct. 15, 2009). Written by Daniel Loflin and Andrew Dabb, directed by Charles Beeson.

5.07, "The Curious Case of Dean Winchester" (Oct. 29, 2009). Written by Sera Gamble, story by Sera Gamble and Jenny Klein, directed by Robert Singer.

5.08, "Changing Channels" (Nov. 5, 2009). Written by Eric Kripke, directed by Charles Beeson.

5.09, "The Real Ghostbusters" (Nov. 12, 2009). Written by Eric Kripke, directed by James L. Conway.

5.10, "Abandon All Hope…" (Nov. 19, 2009). Written by Ben Edlund, directed by Phil Sgriccia.

5.12, "Swap Meat" (Jan. 28, 2010). Written by Julie Siege, story by Julie Siege, Rebecca Dessertine, and Harvey Fedor, directed by Robert Singer.

5.13, "The Song Remains the Same" (Feb. 4, 2010). Written by Sera Gamble and Nancy Weiner, directed by Steve Boyum.

5.14, "My Bloody Valentine" (Feb. 11, 2010). Written by Ben Edlund, directed by Mike Rohl.

5.15, "Dead Men Don't Wear Plaid" (March 25, 2010). Written by Jeremy Carver, directed by John F. Showalter.

5.16, "Dark Side of the Moon" (April 1, 2010). Written by Andrew Dabb and Daniel Loflin, directed by Jeff Woolnough.

5.18, "Point of No Return" (April 15, 2010). Written by Jeremy Carver, directed by Phil Sgriccia.

5.19, "Hammer of the Gods" (April 22, 2010). Written by Andrew Dabb and Daniel Loflin, directed by Rick Bota.

5.20, "The Devil You Know" (April 29, 2010). Written by Ben Edlund, directed by Robert Singer.

5.22, "Swan Song" (May 13, 2010). Written by Eric Kripke, directed by Steve Boyum.

Season 6

6.01, "Exile on Main Street" (September 24, 2010). Written by Sera Gamble, directed by Phil Sgriccia.

6.03, "The Third Man" (Oct. 8, 2010). Written by Ben Edlund, directed by Robert Singer.

6.04, "Weekend at Bobby's" (Oct. 15, 2010). Written by Andrew Dabb and Daniel Loflin, directed by Jensen Ackles.

6.05, "Live Free or Twihard" (Oct. 22, 2010). Written by Brett Matthews, directed by Rod Hardy.

6.06, "You Can't Handle the Truth" (Oct. 29, 2010). Written by Eric Charmelo and Nicole Snyder, directed by Jan Eliasberg.

6.10, "Caged Heat" (Dec. 3, 2010). Written by Brett Matthews, story by Brett Matthews and Jenny Klein, directed by Robert Singer.

6.13, "Unforgiven" (Feb. 7, 2011). Written by Andrew Dabb and Daniel Loflin, directed by David Barrett.

6.14, "Mannequin 3: The Reckoning" (Feb. 18, 2011). Written by Eric Charmelo and Nicole Snyder, directed by Jeannot Szwarc.

6.15, "The French Mistake" (Feb. 25, 2011). Written by Ben Edlund, directed by Charles Beeson.

6.17, "My Heart Will Go On" (April 15, 2011). Written by Eric Charmelo and Nicole Snyder, directed by Phil Sgriccia.

6.18, "Frontierland" (April 22, 2001). Written by Andrew Dabb and Daniel Loflin, directed by Guy Norman Bee.

6.20, "The Man Who Would Be King" (May 6, 2011). Written and directed by Ben Edlund.

6.21, "Let It Bleed" (May 20, 2011). Written by Sera Gamble, directed by John F. Showalter.

6.22, "The Man Who Knew Too Much" (May 20, 2011). Written by Eric Kripke, directed by Robert Singer.

Season 7

7.01, "Meet the New Boss" (Sept. 23, 2011). Written by Sera Gamble, directed by Phil Sgriccia.

7.03, "The Girl Next Door" (Oct. 7, 2011). Written by Andrew Debb and Daniel Lofflin, directed by Jensen Ackles.

7.08, "Season 7, Time for a Wedding!" (Nov. 11, 2011). Written by Andrew Dabb and Daniel Loflin, directed by Tim Andrew.

7.09, "How to Win Friends and Influence Monsters" (Nov. 18, 2011). Written by Ben Edlund, directed by Guy Bee.

7.11, "Adventures in Babysitting" (Jan. 6, 2012). Written by Adam Glass, directed by Jeannot Szwarc.

7.12, "Time After Time" (Jan. 13, 2012).

Written by Robbie Thompson, directed by Phil Sgriccia.

7.19, "Of Grave Importance" (April 20, 2012). Written by Brad Buckner and Eugenie Ross-Leming, directed by Tim Andrew.

7.20, "The Girl with the Dungeons and Dragons Tattoo" (April 27, 2012). Written by Robbie Thompson, directed by John MacCarthy.

7.21, "Reading Is Fundamental" (May 4, 2012). Written by Ben Edlund, directed by Ben Edlund.

7.22, "There Will Be Blood" (May 11, 2012). Written by Andrew Dabb and Daniel Loflin, directed by Guy Norman Bee.

7.23, "Survival of the Fittest" (May 18, 2012). Written by Sera Gamble, directed by Robert Singer.

Season 8

8.02, "What's Up, Tiger Mommy?" (Oct. 10, 2012). Written by Andrew Dabb and Daniel Loflin, directed by John F. Showalter.

8.11, "LARP and the Real Girl" (Jan. 23, 2013). Written by Robbie Thompson, directed by Jeannot Szwarc.

8.13, "Everybody Hates Hitler" (Feb. 6, 2013). Written by Ben Edlund, directed by Philk Sgriccia.

8.17, "Goodbye Stranger" (March 20, 2013). Written by Robbie Thompson, directed by Thomas J. Wright.

8.20, "Pac Man Fever" (April 24, 2013). Written by Robbie Thompson, directed by Robert Singer.

8.21, "The Great Escapist" (May 1, 2013). Written by Ben Edlund, directed by Robert Duncan McNeill.

8.22, "Clip Show" (May 8, 2013). Written by Andrew Dabb, directed by Thomas J. Wright.

Season 9

9.01, "I Think I'm Gonna Like It Here" (Oct. 8, 2013). Written by Jeremy Carver, directed by John Showalter.

9.04, "Slumber Party" (Oct. 29, 2013). Written by Robbie Thompson, directed by Robert Singer.

9.08, "Rock and a Hard Place" (Nov. 26, 2013). Written by Jenny Klein, directed by Johnny MacCarthy.

25

9.15, "#thinman" (March 9, 2014). Written by Jenny Klein, directed by Jeannot Szwarc.

9.18, "Meta Fiction" (April 15, 2014). Written by Robbie Thompson, directed by Thomas J. Wright.

9.21, "King of the Damned" (May 6, 2014). Written by Eugenie Ross-Leming and Brad Buckner, directed by P.J. Pesce.

9.23, "Do You Believe in Miracles?" (May 20, 2014). Written by Jeremy Carver, directed by Thomas J. Wright.

Season 10

10.04, "Paper Moon" (Oct. 28, 2014). Written by Adam Glass, directed by Jeannot Szwarc.

10.05, "Fan Fiction" (Nov. 11, 2014). Written by Robbie Thompson, directed by Phil Sgriccia.

10.09, "The Things We Left Behind" (Dec. 9, 2014). Written by Andrew Dabb, directed by Guy Norman Bee.

10.11, "There's No Place Like Home" (Jan. 27, 2015). Written by Robbie Thompson, directed by Phil Sgriccia.

10.13, "Halt & Catch Fire" (February 10, 2105). Written by Eric Carmelo and Nicole Snyder, directed by John F. Showalter.

10.17, "Inside Man" (April 1, 2015). Written by Andrew Dabb, directed by Rashaad Ernesto Green.

10.18, "Book of the Damned" (April 15, 2015). Written by Robbie Thompson, directed by P.J. Pesce.

10.21, "Dark Dynasty" (May 6, 2015). Written by Eugenie Ross-Leming and Benjamin Buckner, directed by Robert Singer.

10.22, "The Prisoner" (May 13, 2015). Written by Andrew Dabb, directed by Thomas J. Wright.

Season 11

11.05, "Thin Lizzie" (Nov. 4, 2015). Written by Nancy Won, directed by Rashaad Ernesto Green.

11.09, "O Brother Where Art Thou?" (December 9, 2015). Written by Eugenie Ross-Leming and Brad Buckner, directed by Robert Singer.

11.14, "The Vessel" (Feb. 17, 2016). Written by Robert Berens, directed by John Badham.

11.15, "Beyond the Mat" (Feb. 24, 2016). Written by John Bring and Andrew Dabb, directed by Jerry Wanek.

11.17, "Red Meat" (March 30, 2016). Written by Robert Berens and Andrew Dabb, directed by Nina Lopez-Corrado.

11.20, "Don't Call Me Shurley" (May 4, 2016). Written by Robbie Thompson, directed by Robert Singer.

11.21, "All in the Family" (May 11, 2016). Written by Eugenie Ross-Leming and Brad Buckner, directed by Thomas J. Wright.

11.23, "Alpha and Omega" (May 25, 2016). Written by Andrew Dabb, directed by Phil Sgriccia.

Season 12

12.01, "Keep Calm and Carry On" (Oct. 13, 2018). written by Andrew Dabb, directed by Phil Sgriccia.

12.04, "American Nightmare" (Nov. 3, 2016). Written by Davy Perez, directed by John F. Showalter.

12.05, "The One You've Been Waiting For" (Nov. 10, 2016). Written by Meredith Glynn, directed by Nina Lopez-Corrado.

12.06, "Celebrating the Life of Asa Fox" (Nov. 17, 2016). Written by Steve Yockey, directed by John Badham.

12.07, "Rock Never Dies" (Dec. 1, 2016). Written by Robert Berens, directed by Eduardo Sánchez.

12.08, "LOTUS" (Dec. 8, 2016). Written by Eugenie Ross-Leming and Brad Buckner, directed by Phil Sgriccia.

12.13, "Family Feud" (Feb. 23, 2017). Written by Brad Buckner and Eugenie Ross-Leming, directed by P.J. Pesce.

12.17, "The British Invasion" (April 6, 2017). Written by Eugenie Ross-Leming and Brad Buckner, directed by John F. Showalter.

12.22, "Who We Are" (May 18, 2017). Written by Robert Berens, directed by John F. Showalter.

Season 13

13.06, "Tombstone"(Nov. 16, 2017). Written by Davy Perez, directed by Nina Lopez-Corrado.

13.11, "Breakdown" (Jan. 25, 2018). Written by Davy Perez, directed by Amyn Kaderali

13.16, "Scoobynatural" (March 29, 2018). Written by Jeremy Krieg and James Adams, directed by Robert Singer and Spike Brandt.

13.18, "Bring 'Em Back Alive" (April 12, 2018). Written by Brad Buckner and Eugenie Ross-Leming, directed by Amyn Kaderali.

13.20, "Unfinished Business" (April 26, 2018). Written by Meredith Glynn, directed by Richard Speight, Jr.

13.22, "Exodus" (May 10, 2018). Written by Eugenie Ross-Leming and Brad Buckner, directed by Thomas J. Wright.

13.23, "Let the Good Times Roll" (May 17, 2018). Written by Andrew Dabb, directed by Robert Singer.

Season 14

14.04, "Mint Condition" (November 1, 2018). Written by Davy Perez, directed by Amyn Kaderali.

14.09, "The Spear" (December 13, 2018). Written by Robert Berens, directed by Amyn Kaderali.

14.14, "Ouroboros" (March 7, 2019). Written by Steve Yockey, directed by Amyn Kaderali.

14.15, "Peace of Mind" (March 14, 2019). Teleplay by Meghan Fitzmartin, story by Meghan Fitzmartin and Steve Yockey, directed by Phil Sgriccia.

14.16, "Don't Go in the Woods" (March 21, 2019). Written by Davy Perez and Nick-Vaught, directed by John Fitzpatrick.

Appendix Two
Main and Major Characters

Brief information about all major characters and about secondary ones who are relevant to the essays in this volume appears below.

Main Cast (Regulars)

Dean Winchester*	Jensen Ackles
Sam Winchester**	Jared Padalecki
Ruby (Season 3)†	Katie Cassidy
Bela Talbot (Season 3)	Lauren Cohan
Castiel	Misha Collins
Crowley	Mark Sheppard
Lucifer/Nick***	Mark Pellegrino
Jack Kline	Alexander Calvert

*Young Dean was played by Dylan Everett (9.07, 10.12, 11.08), Ridge Canipe (1.18, 3.08), Brock Kelly (4.13), Nicolai Guistra (5.22, 7.10), Anthony Bolognese (12.22), and Elderly Dean was played by Chad Everett (5.07).

**Young Sam was played by Colin Ford (3.08, 4.13, 4.21, 5.16, 7.03, 11.10), Alex Ferris (1.18), Nathan Smith (5.22), Hunter Dillon (9.07), and Dylan Kingwell (11.08).

***Lucifer has also been played briefly by Bellamy Young (5.01) Jared Padalecki (5.04, 5.22), Misha Collins (11.10, 11.11, 11.14, 11.15, 11.18, 11.21, 11.22), Rick Springfield as Vince Vincente (12.02, 12.03, 12.07), and David Chisum as President Jefferson Rooney (12.08), Michael Querin (12.08), Emma Johnson (12.02), and Adrianne Palicki (5.03).

†Ruby was recurring and played by Genevieve Padalecki (nee Cortese) in Season 4 and Anna Williams (4.09) and Michelle Hewitt-Williams (4.09). Padalecki also played herself in (6.15).

Major Recurring Characters/Characters Referenced

Abaddon/Josie Sands	Alaina Huffman
Adina	Jud Tylor
Ajay	Assaf Cohen
Alastair°°	Christopher Heyerdahl
Alpha Vamp	Rick Worthy
Alice	Kelli Ogmundson
Amara°†	Emily Swallow
Antichrist	see Jesse Turner below
Ash	Chad Lindberg
Asmodeus	Jeffrey Vincent Parise
Azazel	Frederic Lehne
Balthazar	Sebastian Roche
Alicia Banes	Kara Royster
Max Banes	Kendrick Sampson
Barnes	Ernie Grunwald
Pamela Barnes	Traci Dinwiddie
Aaron Bass	Adam Rose
Tara Benchley	Elizabeth Whitmere
Doc Benton	Billy Drago
Lady Toni Bevell	Elizabeth Blackmore
Billie	Lisa Berry
Stuart Blake	Kurt Ostlund
Lou Bollo	Himself
Boltar	Hank Harris
Boris	Joseph D Reitman
Charlie Bradbury	Felicia Day
Ben Braeden	Nicholas Elia
Lisa Braeden	Cindy Sampson
Sherriff Al Britton	Jack Conley
Cain	Timothy Omundson
Jimmy Caldwell	Connor Levins
Calliope	Hannah Levien
Christian Campbell	Corin Nemec
Deanna Campbell	Allison Hossack

Gwen Campbell

Samuel Campbell

Edward Carrigan

Madge Carrigan

Mrs. Chandler

Chet

Terrance Clegg

Ben Collins

Haley Collins

Tommy Collins

Samuel Colt

Alan J. Corbett

Cronos

Freeman Daggett

Dagon

Daphne

Mick Davies

Death

Demian

Frank Devereaux

Dirk

Walter Dixon

Cyrus Dorian

Dorothy

Dracula

Edgar

Eve°°°

Fate/Atropos

Fenrir

Len Fletcher

Garth Fitzgerald IV

Marty Flagg

Gabriel/Trickster

Gadreel

Dr Gaines

HH Holmes

Jessica Heafey

Mitch Pileggi

Spencer Garrett

Merrilyn Gann

Alberta Mayne

Sean Owen Roberts

Chris William Martin

Alden Ehrenreich

Gina Holden

Graham Wardle

Sam Hennings

Dustin Mulligan

Jason Dohring

John DeSantis

Ali Ahn

Grey Griffin (voice)

Adam Fergus

Julian Richings

Devin Ratray

Kevin McNally

Aaron Paul Stewart

Benjamin Ratner

Dee Jay Jackson

Kaniehtiio Horn

Todd Stashwick

Benito Martinez

Julie Maxwell

Katie Walder

Sandy Robson

Jared Gertner

DJ Qualls

Michael B Silver

Richard Speight Jr.

Tahmoh Penikett

Cameron Bancroft

Stephen Aberle

Convention Host	Jonathan Bruce
Game Show Host	Hiro Kanagawa
Sera Gamble	Hilary Jardine (voice)
Gandhi	Paul Statman
Dr. Garrison	Christopher Cousins
Father Gil	Robert Curtis Brown
Gilda	Tiffany Dupont
God/Chuck Shurley	Rob Benedict
The Golem	John DeSantis
Guy/Demon	Leslie Odom Jr.
Hannah	Erica Carroll
Donna Hanscum	Briana Buckmaster
Ellen Harvelle	Samantha Ferris
Jo Harvelle	Alona Tal
Hatchet Man	Barry Nerling
Victor Hendrickson	Charles Malik Whitfield
Dr. Hess	Gillian Barber
Adolf Hitler	Gil Darnell
Isaac	Peter Macon
Jamie	Melinda Sward
Jay	Peter New
Alex Jones	Katherine Ramdeen
Fred Jones	Mike Farrell
Joshua	Roger Aaron Brown
Kali	Rekha Sharma
Jacob Karns	Sean Millington
Kate	Brit Sheridan
Katie	Vivien Elizabeth Armour
Arthur Ketch	David Haydn-Jones
Kelly Kline	Courtney Ford
Eric Kripke	Micah Hauptman
Kristen	Nina Winkler
Clif Kosterman	Philip Maurice Hayes
Kubrick	Michael Massee
Serge Ladouceur	Art Kitching
Benny Lafitte	Ty Olsson

Russell Lemmons	Kadeem Hardison
Lenore	Amber Benson
Leshii	Paris Hilton
Lilith°	Katherine Boecher
Abraham Lincoln	David Livingstone
Lucy	Holly Elissa
Gavin MacLeod	Theo Devaney
Madison	Emmanuelle Vaugier
Marlon	Steven Yaffee
Maeve	Joy Regullano
Marie	Katie Sarife
Meg Masters	Nicki Aycox (seasons 1 and 3)
Meg Masters	Rachel Miner (seasons 5–8)
McG	Regan Burns
Molly McNamara	Tricia Helfer
David McNamara	Dan Gauthier
Metatron	Curtis Armstrong
Michael††	Christian Keyes
Jim Michaels	Garwin Sanford
Jody Mills	Kim Rhodes
Anna Milton	Julie McNiven
Jack Montgomery	Dameon Clarke
Jessica Moore	Adrianne Palicki
Missouri Moseley	Loretta Devine
Nate Mulligan	David Quinlan
Mordechai Murdoch	Nick Harrison
Naomi	Amanda Tapping
Narfi	Michael Adamthwaite
Nicky Mermaid	Ida Segerhagen
Eliot Ness	Nicholas Lea
Nicole/Demon	Nicole "Snooki" Polizzi
Noah	Philippe Bowgen
Claire Novak	Kathryn Newton
Odin	Duncan Fraser
Kevin Parks	Jason Bryden
Jerry Penowski	Brian Markinson

Magda Peterson	Paloma Kwiatkowski
Pestilence	Matt Frewer
Phoenix/Elias Finch	Matthew Armstrong
Amy Pond	Jewel Staite
Young Amy Pond	Emma Grabinsky
Carmen Porter	Michelle Borth
Raphael†††	Demore Barnes
Brad Redding	Gary Cole
Amelia Richardson	Liane Balaban
Dr Robert	Robert Englund
Cassie Robinson	Megalyn Echikunwoke
Dick Roman	James Patrick Stuart
Ronnie (Santa)	Alex Bruhanski
Roseleen	Crystal Allen
Becky Rosen	Emily Perkins
Rowena	Ruth Connell
Roy	Kerry Van Der Griend
Samandriel	Tyler Johnston
Samantha	Genevieve Buechner
Samhain	Don McManus
Scooby-Doo	Frank Welker (also the voice of Fred Jones)
Dr Sexy	Steve Bacic
Delphine Seydoux	Weronika Rosati
Shaggy	Matthew Lillard (voice)
Sara Siege	Keegan Connor Tracy
Cuthbert Sinclair	Kavan Smith
Bobby Singer	Jim Beaver
Karen Singer	Carrie Ann Fleming
Robert Singer	Brian Doyle-Murray
Siobhan	Alyssa Lynch
Sleipnir	Fletcher Donovan
Sparkle	Everett Shea
Harry Spengler	Travis Wester
Kenny Spruce	Austin Basis
Starla	Elena Esovolova

Eldon Styne	David Hoflin
Eli Styne	Matt Bellefleur
Monroe Styne	Markus Flanagan
Sully	Nate Torrence
Jake Talley	Aldis Hodge
Tamara	Caroline Chikezie
Tammy	Rachel Warkentin
Tara	Rachel Hayward
Tasha	Emily Tennant
Tessa/Reaper	Lindsey McKeon
Clay Thompson	Troy Ruptash
Corbin Tilghman	Blair Penner
Tiny	Clif Kosterman
Tooth Fairy	Mark Acheson
Kevin Tran	Osric Chau
Linda Tran	Lauren Tom
Travis	Ron Lea
Cole Trenton	Travis Aaron Wade
Jesse Turner	Gattlin Griffith
Rufus Turner	Steven Williams
Uriel	Robert Wisdom
Velma	Kate Micucci (voice)
Veritas	Serinda Swan
Eleanor Visyak	Kim Johnston Ulrich
Vince Vincente	Rick Springfield
Gordon Walker	Sterling K Brown
Walt	Nels Lennarson
Ms. Watt	Bronagh Waugh
Constance Welch	Sarah Shahi
Michael Wheeler	Brandon W Jones
Brian Wilcox	Leigh Parker
John Winchester	Jeffrey Dean Morgan
Young John	Matt Cohen
Henry Winchester	Gil McKinney
Mary Winchester	Samantha Smith
Young Mary	Amy Gumenick

Ava Wilson	Katherine Isabelle
Zachariah	Kurt Fuller
Ed Zeddmore	AJ Buckley
Maggie Zeddmore	Brittany Ishibashi

††Michael was also briefly played by Jake Abel (5.22), Matthew Cohen (5.13), Felisha Terrell (14.09) and Jensen Ackles (13. 23 and in Season 14).

†††Raphael was also played by Lanette Ware in (6.15).

°Lilith was also played by Sierra McCormick and Katie Cassidy in (3.16).

°°Alastair was also played by Mark Rolston in (4.10) and briefly by Andrew Wheeler in (4.15).

°°°Eve was also played by Samantha Smith in (6.19).

°†Amara was also played by Gracyn Shinyei (11.02), Yameene Ball (11.05), and Samantha Isler (11.06).

About the Contributors

Laurena **Aker** is an independent author and editor and the managing editor for *The Winchester Family Business*. Her *Supernatural* publications include a chapter in *Family Don't End with Blood*, over 200 feature articles, *TV Fanatic* weekly reviews, and the paper "Sparking and Sustaining Superfandoms." Her book *Fan Phenomena* combines behind-the-scenes interviews with expert analysis to document *Twilight*'s 10-year impact on literature, the entertainment industry and opportunities for women.

Cait **Coker** is an associate professor and curator of rare books and manuscripts at the University of Illinois at Urbana–Champaign. Much of her research focuses on the history of science fiction fandom and popular culture. Her other writings include, with Candace Benefiel, "The Hunter Hunted" in *Supernatural, Humanity, and the Soul* (2014) and "'It's a Guilty Pleasure': Gendering Cultural Consumption, Masculine Anxiety, and the Problems of Dean Winchester" in *Metafiction, Intertextuality, and Authorship in Supernatural* (forthcoming).

Camille **DeBose** is a lecturer and award-winning filmmaker in the College of Computing and Digital Media at DePaul. With a master's degree in sociology and an MFA in cinema, she takes an academic approach to the exploration of social forces through the analysis and production of film. All three of her films have been official selections at various film festivals. She has popular writings published on *Flow TV* by the University of Texas at Austin and *In Media Res*.

Megan **Genovese** is a Ph.D. candidate at the Annenberg School for Communication at the University of Pennsylvania. Her research examines fandom as a critical site of interaction between popular media cultures and the development and expression of political beliefs. Her dissertation will study the use and rhetorical effect of fantastic media metaphors in grassroots political talk both on- and offline.

Dominick **Grace** is a professor of English at Brescia University College and the author of *The Science Fiction of Phyllis Gotlieb*, coeditor with Eric Hoffman of *Approaching "Twin Peaks"* as well as coeditor of several other books and author of numerous articles on popular culture. With Lisa Macklem, he is also coeditor of Supernatural *Out of the Box: Essays on the Metatextuality of the Series*.

Paula S. **Kiser** is an assistant professor and digital scholarship librarian at Washington & Lee University. She earned a master's degree in history from James Madison University and a master of science in information science from the University of Tennessee, Knoxville. She teaches and presents on information literacy in higher education. She has published entries in the *Encyclopedia of Japanese Horror*, *Reforming America*, and *The World of Antebellum America*.

Lisa **Macklem** is a Ph.D. candidate in law at the University of Western Ontario. In addition to a BA in English, she has a JD with a specialization in IP and IT, an LLM in entertainment and media law and an MA in media studies. Her MA thesis is "We're On This Road Together: The Changing Fan/Producer Relationship in Television as Demonstrated by *Supernatural*" (2013).

Keshia **Mcclantoc** is a Ph.D. student in composition and rhetoric at the University of Nebraska–Lincoln. She holds a master's degree in English and a certification in women and gender studies from the University of Nebraska–Lincoln. Her areas of interest include rural and community literacies, especially of women and queer peoples in those spaces. Her research focuses on the ways digital communities interact with marginalized identities in rural spaces.

Leanne **McRae** is a research officer in the School of Media, Creative Arts and Social Inquiry at Curtin University in Western Australia. She works in disability studies on a range of projects including audio description and navigating urban spaces. Her first book, *Terror, Leisure and Consumption: Spaces for Harm in a Post-Crash Era*, was released in 2018 by Emerald Publishers.

Tatiana **Prorokova-Konrad** is a postdoctoral researcher at the Department of English and American Studies, University of Vienna, Austria. She holds a Ph.D. in American Studies from the University of Marburg, Germany. She was a Visiting Researcher at the Forest History Society (2019), an Ebeling Fellow at the American Antiquarian Society (2018), and a Visiting Scholar at the University of South Alabama, USA (2016). She is the author of *Docu-Fictions of War: U.S. Interventionism in Film and Literature* (University of Nebraska Press, 2019), the editor of *Transportation and the Culture of Climate Change: Accelerating Ride to Global Crisis* (West Virginia University Press, 2020) and *Cold War II: Hollywood's Renewed Obsession with Russia* (University Press of Mississippi, 2020), and a coeditor of *Cultures of War in Graphic Novels: Violence, Trauma, and Memory* (Rutgers University Press, 2018).

Emily E. **Roach** is a Ph.D. candidate at the University of York, specializing in queer performance poetry on YouTube, theorizing online space and post–Stonewall LGBT American fiction. Her research on queer online fiction extends to work on fan communities and queering pop culture. She has published papers on Harry Potter, fandom platform migration, *Stranger Things* and RPF pop music fandoms. She is an active fanfic writer in multiple fandoms, a pop culture blogger and freelance writer and an LGBT activist.

Angélica **Varandas** is an assistant professor in the Department of English Studies of the School of Arts and Humanities, University of Lisbon, where she teaches medieval culture and literature, as well as English linguistics and science fiction and fantasy. Her main area of research is English medieval literature and culture, on which she has published widely. She is the author of two books about Celtic mythology: *Mitos e Lendas Celtas: Irlanda* (2006) and *Mitos e Lendas Celtas: País de Gales* (2007). She is translating the Old English poem *Beowulf* into Portuguese.

Kimberly Lynn **Workman** completed a master of arts degree in technology and communication at UNC–Chapel Hill, with a specialization in media fandom. She researches fair use, media ownership, fan identification, and fandom community structures. Additionally, she has been the *Supernatural* reviewer for *Fandomania* since 2010 and has followed the Winchesters' journey since the show first aired.

Index